PLAYING THE PRICE CONTROLS GAME

How Some People Will Profit from the Coming Controls

Mark Skousen

ARLINGTON HOUSE·PUBLISHERS
NEW ROCHELLE, NEW YORK

To Jo Ann

Manufactured in the United States of America

Library of Congress Cataloging in Publication Data

Skousen, Mark.
  Playing the price controls game.

  Bibliography: p.
  Includes index.
  1. Price regulation—United States. 2. Wage-price
policy—United States. I. Title.
HB236.U5S54   338.5′26′0973   76-48292
ISBN 0-87000-374-7

Contents

Foreword by Gary North, Ph.D. 9

Acknowledgements 13

1. Who's in Control? 15

Who Gains and Who Loses under Controls? 16
What This Book Is About 18
How This Book Is Organized 18
A Personal Note 26
A Moral Judgment 26
Are Controls Constitutional? 27
Civil Disobedience? 29
Is This Book Unpatriotic? 31
Changing Winds in America 31
Turning Political Defeats into Economic Gains 34
Looking Ahead 35

Part I

The Economics and Politics of Price Controls

2. Why Price Controls Are Coming 39

The View from Government: Preparing for the Next
    Round 40

The Views of Economists 43
Economic Studies Favoring Controls 45
The Economic Case for Price Controls: The View of
   John Kenneth Galbraith 47
Will Business again Support Controls? 52
Labor Support 53
The Public Favors Controls 53
Controls without Rapid Inflation? 55
The Prospects for Inflation 56
What Now? 65

3. **Price Controls, Past and Present** 67

Early History of Controls 67
Nazi Germany, 1936–45 71
Postwar Germany under Allied Control 72
China 74
U. S. Experiences during World War II 74
The Korean Controls 77
Other Western Experiences with National Incomes
   Policies 77
Nixon's Stabilization Program, 1971–74 81

4. **What Kind of Controls Are Coming?** 87

The Overall Program: Freeze, Rollback, or Formula
   Pricing? 88
Rationing 93
Production: Free from Controls? 95
Trade Restrictions: A Different Story 96
A Test for Exemptions and Exclusions 97
Price Exemptions 97
Rent Controls and Exemptions 103
Wage Exemptions 105
Profit Controls 106
Restrictions on Interest and Dividends 107
Grayson's Recommendations for Future Controllers . 108

5. **The Consequences of Price Controls** 109

Why Controls Cannot Stop Inflation 110

Problems with a Freeze 113
The Effects of Below-Market Ceilings 118
Price Controls Lead to Socialism 121
Other Forms of Controls 124

6. The Government as Regulator 127

The Bureaucracy 127
Costs of Controls Programs 128
The Folly of Government Bureaucracy 128
Characteristics of Government Controllers 130
Can You Rely on Government Predictions? 130
Are Controls Constitutional? 131
How Government Regulates 135
Government Biases 137
How Government Enforces Controls 137
Dealing with Evasive Acts 139

Part II

The Citizen versus Price Controls: A Practical Guide

7. The Consumer Faces Price Controls 145

How to Deal with Shortages 145
Making Preparations in Advance 146
Preparations for the Next Energy Crisis 147
The Need for Food Storage 149
Joining a Food Co-op 152
Food Terminals 153
The Role of Churches 153
Personal Contacts and Barter Arrangements 155
Use of Gold and Silver Coins 158
Repairs during Controls 159
Taking Advantage of Exempt Markets 160

8. The Worker Faces Wage Controls 164

Exemptions from Wage Controls 164

Circumventing Wage Controls 166
Changing Jobs as a Way of Increasing Income under
    Controls 171
Moonlighting 175

9. **The Businessman Faces Price Controls** 178

How to Prepare for Controls 178
Circumventing Controls 183
Legal and Quasi-Legal Methods of Eluding Controls .. 190
Getting around Markup Regulations 194
Escaping the Profit-Margin Test 195
How Important Is Company Size?................. 198
The Silver Coin Ploy 199
How Businessmen Profit from Controls 201

10. **The Landlord Faces Rent Controls** 205

How to Prepare for Rent Controls 205
Taking Advantage of Exemptions 206
Rent Controls, Political Battles, and Evasive
    Methods: The Case of New York City 208
Cooperative and Condominium Apartments 209
Rent-Control Violations 210
Profiting from Rent Controls 213

11. **The Investor Faces Price Controls** 216

The Stock Market 216
The Bond Market and Interest Rates 222
The Commodity Futures Market 223
Gold and Silver 226
Collectables..................................... 227
Foreign Currency Profits during Controls 229

12. **The Black Market** 232

America's Black Market in World War II 232
Who Ran the Black Market? 234
Sanctions against Black Marketeers 235
How the Black Market Works 236

Rules of the Game 238
Economics of the Black Market 238

13. What Now? 244

Suggested Readings 247

Index 251

Foreword

One of the standard introductions to any new book is "This is one of the most important books of the past ten years." Frankly, I haven't read most of the books published in America over the past ten years, since about 40,000 get published annually. But I can say one thing more confidently: this book may well prove to be the most important book *you* will read over the *next* ten years. The tragedy—and I don't use the word lightly—is that so few people will read this book, and even worse, of those who do read it, so few will actually follow its recommendations. Follow them in time, that is.

Obviously, no one can easily follow every suggestion found in any given investment book. Nevertheless, the investment *approach* of this book is crucial to a sane, objective, and realistic investment program over the next decade. The political popularity of price and wage controls has been a constant factor in man's history for several thousand years. Anyone who doubts this assertion simply has not examined economic history very carefully. Whenever the State holds a legal monopoly over the control of the money supply (which is always), the temptation to escape the limits of a *visible* taxation system invariably lures politicians (or their henchmen, central bank officials) into policies of *invisible* taxation, namely, the expansion of the money supply. Sooner or later, the monopoly of money leads to monetary inflation, and monetary inflation leads to the "boom-bust cycle" of price inflation and economic depression. To escape this cycle, politicians attempt to prolong the inflationary boom, and if they are temporarily successful in their efforts, the policy leads directly to mass inflation. To avoid the effects of mass inflation, politicians are then tempted to impose price and wage controls, and these inevitably and invariably produce shortages of supply, especially shortages of the more widely used goods and services, i.e., economic necessities.

Price controls also lead to the so-called black market. (I don't like the phrase "black market." If professional economists, in their pathological quest for hypothetical neutrality, can label policies of immoral and socially disastrous wealth redistribution as "transfer payments," then I see no logical reason not to call black markets "alternative zones of supply.") We are headed for black markets. There may be some readers who have moral objections or fears about participating on a black market. For such readers this book is doubly important. The information here can be used to help a family stay out of black markets. There may come a time when the author is criticized for having written a book that "encourages" people to enter black markets, but will the criticism be valid? Given the timing of the book's original publication (or at least the final draft of the manuscript), it should be obvious that the author is not advocating any illegal activities. On the contrary, he is recommending steps that will help a person to *avoid* the economic pressures that will eventually lure others into the illegal markets. This assumes, however, that the reader acts *prior* to the imposition of price controls, rationing, and legislation against black markets and "hoarding." (When laws against hoarding are passed, you will notice one peculiar feature of such laws: there will be no *theoretical* explanation of just what constitutes a "hoard," or how the authorities arrived at such a definition. From the point of view of economic theory, there is absolutely no way to distinguish hoarding from saving.)

There is no doubt that the information found in this book could be used to establish illegal markets in the future, thereby relieving some of the crippling pressures and bottlenecks in production and distribution during a future regime of price and wage controls. There is no doubt that some of the steps recommended here will eventually be declared illegal. There is no doubt that those who read this book too late will have to take far more risks and give up far more wealth to follow the author's recommendations. And there *is* some doubt that the political authorities will allow a book like this one to be published three or four years down the price-controls road. (Or, what amounts to the same thing, governments may refuse to allocate paper to any company that tries to publish such a book.) So if you think the book makes sense, you ought to establish a systematic policy of buying "hard" goods, week by week, and the day that controls are declared, you should indebt yourself and buy anything that you think you will have to have over the next half decade or longer. But don't criticize Mark Skousen as having written a handbook for black marketeers. His book will undoubtedly be a useful handbook for black marketeers, but more important, it is *presently* another kind of handbook—a handbook for those who would prefer to avoid becoming black marketeers. What the book becomes in the future is beyond the control of both author and publisher.

The chief problem with most so-called investment books is not simply that it is difficult for a reader to know if the investment advice is sound. Rather, it is the psychological paralysis of readers who actually believe that a course of action is logically correct but who steadfastly refuse to take the first step. Very few readers ever take the necessary first steps. Since the author was too polite when he wrote his manuscript, let me play the role of chief tail-kicker. If you actually take the time and effort to read this book (and many buyers of the book won't), and if you find yourself in basic agreement with its perspective and general analysis, then you owe it to yourself and to all those for whom you are economically responsible to take the following steps:

(1) Begin to draw up a list of tools and durable consumer goods that are likely to be the first goods in short supply within six months after the imposition of price and wage controls. This means the low-profit-margin, high-volume, price-competitive necessities.

(2) Discipline yourself to set aside at least 10 percent of your after-tax income, month by month, for a program of investment in hard goods or in education leading to the ability to repair hard goods.

(3) Watch for the announcement that the Congress has passed

11

a bill permitting the president to impose price and wage controls "at his discretion," meaning without long debates that would tip off potential "hoarders" of the disaster to come, and without tipping off "economic exploiters" (businessmen and laborers) who might raise prices immediately, before the debates in Congress are over. At this point, you should devote at least 20 percent of your after-tax income to systematic purchases of hardware and durable goods.

(4) When the announcement of the "temporary" price freeze comes, you must intensify your efforts to amass a supply of goods (e.g., a complete set of new automobile tires and spare parts, such as spark plugs, points and condensers, et cetera). At this point, you will be racing against time.

Admittedly, these specific percentages are arbitrary. They should serve as general guidelines. But they are representative of what seem to me to be the minimum figures required for a successful program of shortage-hedging. *There is not much time remaining*. Controls could come at any time, and shortages will appear within six months after controls are imposed. Within eighteen months after controls arrive, the shortages will be far more than merely inconvenient. There will be bankruptcies, both personal and corporate, that are the direct products of the controls. The man who reads this book, takes no action, and finds himself in deep trouble in the future really has no excuse. He who has ears to hear, as the Bible says, let him hear.

The most important hedges against a control-induced shortage economy are ethical and personal: personal integrity, charity, faith in one's capacities, a willingness to survive, and an unwillingness to become depressed about the daily pressures of life. These pressures will increase inexorably under price controls. We will be reminded of the slogans of an earlier, less prosperous, more self-reliant, more responsible America. "Make do with less." "Root, hog, or die." And so, my friend, you must "fish or cut bait."

GARY NORTH, PH.D.
President, Institute for Christian Economics
Editor, Remnant Review

Acknowledgements

I would like to take this opportunity to acknowledge the help of Murray Rothbard; Roger Leroy Miller; Larry Wimmer; my editor, Karl Pflock; and especially Gary North. In addition to writing the foreword, Dr. North read the manuscript and provided many useful comments and suggestions. Needless to say, I alone am responsible for the final result.

I also want to thank my wife and family for helping me get through my first book in one piece. My wife, Jo Ann, was extremely helpful in editing the manuscript, and she offered a number of useful suggestions for the latter part of the book.

I was about to write that without my family, this book could not have been written. But on second thought, I will leave that honor to the federal government, without which this book would never have become even a gleam in my eye.

If the U.S. ever succumbs to collectivism, to government control over every facet of our lives, it will not be because the socialists win any arguments. It will be through the indirect route of wage and price controls.—MILTON FRIEDMAN

Chapter One

Who's in Control?

In August, 1974, I was traveling to Denver on a commercial airliner. Sitting next to me was a corporate executive in charge of purchasing computer parts for his company. Wage and price controls had recently been phased out, and so our conversation turned to the problems and distortions that had been created by Nixon's controls program. I expressed a number of reasons why I regarded controls as destructive, but as an economist my views were based entirely on economic principles rather than on any real experiences in the business world.

In response, my acquaintance said, "Well, I'll tell you why I'm opposed to price controls." He then told me about the time he made a call to a supplier to obtain a vital computer component. Much to my seat-mate's consternation, his supplier announced, "Oh, sorry, but we don't make that component any more."

"What!" exclaimed the purchaser. "You've got to be kidding. I simply have to have that part—why, without it the computer can't operate!" The supplier was sympathetic, but his hands were tied. "Look, it's simple economics. Under price controls, it just doesn't pay to make them any more. We concentrate on producing components with higher profit margins."

I could see why my friend was glad to see the end of controls. But what about the future? What would a computer-parts purchaser do if price controls returned? What steps would he take in anticipation of the next round of government price-fixing?

"Well, for one thing," responded the businessman, "I certainly wouldn't depend on just one supplier for computer parts.''

This story illustrates not only the folly of price fixing in general, but also the challenge that businessmen face if they wish to avoid the pernicious effects of a controls program.

Who Gains and Who Loses under Controls?

Of course, businessmen are not the only ones who suffer from the ills of a government price-controls program. Depending on the type of program, consumers can be confronted with empty supermarket shelves, ration booklets, and black markets. Wage- and salary-earners may be forced to accept lower income in real terms and a decrease in their standards of living. Landlords can be severely limited in raising rents, while tenants find it even more difficult to find the right kind of apartment. Investors and speculators may see their stocks drop precipitously as profits dwindle, or find themselves ''locked'' in a declining market. These are just some of the problems that people everywhere and in every walk of life will face when controls are reimposed.

At the same time, though, it is important to remember that not everyone will suffer under controls. Some people, those who are shrewd enough to make the proper preparations in advance, will be in a position to protect themselves from the ill effects of wage and price regulations. And once these restrictions are promulgated, they will be able to take legal steps to circumvent them.

Some people will even be able to profit from the next round of controls, just as they were able to take advantage of past programs. Businessmen are not the only ones who will be able to do this. That is why this book includes separate chapters devoted to the particular circumstances of the consumer, the wage-earner, the investor, and the landlord, as well as the businessman. Each has a different role and an alternative way of looking at his own situation, and all should be able to find perfectly legal ways to prepare for, survive the impact of, and even profit from a controls program. The chief purpose of this book is to show *you* how it is done.

I do not wish to imply that I somehow glory in the coming of price controls. Neither I nor other investors need price controls to find profitable opportunities. Economic gain is available under all kinds of conditions, whether bull or bear markets, falling or rising prices, boom or depression. Price controls, though, like other products of government intervention, create artificial opportunities for profit (and loss!) that would not exist otherwise.

Although there are both winners and losers under government price-fixing programs, it is important to point out that, overall, society is worse off because of them. There are several reasons for this, which we will examine in later chapters. But the primary ill effects are a general reduction in the standard of living and the range of individual choices, increased confrontations between social classes, and the growing usurpation of power by government. (Interestingly enough, all of these effects are characteristic of inflation as well.)

Of course, an "incomes policy" (a euphemism for government suppression of wages, prices, and rents) will affect some groups more than others, depending on its severity. Under Nixon's program of 1971–74, for example, businessmen were undoubtedly hurt most, and eventually they became the most vociferous opponents of controls. Initially, only labor criticized the program. Consumers did not complain much, although their anger was voiced when spot shortages appeared. (Some people went without ground beef for a couple of weeks—though it was always available at restaurants and fast-food chains—but there were no widespread shortages at the retail level.)

Let's face it: For thirty years Americans have not seen first-hand the effects of widespread price controls. Fading memories seem to have softened the bitterness of shortages, long lines, black-market purchases—or no purchases at all. Fortunately, after World War II the American economy returned for the most part to a free market system, and the distortions and shortages disappeared quickly (excluding rent controls in New York City, of course). Not since the war has government-enforced rationing been necessary, although we came close during the "energy crisis" in early 1974—and I am still amazed that Nixon somehow held the line, much to his credit. In countries where government interference continued after World War II, black markets became a way of life. This was especially true in postwar Germany.

Someday the telltale signs of black markets will appear in the United States. A stranger will come up to you on the street with perhaps a shining gold watch hidden in his hand, ready to sell at some forbidden price. All of a sudden door-to-door salesmen will start knocking on your *back* door . . .

What This Book Is About

This book is not devoted to the black market, however. Nor is it a recommendation to become involved in illegal activities. Instead, I first examine in detail the kinds of controls programs you can expect in the near future. This includes a review of past programs, a discussion of the underlying economic factors that will lead to controls (e.g., a resurgence of inflation), and a consideration of the economic consequences of controls.

Second, I will report on some generally unpublicized ways that can help you prepare for controls, outlining the steps you are free to take to protect yourself, your income, or your business once controls are reimposed. Hopefully, therefore, you will not be required to face the difficult decision to buy (or sell) in an illegal—black—market.

How This Book Is Organized

Chapter 2, "Why Price Controls Are Coming," is a close look at the prospects for price controls in the near future. Price controls do not come about naturally in a free market. (There may be cases when stores voluntarily ration supplies rather than raise prices in the face of an unexpected increase in demand; the toilet paper "shortage" of a few years back is a good example of retailers limiting the number of items sold to a customer.)

Wage and price controls are created by government edict, by the whims of Congress and the White House, and they usually have widespread public support—at the outset. In chapter 2 I critically examine the underlying causes for supporting such a government program, from the viewpoints of government officials, businessmen, labor, and the public in general. Controls are almost exclusively a *political* decision. There are a few economists that present economic arguments in favor of controls, and I examine the basis of their arguments. (At least three prominent economists favor limited controls: John Kenneth Galbraith, Walter Heller, and Arthur F. Burns.)

The state of the economy always plays a major role in influencing the minds of most men. And rapidly rising prices will do more than anything else to bring back cries for government "jawboning," guidelines, and outright price-fixing. Consequently, chapter 2 also includes a review of the outlook for wage gains, prices of commodities, and wholesale and retail prices.

Chapter 3, "Price Controls, Past and Present," is an important chapter. In the words of George Santayana, those who do not remember the past are condemned to relive it. The most recent example of this truism is Canada. The Canadian government apparently failed to learn from the Nixon controls, for less than two years after U.S. controls were dropped, Canada imposed its own form of wage and price limits.

The history of controls goes at least as far back as the Code of Hammurabi. The Roman emperor Diocletian and Kublai Khan had their controls programs, too. Modern-day programs have almost always existed only during wartime. (France is an exception; it has had rent controls during both war and peace since 1914.) In World War II Americans experienced their broadest and most stringent program, and it was one of the few times they were subject to rationing.

Chapter 3 not only reviews the history of controls in the U.S., but in Europe and Canada as well. The Nixon program, 1971–74, is highlighted because it is our most recent experience and, according to many experts, will be duplicated in large part the next time around. Some controls in the U.S., of course, have never been lifted—such as those on petroleum products and natural gas—and they are looked at, too. This is especially worth noting, because you never know which "basic public necessity" will next be placed under a price ceiling.

It is interesting to note that in Latin America, where high rates of inflation have been commonplace for decades, few price controls have been instituted. Inflation seems to be a way of life

19

there, and Latins have learned to live with it by means of "indexation" and other methods. Perhaps this suggests that government programs that repress rapidly rising prices cannot be tolerated for long. Only under moderate inflation can a controls program last for any length of time.

Chapter 4, "What Kind of Controls Are Coming?," relies heavily on the preceding chapter on the history of controls. Experienced government bureaucrats know that controls on certain products and services simply do not work. The Nixon ninety-day freeze in 1971 immediately exempted "raw agricultural commodities," for example. Other areas of the economy were later excluded from regulation, but farm products were first. Why? Because supply and demand conditions can change so rapidly in this area that shortages can erupt almost overnight. Farm goods were also exempted during World War II and the Korean War. Controls officials will often follow a tradition, and the exemption of raw agricultural goods is one of them.

Other products and services are invariably excluded from controls, too. Under Phase II of Nixon's program, literally hundreds of economic units were exempted. And so were certain types of wages. In fact, under every controls program that has ever existed, exceptions have been made. And so I ask the question: In the future, what is the likelihood of controls on profits? Dividends? Interest? Rent? Educated responses to these types of questions should help you prepare for and even profit from controls once they are imposed.

It is my firm conviction that we can learn from the past. By becoming familiar with the kinds of controls imposed and how they were administered, we will have a pretty sure guide to what to expect in the future. Can the government be relied upon to set up controls based on the past? Apparently so. Bureaucrats are not complete fools! They do not want to be utterly ineffectual. I suppose that is one reason the last stages of Nixon's program were so loosely administered, giving the facade of fighting inflation yet not creating horrendous shortages and bottlenecks.

This does not mean that times cannot change and that strict controls cannot be instituted. During the Nixon era, rent controls were imposed largely because of labor-union pressure, even though they were opposed by the Cost of Living Council, the Council of Economic Advisers, and the Price Commission. The political climate may change again and force a new set of rules under which the next controls program will operate.

Chapter 5, "The Consequences of Price Controls," is based on economic analysis and practical experience. Using supply and demand curves, economists have been able to show quite clearly how controls reduce output and create shortages. Even if we accept the notion that big business engages in monopolistic practices, it can still be demonstrated that controls cause shortages of labor and products.

Interestingly enough, price *freezes* are seldom analyzed in economics textbooks. Yet it is precisely such freezes that have the greatest popular appeal. Almost every recent example of an incomes policy has started with a freeze. In chapter 5 I explain how a price freeze can eventually cause severe distortions in a dynamic economy. Freezes can, among other things, create permanent dual-pricing (even in the same locality), widen price differentials between domestic and international prices, and lock companies into unprofitable production of certain goods.

Shortages are the offspring of price controls. In fact, the more stringent the government program, the more widespread the shortages. The number and extent of shortages are the best indicators government can have of how well its plans are going. I once facetiously suggested this "shortage indicator" to the Bureau of Labor Statistics, and they said they would take it into consideration when controls were reimposed!

We can demonstrate the existence of shortages using supply and demand curves, but just how are these shortages created? After studying numerous cases, I have found that, under controls, companies find it to their advantage to *reduce* the production of high-volume, low-profit-margin goods ("basic necessities") and *expand* the production of low-volume, high-profit-margin goods ("luxuries"). I believe this phenomenon is one of the chief forces behind the gradual disappearance of goods and services, especially the cheap and popular varieties.

Chapter 5 also includes a discussion of other distortions that take place in a controlled economy: the artificial creation of "new" products, extravagant waste in business expenses, under-

21

investment due to uncertainty, the production of "useless" goods, and the increasing importance of time.

Shortages are what bother the public most, however. Favored customers, bribes, queues, and black markets naturally follow. In chapter 5 I explain how distortions under wage and price controls naturally lead to further intervention by the government. Government finally ends up imposing rationing, extends controls to exports and imports and other previously uncontrolled items (even farm products), subsidizes production of certain items deemed essential to the "public" interest, and so on. Economist Ludwig von Mises appropriately foresaw this situation in his famous article "Middle of the Road Policies Lead to Socialism."

Chapter 6, "The Government as Regulator," is a consideration of the all-important question of how the federal government enforces its controls programs, what forms of punishment it inflicts for "economic crimes," and the growth of the bureaucracy during such programs. Next to income taxes, price controls do more than any other government scheme to expand the role of government in the lives of practically everyone. Freedom in a very real sense is deeply wounded. The similarity between price controls and taxation is a very close one in this regard. Both involve numerous, often contradictory, and sometimes incomprehensible rules. Is it not interesting that the enforcement and reporting arm of the Nixon "stabilization program" was the Internal Revenue Service?

In chapter 6 I look into what kinds of biases government bureaucrats have in dealing with various groups around the country. For example, do they favor big business or small firms? I also examine the cost of controls, IRS compliance rules, and the allegation that at times the government condones black market activities. Finally, I review past court cases and the evidence regarding the constitutionality of wage and price controls.

Chapter 7, "The Consumer Faces Price Controls," is devoted to courses of action that will prepare consumers for controls and aid them in obtaining the goods and services they need when shortages appear. Topics discussed include the advantages of food co-operatives, foreign buying clubs (since imports are generally exempt, foreign consumer goods should be in plentiful supply), tips on buying used goods and purchasing at auctions (another exempt area), and how to deal with rationing by either retail stores or the government.

The consumer often feels helpless when waiting in long gasoline lines or upon finding empty shelves at the supermarket. The only course of action may seem to be to write a letter to a congressman. Fortunately, however, there are more promising recourses, and they are outlined in this chapter.

Chapter 8, "The Worker Faces Wage Controls," is for the wage- and salary-earner. Like consumers, workers, white or blue collar, may feel powerless when confronted with a freeze on income, a cutback in the workload, or layoffs and unemployment. In this chapter I report on legal methods used in the past to obtain raises and other benefits—despite the existence of controls. I also suggest ways that an employer can increase benefits for his employees to keep them from looking elsewhere for work (this has been a major problem in the past). Finally, I show how an employee can start his own business as a way of adding to his income.

Chapter 9, "The Businessman Faces Price Controls," is perhaps the most lucrative section for study. Businessmen are generally much more flexible than most employees in their ability to shift capital and resources into different, more profitable avenues of production. In addition, hundreds of exemptions have existed in the past under controls programs for products and services, and it has been relatively easy for businesses, both large and small, to take advantage of these uncontrolled market areas. Of particular interest is the "small business exemption," which existed under the Nixon stabilization program.

In chapter 9, I report on some of the more unusual ways businessmen have circumvented government regulations, such as changing products, tie-in agreements, barter arrangements, elimination of discounts or rebates, shifting of discretionary costs, and reductions in services or quality. There is always an element of legal uncertainty in these methods; it is a "gray" area. Some of these methods have been decreed illegal after the fact: a reduction in quality, for example, has been determined by government bureaucrats to be the same as a price increase for all practical purposes. It is really amazing how far the government has gone in past programs to eliminate any and all methods of shirking regulations. The Office of Price Administration during World War II published a *Basic Manual* for all of its investigators. Under "miscellaneous price violations," the manual listed dozens of supposedly illegal methods of getting around controls. Chapter 9 provides a close look at all of them, as well as other such lists from other controls periods.

There are also various ways of preparing for controls in advance, so that when they are imposed, the smart businessman will be in a better position than his competitors to deal with the effects of controls (i.e., shortages in products and labor). "Stocking up" is just one possibility. Raising prices in advance is another, although this is difficult to do when your competitors maintain their prices. Fortunately there are ways to raise prices and *still* remain competitive, e.g., discounting, rebates, et cetera. In order for the businessman to fully take advantage of the ideas presented in this chapter, he must be prepared to implement some of them long before controls return, thus establishing a "customary business practice," often the basis of exemption during the Nixon controls. I provide some examples in chapter 9.

There are also many ways in which businessmen can profit from artificial shortages and other distortions in the economy. Examples include buying goods at *controlled* prices and selling them at *uncontrolled* prices ("arbitrage"), acting as a middleman in buying and selling scarce goods, shifting production from domestic to company-owned foreign plants and then importing the goods produced (which would usually exempt them from controls), and so on. Needless to say, this is one of the most fascinating areas of study, and chapter 9 includes much useful information on it.

Chapter 10, "The Landlord Faces Rent Controls," is written to aid primarily the landlord. However, tenants can also gain insights from it. Because rent is the largest single item in the budget of many Americans, rent control has become a popular policy on the local as well as the national level. But effective rent control is not only harmful to the landlord, who suffers losses in income, but to the apartment dweller who faces a housing shortage and higher occupancy rates. New York City's lengthy experience with rent controls (since World War II) is proof enough of the damage that can be done.

Still, landlords have become notorious for devising ingenious methods to avoid the pains and losses of rent ceilings. Typical strategies have included tying agreements ("You can rent this apartment for $200 a month if you buy my child's 'Picasso' for $100"), shifting of apartment ownership to co-ops or condominiums, charging for superficial services, and restructuring of apartments to allow more tenants with less space per occupant. Once again, government controllers have disallowed some of these techniques, declaring them illegal. Obviously, it pays to make a careful study in this area.

Chapter 11, "The Investor Faces Price Controls," should prove helpful to investors and speculators. Like inflation, international crisis, and depression, price controls can have a devastating impact on the price of stocks, commodities, the futures market, precious metals, foreign exchange, government and corporate bonds, and so on. Though in many cases the impact is uncertain or unforeseen, there are at times clear and inevitable results in investment areas. For example, price controls invariably increase the demand for *uncontrolled* goods, and the wise investor will shift his investments away from controlled markets into uncontrolled areas. Since the effects of inflation are repressed in controlled markets, price rises are greater than they otherwise would be in uncontrolled areas—antiques, rare books, coins, art, imports, et cetera.

Profitable opportunities are not always that simple for the investor, however. The profits of a large corporation may temporarily rise if, for example, the government imposes strict wage controls but lax price controls. This could result in favorable stock prices for these companies. (This is what happened during World War II and Phase II of Nixon's program.) Clearly, there is no substitute for keeping informed about the latest economic news and government policy.

In chapter 11, the effects of controls on stocks, bonds, options, and other investment alternatives are considered in light of recent history. I also examine in detail the effects of controls on the commodity futures market, which can be virtually paralyzed under tight controls.

Chapter 12, "The Black Market," is a revealing chapter. For obvious reasons, little concrete information has been gathered on the black market. It has quite a history, though, and I would be remiss not to deal with it. Black markets go hand in hand with price controls, though it is possible for black or "gray" markets to exist under unusual uncontrolled market conditions. For example, shortages can arise under rapidly rising demand (such as during a runaway inflation), creating the temporary establishment of middlemen who buy and sell goods and machinery at "outrageous" prices. Ticket "scalpers" are a good everyday example.

The black market has been referred to as *the* market, since supply and demand do not operate freely under controls. But it would be seriously misleading, I believe, to ignore the illegal aspects of the black market, which can undermine public respect for law.

Chapter 12 includes a short history of the black market, with particular reference to the black markets that were so pervasive for several years in post–World War II Germany. The illegal market was so prevalent in Germany during this time that some estimate that 50 percent of production ended up in illegal channels!

A Personal Note

Now that I have completed a roundup of all the chapters in this book, permit me one personal note. I am sure that my coverage of various legal schemes used to avoid controls is incomplete. There are probably hundreds of useful methods that I have somehow overlooked. I would be very grateful to anyone kind enough to share such information with me. Please write to me at P.O. Box 8233, Washington, DC 20024.

A Moral Judgment

One of the most important issues facing Americans is our moral attitude toward controls. Unfortunately, this question is often buried under the day-to-day battles that go on concerning the operations of a controls program. Considering the results of past Gallup and Harris polls, though, Americans in general seem to have no apparent scruples about the imposition of controls for the "good of the nation."

Is it morally just for government to tell individuals or companies what prices they must charge for their services and goods? In *There's No Such Thing As a Free Lunch,* Milton Friedman aptly observed: "The [Nixon] controls are deeply and inherently immoral. By substituting the rule of men for the rule of law and for voluntary cooperation in the marketplace, the controls threaten the very foundations of a free society. By encouraging men to spy and report on one another, by making it in the private interest of large numbers of citizens to evade the controls, and by making actions illegal that are in the public interest, the controls undermine individual morality."

Are Controls Constitutional?

Another important and related question (which is discussed in more detail in chapter 6) is: Are wage and price controls an infringement on your constitutional rights? If they are, then it should not make any difference how many Americans favor price regulations. Nor should it matter if a democratically elected Congress votes overwhelmingly for controls (though this would complicate the issue and would sooner or later call for turning the question over to the federal courts).

It is worth noting that federal courts have generally upheld the constitutionality of wage and price regulations. And understandably so. Federal judges are, after all, part of the government themselves. ("Don't bite the hand that feeds you.") Because judges are salaried by the government many tend to support most (though certainly not all) *fundamental* legislative decrees. There never has been nor will there ever be a wholesale repudiation of legislative law under this judicial system.

The constitutionality of federal taxation is a case in point. Federal judges almost to a man have ruled in favor of the IRS against citizens who have recently refused to pay their income taxes. In doing so, many of the judges have made a mockery of the Bill of Rights. One federal judge actually said that *regardless of the constitutional rights* of the citizen, he was "going to make an example out of any tax protestors" (which he did, by the way).

Why is this the case? For the simple reason that if the courts upheld the view that taxation is unconstitutional, it would mean the end of government as we know it. And neither the courts nor Congress will ever allow that—nor would the great majority of Americans want it!

Wage and price controls are not as central or potent an issue as taxes, however. Nevertheless federal judges know that rulings in favor of "evaders" of price controls would counter national policy. It is worth noting that in *every single court case* that could have resulted in overturning past government controls programs, the federal courts ruled in favor of the government's position.

There are a number of ways that wage and price controls infringe on the rights of Americans, notwithstanding rulings by the federal courts. For example, they violate the First Amendment. Controls on newspaper prices clearly interfere with freedom of the press. During World War II, the government did not try to interfere with the price of newspapers for fear of infringing on First Amendment freedoms. But more recently, during the Nixon controls, the government forced the *Washington Post* and the *Washington Star* to rescind their fifteen-cent newsstand price. Federal bureaucrats are apparently becoming more bold now (as they are in virtually all other areas).

Using a broad interpretation, controls are also contrary to the Fifth Amendment, which states ". . . nor shall private property be taken for a public use without just compensation." In addition, due to their inherently capricious and discriminatory nature, controls constitute a denial of equal protection under the law (particularly when certain companies, wage-earners, and products are exempt) and due process under the Fifth and Fourteenth amendments.

Perhaps the most fundamental reason why controls are unconstitutional is that by their very nature they deny both buyer and seller their choices to charge and accept higher prices.

Controls are imposed in the first place because people of *their own choice* are not agreeing to stable prices. Wage and price regulations, then, clearly violate voluntary agreements and contracts between citizens. Even John Kenneth Galbraith, who is no enemy of controls, admits to this fatal flaw of controls programs. "Price-fixing," Galbraith admits, "is clearly a case of government without the consent of the governed." How can any government program that fails to obtain the consent of the governed be constitutional?

Civil Disobedience?

If controls are an infringement on the rights of Americans—as I believe they are—what should be our attitude toward them? Are we morally obligated to disobey these laws?

Of course, if you want the courts to make a constitutional judgment on controls, committing a flagrant violation may be the first step. It is not the only step, however. A suit questioning the constitutionality of a federal law can be filed in a federal court without breaking the law. But assuming that the judge rules in the government's favor, what then? Should citizens who still regard the controls as conflicting with their own sense of justice comply with "unjust" laws?

There is no simple answer. It all depends on the situation. For example, during the postwar period in Germany, every business (yes, *every* business) engaged in the black market from time to time to obtain necessary materials, no matter how distasteful it seemed. Even the Allies in control condoned buying in the black market.

Under less severe conditions, illegal activities cannot be recommended. But who is to decide how severe a situation is? For example, while most companies were doing fairly well under Nixon's stabilization program, a few companies actually faced the prospect of bankruptcy as a direct result of controls. (In many cases, companies were about to raise prices due to increased costs, but were prohibited from doing so by the 1971 freeze. Consequently, some companies were forced to sell their goods below cost.) The Cost of Living Council adopted an exception rule in order to "prevent gross inequities," but believe it or not, they ruled that impending bankruptcy was not a sufficient condition for making an exception! Under such conditions, it would be extremely difficult to live within the rules.

There are other moral questions, too. The businessman is, once again, faced with a serious dilemma under price controls. Under strict below-market ceilings, should he try to maintain quality at the risk of losing profits or going bankrupt, or should he reduce quality in some legal or quasi-legal way to maintain his prices and stay in business? But even then he may lose customers who complain of shoddy goods! So, finally, should he seek out surreptitious ways to get around the price ceiling while maintaining quality?

After exhausting all the legal and political channels under which controls have been judged legal, I do not believe advocating continued disobedience of the law can be justified, except as noted above. If all of us disobeyed laws that we regarded as unjust, there would be little room for compromise and orderly conduct in society. Society would disintegrate. Such a situation would "render evil for evil."

The major theme of this book is that there are numerous *legal* ways to "beat the system." Ignoring for now the major problem of deciding what is and what is not legal, there can be no problem here. In taxation, for example, tax *evasion* is illegal, but tax *avoidance* is not. The IRS has no objection to using perfectly legal loopholes to reduce tax liability.

Similarly, controls *avoidance* is entirely lawful, while *evasion* of controls is illegal. Unfortunately, the terms *avoidance* and *evasion* have often been used interchangeably. But the distinction is an important one.

Legally avoiding controls or even profiting from them can in many ways be considered "rendering good for evil." Such practices are socially desirable in the sense that they make it possible for customers to enjoy a greater supply of goods and services.

Not everyone would agree with this viewpoint, of course. Many might feel that avoiding and profiting from a price controls program may not be illegal, but it is contrary to the "spirit of the law." This has been the traditional wisdom for years. During World War II, for example, "profiteers" were social outcasts.

OPA Commissioner Leon Henderson called them "unpatriotic." Chester Bowles referred to them as "unscrupulous businessmen who will do anything for their own personal profit." During the Nixon administration they were characterized as the "spoilers." In a *Wall Street Journal* article, former chairman of the Council of Economic Advisers under Nixon, Paul W. McCracken, stated, "A freeze inherently penalizes the good guys, who tried to be modest with price adjustments, and the guy who went for all he could get while the getting was good is rewarded."

Is This Book Unpatriotic?

No doubt people with such views will see this book as unpatriotic. But I do not see it that way. To me, *controls* are unpatriotic, not the people who try to beat them. This gets back to the old question of causes and symptoms. Are the economic distortions the evil, or is it that which caused the distortions in the first place? Is the shrewd entrepreneur who takes advantage of the controls unpatriotic, or are the controls themselves? Or, to make the comparison more clearly, who killed the deceased victim? Was it the bullet? Or was it the murderer? I think the answer is obvious. Let us lay blame where blame is due.

During the energy crisis, petroleum companies were blamed for *exporting* petroleum to gain higher prices and profits in the international market. What brought on this seeming distortion? Who was at fault? In reality, price controls on domestic oil were responsible for this perverse situation. Without government restrictions, these distortions would never have occurred.

Unpatriotic? Spoilers? Profiteers? Bad guys? I do not think so. I tend to side with Milton Friedman in calling them "ingenious" men, who circumvented controls that "conflicted with their individual sense of justice."

Changing Winds in America

But the philosophical underpinnings of this book go beyond an assessment of patriotic motives. In many ways, this book re-

31

flects the "signs of the times." Dramatic changes have taken place in the United States over the past decade. For one thing, disillusionment and frustration with the political system have become widespread. Time and time again citizens who favor limited government have lost election after election and vote after vote in Congress. Socialistic programs are being imposed by Congress and national administrations of both political parties.

Nothing is more demoralizing than being faced with defeat after defeat. Many people have simply given up any hope of transforming the social, economic, and political Welfare State of today. Their only hope is to stem the tide and *slow down* the growth of government. But it seems that it can never be reversed. The goal is no longer to reduce spending and social programs. Political leaders today only speak of what is politically possible, not what is rationally justifiable. Few if any statesmen run for office anymore.

Electing a "conservative" president or even a "conservative" Congress will not do much to change the course or size of the bureaucracy. Anyone who has worked for government or who deals with government on a daily basis knows that. Anyone who has visited Washington and has seen the never-ending number of government buildings and the continuous construction of new buildings knows that they will never be torn down or sold to private concerns. Even if the economy does not grow, the government will. Just look what happened when the U.S. Postal Service, supposedly now a quasi-private corporation, tried in 1976 to close down a few insignificant post offices. Congress refused to let it happen.

For two years I worked as a Central Intelligence Agency economic analyst. I know what it is like to become involved in the inner workings of government. Boring! A waste of time! Oh, sure, there are legitimate areas of concern for the federal government, but oftentimes they are hard to find. I remember literally hundreds of days when there was simply nothing of any consequence to be done. I would end up reading page after page of the *Washington Post* and the *New York Times,* and believe me, things have to be pretty boring to read both these papers front to back. There were many mornings when I found myself dozing at my desk. Now I know why government workers drink so much coffee.

Most of the time we produced trivia. There was a built-in point system to see who could produce the most trivia. There were a dozen analysts in my office being paid $12,000 to $25,000 a year to keep tabs on economic developments in Latin America. At the same time, I knew of several other government agencies that had dozens more paid to do practically the same thing. I considered my job a waste of taxpayers' money, and when I left, I recommended that the number of analysts in our office be cut to four. It was not, of course, and they even had a replacement for me when I left.

What was most appalling was the duplication, especially with other government agencies. I remember working months on a memorandum on the world beef outlook (yes, Virginia, the CIA *is* into everything!). One of the reasons for this project, I was told, was that the White House did not trust the views of the Department of Agriculture; we were doing independent studies to confirm or deny what Agriculture felt about the situation. After eight months of hard work and"co-ordinating" (a favorite word in government), the paper was published. The results? We came to the very same conclusions as Agriculture. Then, after all that, the Council of Economic Advisers wanted to suppress public release of the document because it did not agree with our findings. (Two years later, we were proven right about the price of beef. It went down.) To me nothing was more frustrating than to see work like that shoved under the table.

Bureaucracies have a life of their own. No president or Congress is going to rock the boat. The president may order a 10 percent reduction in staff, but it never gets that far. Some temporary reduction is made through attrition and maybe a few "rifs" (reductions in force), but sooner or later the desks are all filled again. These are professional, full-time bureaucrats who have years invested in their own pension funds. Even when waste is flagrantly apparent in government, there is no real possibility for radical change.

In addition to the inherent immobility of bureaucracy, the political influence of an individual citizen is on the wane. Today's Congress is influenced more and more by lobbyists and pressure groups. The lone individual has little chance of making any kind of impact. I can well recall the one time I was motivated enough to write my congressman about the energy crisis. But to no avail—the "answer" came as a form letter wherein the congressman stated his own views on energy without any reference to what I had written to him.

But can you really expect anything different? Members of Congress are already swamped with thousands of letters. How could they possibly answer each one individually? In fact, they do not even read them, let alone answer them.

All of this confirms my suspicions that effective political action is near the end of its rope. "Politics is dead," said Karl Hess. If it is not dead, it is at least moribund.

Turning Political Defeats into Economic Gains

Even so, we must not despair. If I felt that the economic and political conditions facing this country were hopeless, I would not have written this book.

We are entering a different, new era—one in which political defeats can be replaced by or turned into economic gains! Losing political battles does not mean we have lost the war. It should be comforting to know that it is possible to profit from the very economic policies that were instituted by Congress.

Irresponsible policies of Congress and the White House do not run their course without paying a toll. Governments reap what they sow, like everyone else. When the Federal Reserve inflates the money supply at double-digit rates, the stage is set for an inflationary boom to be followed by a depression. In the past several years, wise investors have been able to take advantage of these actions by buying gold and other related investments generally regarded to be inflation hedges.

When governments choose to establish fixed exchange rates while at the same time inflating their currencies at a greater rate than in other countries, the inevitable result is devaluation. The economic crisis that follows becomes a heyday for foreign-exchange speculators.

When governments impose economic embargoes (such as

OPEC's 1973 oil embargo), effects are felt not just at the retail level, but in stocks, commodities, precious metals, and foreign currencies. Investors and traders who understand the effects of the embargo are able to profit handsomely.

The same is true with wage and price controls. We can do all we can to dissuade Congress from enacting this kind of legislation. We can write letters, join lobbying groups, vote, and make personal contacts. But if controls are still legislated, all is not lost. This book can be instrumental in helping you prepare for the worst and possibly even profit at the same time—all with perfectly legal methods.

Looking Ahead

One of the most important insights to be gained from a study of wage and price controls is the importance of using history to put things in proper perspective. With history as a reference, we can better see the future. Remember that it was only a couple of years ago that double-digit inflation was at its peak. And for most Americans—including some experts—it came as a complete surprise. People should have been preparing for the coming high prices, controls, and shortages in late 1972, before it was too late and when shortages were not obvious.

Now is the time to prepare for the next time around.

Part I

The Economics and Politics of Price Controls

Chapter Two

Why Price Controls Are Coming

On August 15, 1971, President Richard M. Nixon made his surprising announcement imposing a ninety-day freeze on wages, prices, and rents. It was exactly one year to the day after he had received authority from Congress to establish controls at will under the Economic Stabilization Act of 1970.

The decision was not a complete surprise to those who had been watching closely. Nixon's administration had already taken a number of steps to "control" inflation, including the establishment of a board to oversee wages and prices. An election year was approaching, and the Democrats were mounting a major attack on the Nixon administration, blaming it for the twin evils of inflation and recession, especially during the summer of 1971.

Yet Nixon denied a thousand times that he would ever use the authority he was given by Congress. One wonders, then, why he signed the legislation in the first place. We will probably never know for sure. The administration said that it was because stand-by authority for controls was attached to an important defense production bill; one could not be rejected without the other. But since "riders" are a common means used by Congress to pass controversial laws, the administration's reasoning is unconvincing.

After the president's speech, Senator William Proxmire made a sage comment, "Things will never be the same."

And so they will not. For the first time in modern American history, national controls were tried in the absence of a general war. Such a break in economic policy cannot be overemphasized. This pervasive government intervention into the marketplace during "peacetime" signifies a monumental shift toward totalitarian government. (Some commentators have pointed out the fascist implications of such legislation: "ownership" remains in private hands, but control is more and more given over to government bureaucrats.)

C. Jackson Grayson, the head of Nixon's Price Commission, made the following astute remark: "Once controls have been imposed in peacetime—even on a temporary basis as a sort of 'inflation interruptus'—the probability of their being reimposed in the future is increased. . . . The political pressures to freeze and reimpose controls will be much faster and greater if inflation rises again. Every experience with controls lessens our future will to avoid them." Grayson is firmly convinced that controls will return.

Price-fixing by the government is addicting. A staff member of the *Wall Street Journal* compared it to drug addiction. "Any junkie knows how hard it is to fight the temptation of a brief period of euphoria once the habit has become engrained." Controllers during Phase IV of the Nixon controls often bemoaned the difficulty they had decontrolling the economy. Some areas of the economy are still awaiting decontrol, years after the "temporary" program began.

If it is politically expedient, elected officials will find it easier and easier to bring back controls. Let us examine the present state of opinion among the ranks of government officials, economists, labor leaders, businessmen, and the public in general.

The View from Government: Preparing for the Next Round

It is important to realize that the controls apparatus is still in existence in the United States. The Price Commission, the Pay Board, and the Cost of Living Council are gone, but they have been replaced by the Council on Wage and Price Stability. Stand-by authority to impose controls has expired, and the wartime "emergency" powers granted the president by Congress have only recently been repealed.

The attitudes of the men who ran the last round of controls are revealing. C. Jackson Grayson was interviewed by *Business Week* after the Price Commission was dissolved. Asked, "Will we see a return to controls?" Grayson said, "I really fear that this is going to happen, that the nation will be weary of inflation, trying to keep up, each person ineffectively protecting himself. We'll begin to think, well maybe this time we could do it differently—better."

Grayson's experience is interesting. He took a leave of absence from the School of Business Administration at Southern Methodist University to head the Price Commission. He admitted knowing little if anything about controls. He came away from the experience favoring the free market more than ever before. This is not to say that Grayson is optimistic about the future of the free market in the United States. On the contrary, he seems to be more inclined to the pessimistic views of the late economist Joseph A. Schumpeter, whom he quotes in his *Confessions of a Price Controller*. Grayson concludes, "I am personally convinced that our economic system is steadily shifting *away* from private enterprise and a free-market, and toward central direction and public control."

Grayson is the first to point out that part of this centralization is the coming of *permanent* controls. He says, "Inflation is the number one problem for the American people and the world. It disrupts economic, social, and political systems. And if not checked, it increases the cry for a shift from a market-driven economy to one that is more centrally directed—to one where price and wage controls are not intermittent or in phases, but continuous as a part of an overall planned, mixed economy." And, in another part of his book, he states, "Without competition, wage-price controls may become not an option, but a necessity."

Although I agree that this kind of reasoning will lead to controls and that government leaders will justify their policies on these grounds, I take exception to Grayson's statement that a lack of competition necessarily requires controls. As I noted in

41

chapter one, here we are confronted with the problem of whether to treat the symptoms or the causes of a problem. The *symptom* is the lack of competition among many corporate industries and professional groups. The *cause* is federal and state laws that restrict entry of competitors (such as in the airline and trucking industries and the medical and legal professions), limit production in favorable areas, force companies into collective bargaining, and so forth.

The solution is not to make wage and price policies more restrictive, which could lead to additional distortions. Rather, the answer is to take away the legal umbrella, to deregulate the industries, to remove legal support for the restrictive practices of professional groups and labor unions.

Although recent Republican administrations have made some excellent recommendations along these lines, I doubt that they will be implemented. Consequently, the symptoms of monopolistic practices will continue—along with cries for more regulation, including controls on "big business" and "big labor."

Historical Working Papers

There is another very interesting development concerning how the government views the future of controls. After Nixon's program lapsed on April 30, 1974, without renewal by Congress, the Cost of Living Council authorized the publication of a number of research papers on practically every aspect of the controls program. Almost all of these papers were compiled and published under the title *Historical Working Papers on the Economic Stabilization Program, August 15, 1971 to April 30, 1974*. The three-volume, 1500-page (plus appendix) text was compiled at government (your!) expense. The following subjects were covered: policy planning, Congress and controls, price-control mechanisms, wage stabilization policies, economic controls on state and local government, case processing, price exceptions, compliance and enforcement, price data and data systems, removing controls ("The Policy of Selective Decontrol"), the impact of the Economic Stabilization Program on business, fixed investment, advisory committees, litigation under the economic stabilization program, communicating with the public, the history of petroleum price controls, rent controls, organization and management issues, food price controls (published separately), and "who's who."

There is some evidence that the *Historical Working Papers* are intended to serve as more than just historical and economic references. Repeated direct references are made throughout the work as to how the *Papers* will assist future controllers. In the forward, the directors of the *Papers* project note that "many believe that the recent Economic Stabilization Program will not be the nation's last experience with wage and price controls. Thus there may be a time when government personnel must review available historical and scholarly material to determine how to evaluate policy proposals before them or their superiors."

In the preface, the author speaks of the "next time around—should there be a next time." In several of the papers presented, the authors make or list specific recommendations of policies or courses of action for "future wage and price controllers" to either avoid or pursue.

Congress

What is the attitude of Congress toward controls? Now, several years after the expiration of the Economic Stabilization Act, Senator William Proxmire reports that there is virtually no support for controls. It was his Senate committee that drafted legislation for stand-by controls in 1970.

How quickly could the minds of our congressional leaders change? If the economic climate shifts and inflation resurges, Congress will quickly hear from irate constituents, and it will not be long before the president has standby powers again. Remember that today's Congress is essentially the same one that voted 257 to 19 (in the House) in favor of the Economic Stabilization Act in 1970. (Fortunately, that vote may overestimate the support for the program, since it was attached to a defense bill.)

The Views of Economists

Some professional economists see controls as a permanent feature of U.S. economic policy. The Brookings Institution, often referred to as the Democratic government-in-exile, recently published *Phase II in Review, The Price Commission Experience*. One of its conclusions was that "some form of controls or at least prior review of price and wage increases [is] likely to become a permanent feature of U.S. economic policy. . . . A mechanism will be established to keep a watchful eye on prices and wages." Specifically, the authors of the book recommend that the Employment Act of 1946 be amended to include guarantees of price stability. Also, they argue that a "stabilization board" should be permanently established, with periods of tenure for its members, appointment by the president with congressional approval, and so forth. Now that's permanent! (Have you ever heard of a regulatory agency being dismantled?)

More recently, senior Brookings economists have stated (in a recent edition of the *Brookings Papers on Economic Activity*) that some kind of "incomes policy" is inevitable. Economist George L. Perry analyzed inflation in ten major industrial countries, spotlighting the sharp rises in wage rates. He concluded that inflation will continue to be a serious problem in the years ahead, and that "conventional" austerity programs will not cure inflation and will be too painful in terms of unemployment. He concluded that "because the [Phillips] tradeoff curves are very flat in the short run and because the inertia of inflation is strong, slowing inflation with higher unemployment will be very costly. Strong incomes policies, such as those implemented by Harold Wilson's [British Labor] government, may be the only feasible answer to world inflation." (In a later part of this chapter, I will deal with the specific reasons why inflation seems to be a permanent fixture of our economy, as well as with its relationship to unemployment and depression.) In the same edition of the *Brookings Papers*, Arthur M. Okun, former chairman of the Council of Economic Advisers, opts for wage and price intervention, though with some reservations.

Paul Samuelson, probably the most well-known academic economist in the U.S., told *Boardroom Reports* that "a bout with wage-price controls is inevitable for some time in the next decade. Why? Because by then we won't have had them recently. They work in the short run—although admittedly, that short run has to be pretty short. We'll be seeing a stop-and-go economy over the next 10 years: inflation, controls and recession are all in the cards. But I'm uncertain of the timing. These are diseases of affluence, not a terminal economic illness." Certainly here is a self-fulfilling prophecy! Controls are indeed inevitable if the country blindly follows the inflationary policies recommended by Samuelson, something we have done in the past.

Economist Milton Friedman agrees with Samuelson on this point: ". . . it would be premature to suppose that we have truly learned our lesson. Price controls have been imposed repeatedly for more than two thousand years. They have always failed, yet they have been repeatedly resurrected. . . . I doubt that we in the United States have seen the last of price and wage controls."

Arthur F. Burns, chairman of the Federal Reserve Board, favored some form of "incomes policy" even before the Nixon plan was initiated. He was one of the first policy-makers to recommend a watchdog council for wages and prices. Today Burns continues to argue that high unemployment rates are not a practical instrument for producing a quick end to inflation, and consequently, he recommends some form of "incomes policy." Lately he has joined Galbraith in supporting controls over large corporations and labor unions.

Economic Studies Favoring Controls

Some professional economists have used their statistical and mathematical tools to develop models to test the impact of controls on wages, prices, et cetera. These econometric studies relate controls with economic variables.

Some of these models indicate that the Nixon controls were generally successful. One such econometric regression model, entitled "The Impact of the Economic Stabilization Program on Business Fixed Investment," was done by Roland G. Droitsch for the above-mentioned *Historical Working Papers*. According to his model's results, Droitsch concludes that the controls program had a favorable effect on the economy: ". . . the Stabilization Program—by initially strengthening business and consumer confidence—appears to have stimulated investment spending during the controls period. The program initially appeared to have provided a solution to the problem of inflation, and throughout Phase II, the economy experienced strong real growth along with low rates of inflation.''

In the Brookings study of Phase II of Nixon's program, *Phase II in Review,* the authors note that during this period, 1971–72, the consumer price index moderated. There was a modest reduction of price changes in manufacturing and in other areas, and the gross national product grew 6.4 percent.

In a series of articles on the economic impact of wage-price controls presented at the American Economic Association's meeting in December, 1973, economists Robert F. Lanzillotti and Blaine Roberts referred to the following favorable effects of the Phase II controls: a reduction of price inflation of two percentage points, a small reduction in wage increases, an increase in GNP of $15–22 billion, a drop in the rate of unemployment, and an increase in productivity. They concluded that the distortions and regulatory costs were minuscule compared to the benefits!

Other economists and commentators have pointed out similar figures. The rate of inflation was brought down to 3 percent in 1972. Real output rose approximately 6 percent during the same year. The unemployment rate declined slightly and increases in employment were substantial. Profits rose in 1972, and wage earnings also rose in real terms. Wage increases were held down compared to the preceding four years. Finally, controls ''significantly'' reduced inflation in construction wages and health-care costs in 1972–73. Yes, President Nixon was right. It was a ''very good year.''

There are a number of serious if not fatal errors in these econometric studies, however. And by understanding the shortcomings of these models, we might come to the opposite conclusion. After all, if the controls along with monetary inflation caused a major recession in 1974, how could we possibly call it a ''very good year''?

The fundamental problem with econometric models is that they can easily lead to the post hoc ergo propter hoc fallacy: if two events take place at the same time or if one follows the other, then there is a cause and effect relationship. For example, the state of Wisconsin has a high per capita consumption of milk and it also has a high death rate due to cancer. According to the post hoc misapplication of cause and effect, we conclude that drinking milk causes cancer (or perhaps that having cancer makes one drink milk). This is a crude example, but it demonstrates the problem of the post hoc fallacy.

In the case of controls and economic variables (such as prices, wages, GNP), one cannot simply conclude that because controls existed while inflation declined, controls must have *caused* the decline. Without any controls, inflation might have declined anyway, due to other factors. (Inflation *was* already declining when the Nixon controls were imposed!) A good econometric model, of course, is expected to detect these other factors (independent variables), but there never can be any "proof positive" they are the *real* causes (even if the "coefficient of determination," R^2, is 1.00). Actually, a model cannot distinguish between the *dependent* variables (the effects) and the *independent* variables (the causes)! That decision must be made by the model-builder, based on theory and a priori assumptions.

Other problems with these models include a lack of proper data (the consumer price index, for example, probably underestimates the rise in prices), lack of a proper time frame (ignoring the effects of controls later on in Phase IV), and so forth.

Yet, despite these criticisms, the generally accepted view is that under Phase I (the freeze) and Phase II, wage and price inflation abated without too much distortion. Never mind later effects, some say; if we can only duplicate the earlier phases again, perhaps we can end up with the same results.

The Economic Case for Price Controls: The View of John Kenneth Galbraith

There is little support among professional economists for pervasive wage and price controls, especially on a theoretical level. Some economists regard the very use of the phrase "tools of wage-price regulations" as inappropriate. I do not agree. The use of the word *tools* is just as appropriate in this context as it is in connection with monetary and fiscal policy. All are tools of government intervention into the marketplace.

47

Walter Heller, past chairman of the Council of Economic Advisers, has supported controls on a partial basis. He told the *Wall Street Journal* that "in areas dominated by powerful unions and industrial oligopolies, a prod is needed if habitual inflation—inflation with no visible means of support from underlying supply and demand conditions in the economy—is to be broken."

Harvard economist and former U.S. Ambassador to India John Kenneth Galbraith is without a doubt the most formidable proponent of strong government wage-price interventions, and his views are worth examining. While C. Jackson Grayson acquired a distaste for controls after having been involved with them, Galbraith came out in favor of them after working for the Office of Price Administration during World War II. Based on his OPA experiences, he wrote a small book on *A Theory of Price Controls,* outlining his theoretical framework for a workable government scheme. (Galbraith regards this as his best theoretical piece.) Galbraith's *Theory* is a singular contribution to the field in the sense that few if any Western professional economists have written a theoretical treatise on controls (until recently, most would consider it a questionable undertaking at best).

In his introduction, Galbraith makes a sanguine remark: "If real peace continues to elude us and the economies of the United States and other countries of the West remain under tension, the theory of control is fated to become one of the expanding universes of economics."

From the very beginning, it has been Galbraith's contention that "price control . . . does, I am persuaded, have an important and perhaps an indispensable place in the pharmacopoeia of inflation remedies." He specifically pinpoints areas of the economy that need controls, while leaving other areas uncontrolled. Galbraith appears to favor *selective* controls, particularly if government planners wish to avoid rationing. (He has been a strong supporter of a freeze on all wages and prices.)

Shortages during World War II, Galbraith contends, only existed on a widespread basis in areas of near "pure competition," where there were many buyers and sellers, each having little control over prices. Examples include the food and clothing industries. Price controls in these areas necessitate rationing, which the government recognized in World War II. The Office of Price Administration suffered its greatest number of failures in these "purely competitive" markets.

On the other hand, the imperfect, concentrated markets of big business are controllable, according to Galbraith. "In the imperfect market—in particular, in the market of small numbers—price control *qua* price control is a technically workable instrument of economic policy, at least in the short run." These include wages set by collective bargaining with powerful unions and prices set by corporations in industries where these unions exist. The steel, automobile, electrical, and chemical industries would be examples. Galbraith contends that "in the United States, price controls need not apply to more than a few thousand of the largest firms." Freezes of wages and prices are unnecessary from a theoretical point of view. Union wages would be held to productivity gains and corporate prices would be relatively constant—not individual prices, but prices according to a weighted average.

According to Galbraith, powerful unions demand and receive above-market wage rates, and big corporations set monopolistic prices unrelated to the real desires of consumers. In simplified terms, the net result is shown in the following graph.

As can be seen from the graph, unions push up costs, causing an upward shift of the supply curve. Similarly, corporations create greater demand for their products, shifting the demand curve upward. The net result is the same output at higher prices, or, in other words, inflation. The remedy is to restrict these excess wage and price demands without hurting production.

This is the essence of the argument that inflation is cost-push rather than demand-pull. Unions force corporations to pay higher wages and salaries, and the corporations compensate for higher costs by raising prices.

There are a number of criticisms of this interpretation of cost-push inflation. First of all, if it is true that large corporations can raise prices to offset labor costs without penalty, why then should corporations wait for increased labor costs to raise their prices? Why not simply raise prices without regard to labor costs? Why not increase prices unilaterally before labor costs go

A VIEW OF COST-PUSH INFLATION

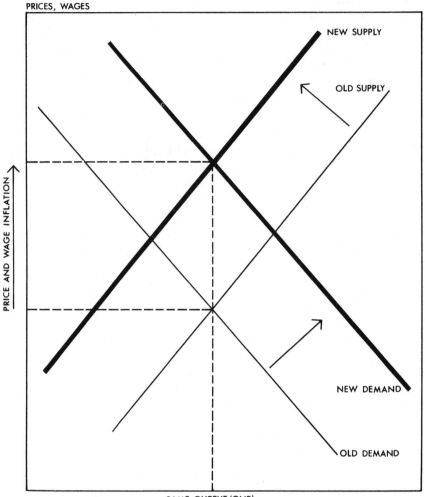

PRICES, WAGES

NEW SUPPLY

OLD SUPPLY

PRICE AND WAGE INFLATION

NEW DEMAND

OLD DEMAND

SAME OUTPUT (GNP)

up? The fact that corporations cannot do this, due to competition and the loss in consumer demand for their products, demonstrates the failure of cost-push to explain what really causes inflation.

Another serious defect in Galbraith's reasoning is revealed by the history of price controls. Why is it that large, "monopolistic" firms have suffered from controls just as much as smaller,

50

"purely competitive" firms? Larger firms have also been faced with product and labor shortages, cutbacks in production, et cetera. If Galbraith's thesis were true, controls on big business should work. Yet they have not for any long period of time.

In *There's No Such Thing As a Free Lunch,* Milton Friedman pointed out another criticism:

> One fairly modern argument given for price and wage controls is that inflation is produced by the concentrated power of business and labor monopolies, so that controlling a small number of strategic prices will suffice to control the price level in general. This argument seems impervious to the evidence that prices in products produced by the concentrated industries have on the average risen less rapidly than other products or indeed may even have fallen. It is equally impervious to the evidence that wages of unionized labor typically lag behind wages of nonunionized labor in the early stages of an accelerated inflation and catch up only later.

This critique of Galbraith is not meant to ignore the power of unions and big business, nor their impact on prices. But what is being questioned is the view that unions and big business set the stage for the rest of the nation. Yes, "wage-push" is a reality, but only for certain areas of an industry. Besides, wage-push may be more a cause of "frictional unemployment" than inflationary pressure.

The solution to this problem is not to impose selective wage controls, as suggested by Galbraith. This treats the symptoms, not the cause. In *Incomes Policy and Inflation: Some Further Reflections,* economist Gottfried Haberler suggests the following remedies:

> Radical solutions have been proposed, such as prohibition of industry-wide bargaining and dissolution of industry-wide unions. It is, however, politically impossible and probably unnecessary to go that far. Fortunately, there are many available measures short of radical solutions that would produce a marked moderation of the wage push, if they were systematically applied. Some examples are withdrawal of the special legal or de facto privileges which unions enjoy and which tilt the scale in collective bargaining in favor of organized labor, modification of minimum wage laws, changes in the policy of subsidizing strikes through welfare payments to strikers (and, in New York and Rhode Island, unemployment benefits also, after a strike has lasted eight weeks). Industrial monopolies or oligopolies are not much of a problem as far as inflation is concerned. (Prices in the public utility area,

51

"natural monopolies," are controlled, and usually over-controlled, anyway.) But any measures that strengthen competition, e.g., more vigorous antitrust action or liberalization of imports, have not only a direct favorable effect on prices but also serve to curb union power. For market power in the product markets always strengthens the market power of labor unions.

Will Business again Support Controls?

At the present time, businessmen are adamantly opposed to controls. So far they have good memories. They were the prime victims of shortages and other controls-created distortions, particularly under Phase III½ (the second freeze) in June-August, 1973, and Phase IV.

Unfortunately, though most big businessmen have good memories, they are also becoming more and more self-serving. They will support the free market only when it benefits them. They are becoming more like the mercantilists of old, seeking legal and financial favors from the government. This includes protection from foreign and domestic competition and labor unions. Businessmen would no doubt vote unanimously for wage controls—if prices were excluded. In the unlikely event this were to happen, businessmen would learn to regret that decision as well. Even for big business, wage controls are not harmless. Under effective wage limitations, labor shortages are inevitable and the results can be devastating. So far, businessmen have not had to learn this lesson. Under Nixon's program, wage restrictions were not stringent, and they did not last very long.

The self-serving nature of businessmen today is shown by the degree of support they rendered to Nixon's stabilization program. Even before controls were imposed, in May, 1970, the Business Council (leaders of top U.S. corporations) voted overwhelmingly for wage controls. The initial freeze in 1971 and Phase II were greeted enthusiastically by the U.S. Chamber of Commerce and the National Association of Manufacturers. During Phase III, when prices were accelerating, officials of the National Small Business Association wrote President Nixon, calling for "a return to the stringency of Phase II controls, in order to quench the fires of accelerating inflation."

Why did business support controls? Former Price Commissioner Grayson has pointed out that industry officials were particularly fearful of union power and its ability to extract huge wage hikes in the face of continued inflation. They generally felt that government intervention could keep down these wage hikes without unduly restricting price adjustments. It was a decision based on a kind of cost-benefit analysis. In the minds of most businessmen, the benefits far outweighed the costs.

Labor Support

Active participation by organized labor was sought by the government during both the World War II and Korean War controls periods, and the Nixon strategy was no different. Nixon's men obtained some support from labor in exchange for the imposition of national rent controls. Labor leaders also pressed for controls on profits, dividends, and interest, but Nixon agreed to this only indirectly, through voluntary participation and monetary and fiscal policy.

George Meany, head of the AFL-CIO, criticized the president's controls package in August, 1971. To him the freeze was "Robin Hood in reverse—robbing the poor to pay the rich." He regarded the Phase I freeze as probusiness and antilabor. After Phase I, Meany called for a freeze on profits and a ceiling on interest rates.

Labor became totally disenchanted with controls in 1973 and walked out of the Pay Board. Some bitterness is still evident. Labor will probably remain cool to any suggestions of wage and price controls, especially when run by Republican administrations.

The Public Favors Controls

As late as summer, 1974, just after the Nixon controls had expired, a Gallup poll revealed that Americans favored the reimposition of controls by a five-to-four margin. The public supported the concept of wage and price controls throughout the period 1970–75. They were particularly enamored of the idea of a freeze. In the latter part of 1973, for example, a Gallup poll showed that 52 percent of Americans sampled favored a return to the freeze, while 32 percent were opposed.

In September, 1972, another Gallup poll showed that only 9 percent of the public wanted price controls removed, 45 percent wanted them to be more strict, and 29 percent said they should remain the same. After controls ended, Jackson Grayson concluded in his book *Confessions* that "the public feels there should be more, not less, control in business and labor."

While controls were still on, Harvard economist Hendrik Houthakker commented, "Most people believe in controls, and in a democracy this is a factor which no one would want to ignore. To some extent the government has given the people what they want." And Grayson noted, "Throughout all the various phases of controls, the public has had, as it should, a strong influence on the direction, shape, and duration of controls. It *is* a political economy. . . ."

Public support for controls is not new. For example, several polls were made during World War II. In spring, 1941, two-thirds of Americans sampled by Gallup favored price controls. Throughout the war, the percentage actually rose, even in the face of widespread shortages and black markets! A few months before controls were imposed, 63 percent were found to approve of the price and wage ceilings. In 1944, during the height of rationing and shortages, 91 percent believed that prices should be held at prevailing levels. In the face of black markets in 1945, another Gallup poll revealed that 20 percent of Americans would condone occasional black market buying.

The extent of public support for wage and price regulations depends mostly upon one factor: the level of price inflation. Throughout the 1971–74 controls period, the call for more stringent controls fluctuated in direct proportion to the rate of inflation (this is no post hoc fallacy; the most common reason expressed by those polled was inflation). In the *Historical Working Papers,* analysts Henry Perritt and Robert Dresser noted, "When prices are stable, the public thinks controls are working and should be maintained; when prices are rising the public thinks lax controls are to blame and urges that controls be tightened." That is why decontrol is difficult. And when decontrol finally comes, if inflation accelerates, the public might tend to blame it on the end of controls rather than the fact that it was created by controls in the first place.

The Harris surveys during Nixon's Phase II (1972) showed that the public perceived that inflation rose at first and then tapered off at the end of 1972. During this same period, public support for stricter controls rose from about 33 percent to between 45 and 53 percent and then, during late 1972, dipped down to 28 percent. There appears to be a direct correlation between a perceived change in the rate of inflation and public support for wage and price controls. I have no doubt that this relationship will continue in the future.

Controls without Rapid Inflation?

From past experience, we can only conclude that a resurgence of inflation will bring with it a strong public demand for renewed controls. But this is not to ignore another definite possibility: the reimposition of wage and price intervention under persistent, "sticky" price inflation of 6 to 9 percent a year.

Even in the face of receding worldwide inflation rates, many countries have adopted "incomes and price policies." Canada has recently established its own "Anti-Inflation Board" and has developed a controls program involving price reductions, profit limitations, and wage guidelines. Also, as I noted above, the U.S. began its most recent controls program when inflation was *decreasing*.

Another country to adopt an incomes policy in the face of receding inflation is Belgium. Its program includes price freezes followed by limits to price increases.

But all of the other Western nations that have started controls programs are doing so in the face of rising inflation; the United Kingdom, New Zealand, and Finland all have double-digit rates of inflation. In the United States, wage and price controls are not likely unless inflation flares again. And if controls are imposed under single-digit inflation, the government plan is likely to be weak (guidelines, jawboning, and other similar measures).

Food-price increases are the most important factor affecting the consumer's perception of inflation. A rapid return to double-digit price increases in food will bring on the calls for a return to controls. The consumer price index is heavily weighted to changes in food prices, and they are always highlighted in the press.

Galbraith suggests that consistently high unemployment rates will also contribute to a consensus that controls are needed, but he does not elaborate.

The Prospects for Inflation

We have concluded that a sharp increase in prices will rekindle desires for controls, at least in the minds of the general public. Consequently, we need to answer this question: what is the outlook for price inflation?

In an effort to predict future prices, we need a clear understanding of the causes of inflation. Once we have established the fundamental causes, we can then look at those areas or institutions that promote inflationary policies.

The Cause of Inflation

There are a number of theories that seek to explain inflation. I have already discussed and largely dismissed one of them, the concentration of major industries and labor unions. Many Americans suspect that there is a direct relationship between inflation and federal deficit spending. Is this belief justified? If so, how do deficits translate into higher prices?

Deficit financing by the federal government has almost been a way of life since 1930. The year 1969 was the last year the federal government ran a small surplus. The total national debt was a little less than $300 billion in 1960. Today it is double that figure. Huge deficits were racked up during the Vietnam War, the recession years of the Nixon administration (1969–70), and during the Ford administration. The following graph vividly portrays the serious nature of the latest shortfall in government revenues. Up until 1974, in relative terms, federal receipts came close to matching expenditures. The deep recession of 1974–75,

FEDERAL BUDGET
(National Income Accounts Basis)

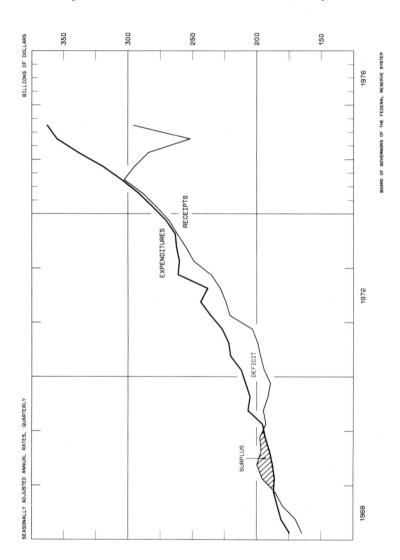

57

the worst since the Great Depression, caused federal income to fall off substantially. Expenditures continued to climb at a rapid rate, however; it was feared that a balanced federal budget would turn the recession into a full-fledged depression.

Serious inflation existed side by side with these deficits. Is there a relationship, or is it some kind of post hoc fallacy of false comparison?

The answer to this question is found in how the deficits were (and are) financed: The U.S. Treasury sells mainly short-term securities (maturing in less than a year) to individuals, banks, and other financial institutions. In other words, the Treasury competes with private business, home-owners, corporations, et cetera, in the capital and money markets for funds to pay for its deficits. In addition to selling new debt obligations, the Treasury often has to refinance old loans that have reached maturity. Moreover, annual interest payments on the national debt amount to over $40 billion and grow faster than the debt itself as interest rates rise. And interest rates tend to rise as a result of the Treasury's activities in the capital markets. In 1974, ninety-day Treasury bills yielded over 9 percent because of the tightness of the money market.

But how does this cause inflation? Interest rates may rise as a result of financing the federal deficit, but what about prices? In reality, it is difficult to see how deficit financing *directly* causes inflation. It is true, of course, that the additional funds the government raises from deficit financing are spent on goods and services. This naturally increases the demand for these particular goods and services—but, remember, at the same time, private markets have been deprived of funds due to the government's deficit financing and are forced therefore to spend *less* on their goods and services. So prices for the goods and services demanded by the private market tend to fall.

What is the outcome? Some prices rise, other prices fall. The net effect? Uncertain. Federal deficits do not in and of themselves increase the nation's money supply and cause generally rising prices of *all* goods and services. In order for federal deficits to have an inflationary impact on all goods and services they need the assistance of the Federal Reserve Board in Washington.

The Role of the Federal Reserve

The Federal Reserve Board, which consists of seven members appointed by the president and approved by Congress, is directly responsible for the supply of money in the United States. Essentially, when the money supply expands, more money is available to businesses, workers, and consumers, and this in turn increases the demand for goods and services. And herein lies the pressure for rising prices. When the money supply grows at a rapid pace (say, over 10 percent a year), prices are likely to accelerate. There is no direct, one-to-one correlation between monetary expansion and inflation, however. This is due to the fact that increases in the money supply affect different sectors of the economy more than others and at different times. Monetary expansion also creates the conditions for a trade cycle, but this will be examined later. The major point is that there is a definite relationship between the money supply and inflation. As Milton Friedman points out, "Inflation is always and everywhere a monetary phenomenon."

In recent years, the money supply has been growing at very high rates from a historical point of view. It even increased during the 1969–70 recession, explaining why we continued to have rising prices even during the recession. Prior to the 1969–70 recession, the money supply *fell* during recessions, and prices tended to fall too. The following graph (which appears here with the kind permission of the *Bank Credit Analyst*—Monetary Research Ltd., Hamilton, Bermuda) shows the movement in the narrowly defined money supply (M_1) and time deposits. Note that 1960 was the last year when the money supply declined for any long period of time. (It was also the last recession coupled with slightly falling prices.)

In 1972, the money supply, M_3 (broadly defined to include currency, checking accounts, and time deposits at banks and savings and loan associations), grew almost 11 percent, and this virtually sustained the inflationary boom of 1972–73. But the rate of growth in the money supply started to decline in 1973, to 9 percent, and then to 7 percent in 1974. As a result, the U.S. experienced its severest depression since the 1930s.

You may wonder why the Federal Reserve has taken such a

MONEY SUPPLY

Banking System Liabilities

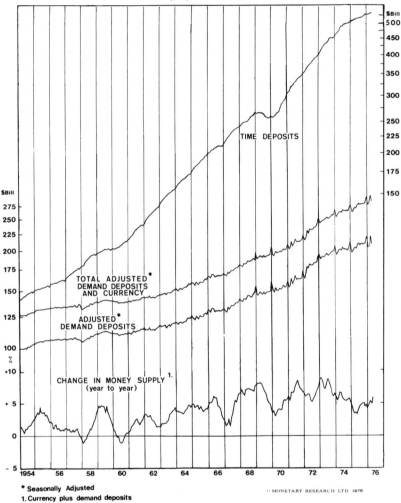

() MONETARY RESEARCH LTD 1976

* Seasonally Adjusted
1. Currency plus demand deposits

reckless course of action. Why did it not allow the money supply
to grow on a more even keel? One of the reasons is that the Fed
cannot control the money supply very precisely, due to the fact
that the money supply is dependent on commercial loans. But
there are two more important reasons. First, the Federal Reserve speeded up growth of the money supply in the early 1970s
to get us out of the 1969–70 recession. Second—and this is where
the role of the Federal Reserve becomes significant—the Fed

helped finance a portion of the large federal deficits of the early 1970s (amounting to $50 billion in 1972–73) by indirectly purchasing new government securities with new Federal Reserve notes.

This had to be done indirectly because the Federal Reserve cannot legally purchase securities *directly* from the Treasury except in extreme circumstances. It must buy them through private sources, individuals, banks, financial institutions, and so forth. The new dollars sold in exchange for government securities are then deposited in commercial banks. In this way the Fed expands the money supply. (When the Fed *sells* government securities, the money supply shrinks.)

Although not required by law, it is the official policy of the Federal Reserve to help finance large federal deficits with the printing of new dollars. (It is interesting to note that the Federal Reserve does *not* actually print these Federal Reserve notes. Rather, it is done by the Bureau of Engraving and Printing, an organ of the U.S. Treasury. Who says the Fed is independent? It is only fair to point out that only a small portion of new money involves the printing of new bills. Actually, most of the money is created through checks and bookkeeping procedures.)

The newly revised edition of the official publication *The Federal Reserve System, Purposes and Functions* states that the Federal Reserve "does not undertake any actions that, by themselves, would severely jolt market attitudes while a large U.S. Government financing is in process and thereby risk great unsettlement in securities markets generally."

Thus, we can conclude that large federal deficits *indirectly* cause inflation through the *direct* actions of the Federal Reserve. I might point out that it would serve as an unforgettable lesson to Congress if the Fed refused to finance a large federal deficit, especially if it did so during an inflationary boom. Perhaps Congress would then be far more reluctant to spend irresponsibly. I am afraid, though, that the only outcome of such a crisis would be for Congress to strip the Fed of its "independence" and to usurp control of the money supply itself.

Inflation and Depression

Cannot Congress reduce its deficit spending and the Fed cut the growth in the money supply to zero or at least to productivity gains (about 3 percent a year)? Would this not eliminate inflation?

The answer is yes, it would eliminate inflation, but for several reasons, neither Congress nor the Federal Reserve is willing to do so. A sharp cut in federal spending coupled with a sharp drop in the money supply would result in a credit crunch, loss of jobs, bankruptcies, and, in short, a major depression. The fact is that inflation and depression are closely interrelated. Moreover, as we shall see, it is the monetary inflation by the federal government that *causes* depression.

In this regard, it is worth noting that neither major "respectable" group of economists (the Keynesians and the monetarists) has really recognized this important relationship. Nor has either been able to develop a plausible explanation for the existence of both recession and inflation at the same time. Such a predicament clearly shows how little most economists know about the workings of our "mixed economy."

There *is* an explanation for the concomitant existence of inflation and recession. In his excellent *America's Great Depression,* economist Murray N. Rothbard argues that

> inflation is not the only unfortunate consequence of governmental expansion of the supply of money and credit. For this expansion distorts the structure of investment and production, causing excessive investment in unsound projects in the capital goods industries. This distortion is reflected in the well-known fact that, in every boom period, capital goods prices rise further than the prices of consumer goods. The recession period of the business cycle then becomes inevitable, for the recession is the necessary corrective process by which the market liquidates the unsound investments of the boom and redirects resources from the capital goods to the consumer goods industries. The longer the inflationary distortions continue, the more severe the recession-adjustment must become. During the recession, the shift of resources takes place by means of capital goods prices falling relative to consumer goods. During the depression of 1974–75, we have seen this occur, with industrial raw material prices falling rapidly and substantially, with wholesale prices remaining level or declining slightly, but with consumer goods prices still rising rapidly—in short, the inflationary depression.

Since Rothbard's explanation of how inflation creates a boom-bust cycle may be new to you (it is not generally taught in college courses, unfortunately), let me explain this theory more fully.

Given a supply of money in an economy, some of the money is spent on consumption goods and the rest is saved. The savings are invested in a chosen *structure of capital*. This structure-of-capital concept is extremely important. An undeveloped society will, for the most part, spend most of its resources on consumption. As a society develops, however, it spends more and more of its time and resources on investing in capital goods in an effort to have more consumption goods in the future. In order to do this, individuals in the society voluntarily reduce their consumption now and invest their savings in more capital goods. *This division between consumption goods and capital goods is the structure of capital.* Ultimately, the structure is based on people's time preferences—their preference for present satisfaction or future satisfaction—and this determines the ratio of consumption to savings in the economy. Time preferences also establish the "natural rate of interest" in the loan market.

The crucial introduction of the business cycle occurs when banks (led by the Federal Reserve in the U.S.) print new money and lend it to business. What is the immediate result? First of all, in the loan market the interest rate falls because of the additional supply of funds for investment purposes. So businessmen expand their investments, particularly in such "higher" orders of production as the capital goods industries, highly speculative investments in real estate, and so on. The boom has begun!

Over time, the new money sifts down through the factors of production in the form of wages, rents, and interest. The people with this new income begin spending it according to their regular consumption/savings habits. Their consumption/savings habits have not changed since the new fiat currency was injected into the economy. Remember that the new money for investment was created out of thin air by the Fed, *not* out of increased savings from the people.

Because there has been no shift in the old consumption/savings pattern, people will continue to spend their higher incomes in the old proportions. Demand will shift *away from* the higher orders of production (where the boom is) and move closer to the "lower" orders of production, consumer goods. The capital goods industries find that their investments were made in error for *lack of demand*. They are found to be wasteful and must therefore be liquidated. This initiates the "bust," or depression, that follows the boom.

The boom period of the cycle must therefore be viewed as a false prosperity. Genuine prosperity would result from a change to a lower time preference by individuals, who would save more, taking savings away from consumption and putting it in higher-order investments. But with bank-credit expansion, the inflationary boom turns out to be a period of wasteful malinvestment.

The depression is the process of adjustment by which the economy adjusts to the wastes and errors of the boom. It includes the rapid liquidation of these wasteful investments. "The depression, then, far from being an evil scourge," writes Rothbard, "is the *necessary* and beneficial return of the economy to normalcy after the distortions imposed by the boom. The boom, then, *requires* a 'bust.' "

For a number of reasons, inflationary prosperity oftentimes lasts for a considerable length of time. First, government may continue to pump new money into the economy to keep bankrupt companies from going under. Second, people's time preferences may change in favor of higher levels of savings.

The latter is a genuine and healthy development. It has often existed at the same time government inflates the money supply. This has led many economists to erroneously conclude that a "little" inflation is good for the economy. It happened in the 1920s and the 1960s, causing many economists to publicly praise the boom period and discount any predictions of a future "bust."

According to the above analysis, the following predictions can be made regarding the effects of a monetary expansion: First, in the expansion stage, there will be a general overexpansion in the production of higher capital goods and underinvestment in consumer goods industries. The prices of capital goods will tend to rise more rapidly than the prices of consumer goods.

Second, in the recession stage, the price of consumer goods always tends to rise *relative* to the price of producer goods.

Production falls more in the capital goods industries than in the consumption goods industries.

Third, the money supply will necessarily have to be expanded by the central monetary authorities at an ever *increasing* rate if they wish to avoid a recession. Contrary to the monetarist point of view, a constant increase in the money supply will inevitably lead to a recession. There is a universal tendency, therefore, for credit expansion to lead to runaway inflation if the government pursues a policy of avoiding a recession at all costs. However, this policy cannot persist forever and will leave no alternative but runaway inflation and eventual depression (such as in Germany in the 1920s).

I am not suggesting that the U.S. is headed for an inevitable bout with runaway inflation. U.S. monetary authorities are apparently willing to accept a recession for some period of time, and this is a good sign. But if the U.S. economy plunges into another full-scale recession due to the restrictive policies of the Fed, with imminent bankruptcies abounding, what the government would do seems obvious. It would reinflate vigorously, far beyond previous double-digit levels. This, coupled with wage and price controls, could only mean further centralization of power in the hands of government.

What Now?

The federal deficit climbed to nearly $70 billion in fiscal year 1976 and was expected to reach over $40 billion in fiscal year 1977. There may never be another budget year ending in a surplus.

Under recent depressed conditions, the Fed has had a fairly easy time of financing federal deficits, even though, as Treasury Secretary William Simon noted, the federal government's 1975 borrowing scheme was the largest ever undertaken in any single year of American history. In 1975, the Treasury accounted for over half of the debt-capital market!

Meanwhile, the Federal Reserve is said to have had a difficult time in stimulating the growth of the narrowly defined money supply. However, if one looks at a broader definition of the money supply, M_3, as discussed earlier, one will note that the money supply grew 12 percent in 1975. In 1976, an election year, it continued to grow at comparable rates.

If the money supply does grow faster—and this is difficult to predict—an inflationary boom of greater dimensions than that of 1972–73 will be under way. The money supply will need to grow extremely fast in order for this to happen, however. Rates would have to exceed the double-digit rates of 1972–73.

Whenever it comes, the next inflationary boom will be followed by even stronger deflationary forces, but in the meantime, a return of wage and price controls is practically inevitable. Perhaps Congress will adopt Congressman Wright Patman's bill, which he introduced in early 1973, calling for automatic mandatory wage, price, rent, interest, and profit controls whenever the consumer price index increased in any quarter at an annual rate of more than 3 percent.

In summary, not all sectors of the economy are favorable to wage and price controls. The 1971–74 experiment was a lesson to some. When inflation flares again—and I am fairly confident that it will—the general public will be the most vocal group calling for new controls. Businessmen and labor leaders in general may be reluctant to give their support, but they will probably give in, hoping for some benefits in return.

Chapter Three

Price Controls, Past and Present

Government intervention into wages, prices, interest and rents has been instituted from time to time since the beginning of civilization. In the United States alone, controls on prices have existed since before the American Revolution and have been tried three times in the past three decades. And now that we have experienced ubiquitous price-fixing by government in peace and war, who could rule out the possibility of its happening again?

In this chapter I will describe the various plans that have been instigated by various governments throughout history.

Early History of Controls

The earliest known case of rigid controls occurred over 3700 years ago in Babylon under the Code of Hammurabi. The code imposed strict limits on wages, prices, production, and consumption.

In the fourth century B.C., Athens placed severe controls on the grain trade and tried to enforce the regulations by hiring inspectors. Violators were subject to the death penalty.

In the ancient world, controls programs were not always responses to public demand. Many rulers were impressed with the philosophical support for these policies. For example, Plato argued in *The Republic* for controls over population as well as exchange. Usury and profit were to be curtailed in a "just" society. Foreign trade should be restricted. Later, Aristotle, although more sympathetic to the desire for private property, spoke out against excessive inequality and called for the control of usury, excess profits, and so forth. Prices in the marketplace should be "just." The Bible also includes references to the evils of usury. The Law of Moses stated, "Thou shalt not lend upon usury to thy brother" (Deut. 23:19). These philosophies were later incorporated into Catholic and Protestant doctrines, and they were used to support legislation limiting prices, wages, and interest.

The Emperor Diocletian, A.D. 301

For centuries, the Roman Empire suffered inflation due to the debasement of the Roman denarius. In a last-ditch effort to curb inflation, the Roman emperor Diocletian "commanded cheapness" of some 800 different goods and spelled out wage limits in his famous "Edict of A.D. 301." Wage ceilings were imposed on teachers, writers, lawyers, doctors, bricklayers, tailors, and almost all other professions. There were over 220 different price schedules for food products, 87 for hides and leather goods, 94 for timber and wood products, 385 for textiles and clothing, 32 for wicker and grass products, 53 for cosmetics, ointments, and incense, and 17 for precious metals.

The penalty for an offense was death. After thirteen years, the program was abandoned with reluctance. A contemporary historian, Lactantius, wrote:

> After that the many oppressions which he put in practice had brought a general dearth upon the empire, then he set himself to regulate the prices of all vendible things. There was also much blood shed upon very slight and trifling accounts; and the people brought provisions no more to markets, since they could not get a reasonable price for them; and this increased the dearth so much, that at last after many had died by it, the law itself was laid aside.

Sixty years later, Emperor Julian made a similar attempt to control prices, but was unsuccessful.

The Medieval Period

Price controls, especially on food and drink, were established by governments from time to time during the Middle Ages. In the twelfth century, Britain placed ceilings on the prices of bread, fish, and wine. Simon Litman in his *Prices and Price Control in Great Britain and the U. S. during the World War* reports:

> An attempt to control both the wholesale and the retail price of wine by fixing a maximum was made by the British Government in 1199. The measure failed and in 1330, after a long period of ineffectiveness, a new law was passed which required the merchants to sell at a "reasonable" price, the latter to be based on import price, plus expenses. This new measure of control proved as futile as the old one.
>
> The first attempt to regulate the price of wheat and bread was made in 1202. The most important ordinance on the matter was by Henry III. This ordinance fixed changing weights for the farthing loaf to correspond to six penny varieties in the price of the quarter of wheat from 12 pence to 12 shillings. The law was enforced locally on sundry occasions, but fell gradually into disuse.

The last laws fixing the price of bread were not repealed until 1815!

An interesting episode took place during the Dutch Revolution in the 1580s. When Antwerp was besieged by the Duke of Parma, the city authorities clamped price controls on nearly everything. Although this move was considered politically excellent, it proved to be a fatal blunder militarily. Because prices were held artificially low, the people inside the city bought up all the food and supplies as quickly as possible and shortages appeared. At the same time, traders and smugglers could not be induced to bring in new supplies for such small rewards. Consequently, Antwerp ended up blockading itself far more effectively than the Duke of Parma ever could have by himself!

Many other instances of price-fixing occurred during the Middle Ages and later in such diverse places as France, India, and Mongolia. In the thirteenth century, Kublai Khan set maximum prices on all kinds of goods. Before and during the French Revolution, mandated maximum prices had become routine.

Early U.S. Experiences

The American colonists several times imposed price ceilings on agricultural products. The historian William B. Weeden wrote:

The colonial history of the United States affords many instances of the failure of fixed prices to remedy the evils they were designed to cure. The governor and council of New England fixed the price of beaver at 6s in fair exchange for English goods at 30 percent profit, with the freight added. The scarcity of corn which was selling at 10s "the strike" led to the prohibition of its sale to the Indians. Under the pressure of this prohibition the price of beaver advanced to 10s and 20s per pound, the natives having refused to part with beaver unless given corn. The court was obliged to remove the fixed rate and the price which ruled was 20s. An equally fruitless attempt was made to regulate the price of labor. These regulations were enforced for about six months and then were repealed.

It is interesting to add that during this period American Puritans who violated the price regulations were classed with "adulterers and whoremongers."

Before the Declaration of Independence, the Continental Congress set price ceilings and fixed the value of the Continental dollar to gold. In 1774, Congress decreed "that all manufactures of this country be sold at reasonable prices" and that retailers "will sell the same at rates we have respectively accustomed to do twelve months last past." The price ceilings were widely ignored, however, and were abandoned in 1780. The Congress wrote the following resolution at that time:

It hath been found by Experience that Limitations upon the Prices of Commodities are not only ineffectual for the Purposes proposed, but likewise productive of very evil Consequences to the great Detriment of the public Service and grievous Oppression of Individuals. . . .

Many state and local governments continued to enforce price controls during the Revolutionary War. Boston, for example, published the names of violators "as enemies to their country, that the public may abstain from all trade and conversation with them, and the people at large inflict upon them that punishment which such wretches deserve." Yet fines, threats, and boycotts did not stem the tide of rising prices and the flood of paper money during this period.

World War I

Production controls and price-fixing of basic commodities were instituted during World War I. The consensus of government leaders has always been that war requires the sacrifice of citizens and that profiteering from war is immoral and unpatriotic. Price controls during war are an integral part of this consensus. The controls imposed during the First World War were not so pervasive as those of World War II. The War Industries Board was established and headed by financier Bernard Baruch. A Price-Fixing Committee was soon set up to regulate basic commodities. Food prices were indirectly suppressed through a vast network of licensing agreements run by the Food Administration under Herbert Hoover. Hoover granted federal licenses only to businessmen who promised to set prices to allow "a reasonable margin of profit." Surprisingly enough, *minimum support* prices were also set in 1917.

The government also sought to coordinate and allocate production during the war. The nation's railroads were seized by the government in 1917, and the Railroad Administration was established to carry out the war effort.

Nazi Germany, 1936–45

The first comprehensive program of wage and price controls was introduced by Adolf Hitler in 1936. Many of the modern techniques used to enforce controls were developed at this time. There is a striking similarity between the Nazi program and programs later used by Western governments, including the U.S.

After using selective controls for some time, Hitler appointed a commissioner for price control. In November, 1936, the commissioner declared a "Price Stop Decree," amounting to what is commonly called a rollback. All prices were made retroactive to October, 1936.

In a short time, in order to eliminate methods of evasion, the Third Reich prohibited the use of "combination sales" and the substituting of inferior goods at old prices. "New commodities" had to be priced according to prices for similar products.

Regulations were soon drafted to allow for the pass-through of costs. Markups were limited to specific maximum percentages for wholesale and retail sales of such goods as furniture, shoes, textiles, and wearing apparel. Base-period pricing was established in the textile industry. (All this sounds very similar to Nixon's Economic Stabilization Program, does it not?)

The purpose of the controls, according to Nazi propaganda, was to push for the social aim of self-sufficiency. "Economic misbehavior," flagrant violations, and evasive action brought the death penalty and the confiscation of property. However, the bureaucratic burden soon became unbearable. To simplify the program, many products were standardized and the production of luxury goods was forbidden. High profit margins were eliminated by decree. Rationing was instituted for food products and other basic necessities. Rations were distributed according to age and type of work. By the end of the war, rationing was widespread throughout Germany.

Postwar Germany under Allied Control

After the fall of the Third Reich, the Allied Control Council took over and decided that immediate economic freedom would bring social chaos. So the Allies continued the Nazi wage and price freeze.

To get some idea of the imbalance between spendable income and availability of goods during this period of Allied control, 1945–48, and why black markets became a way of life, consider this observation by historian Horst Mendershausen:

> In 1947, currency in circulation in the four zones of Germany and Berlin was estimated at about 10 times the amount that circulated in the Reich in 1936—when Hitler imposed the price stop—total currency and deposits at five times the amount of 1936, while the real national income was put at roughly one-half of that of the Reich of 1936. . . .

There were other peculiarities in the German situation. As in the U.S., Germans had substantially increased their savings during the war when consumer goods were not readily available. However, after the war, most Germans knew that their old currency, the Reichsmark, would soon be replaced. There were strong rumors that any future currency conversion would be scaled down to a small fraction of the value of the Reichsmark at the time, as much as a 90 percent devaluation.

As a result of these factors, on top of price and wage controls, it was almost impossible to buy anything—except ration tickets—with Reichsmarks. So the Germans turned to barter. Fixed swap terms developed between industry and agriculture. There was a rush into goods and hoarding; this was even encouraged by such German leaders as Ludwig Erhard. It was estimated that 50 percent of output went into hoards or was used for barter! When it was thought that coins would be converted at better terms than the paper Reichsmark, there was a big rush into coins.

Black markets became pervasive in postwar Germany, and controls were violated openly in many cases. Wages beyond the ceilings were paid in kind. "The compensation trade," as it was called, involved these barter deals and was always transacted at "legal prices." This activity was often condoned by the authorities. One estimate is that between 1945 and 1948 German farmers were able to obtain only one to 2 percent of farm machinery, parts, and fertilizer through legal channels—the rest came through the black market or through barter arrangements. It was reported that, no matter how degrading or disgusting, every person at one time or another participated in the black market.

Without the utility of the Reichsmark, commodities such as cigarettes emerged as currency and frequently bought goods that the Reichsmark could not. Some saw it as a reverse of Gresham's law: the "good" money drove out the "bad"!

Newsmen from the U.S. and England often mistook the widespread use of cigarettes as some kind of "addiction" for cigarettes that was peculiar to the German people. Britain's *Sunday Express,* for example, carried the following story on "How the Cigarette Rules Germany":

> Germany is a land almost run on cigarettes. Seventy-five percent of everyday crime in the country is traceable to cigarettes. . . . You can't throw a cigarette stump away without someone diving into the road to pick it up. Nearly everyone does it, no matter of what social position. . . . A large percentage of the German cigarette buyers are women. At times, they become quite maniacal, selling their children's food, their belongings and even themselves to get cigarettes. One cannot possibly imagine the lengths to which people who lack tobacco will go to get a smoke. It is far worse than hunger.

There is no doubt that many Germans did go to extreme lengths to smoke a cigarette, particularly at the end of the war. This was a major reason that cigarettes became a medium of exchange. But once cigarettes became a general medium of exchange, their nature changed. No longer did cigarettes simply serve as a consumption item. Now, suddenly, Germans who did not smoke demanded cigarettes, not for smoking but for exchange for other goods or services. As a result, the demand for cigarettes skyrocketed in Germany.

China

Price controls played an important though little-known role in recent political developments in Asia. *Libertarian Forum* notes:

> One of the major reasons for the downfall of Chiang Kai-shek was the fact that, due to national deficits and paper money inflation, China had been suffering, before and during World War II, from a runaway inflation, and Chiang had met the problem by imposing severe price and wage controls. The inevitable result of the controls was grave shortages throughout the country, and, as in so many cases in the past since the Edict of Diocletian in ancient Rome, the government met the problem by escalating the penalties for evading controls. Chiang, in fact, ended by making an example of black marketeers by executing them publicly in the streets. In this way, he lost his merchant and middle-class support; in contrast, the Communists, whenever they occupied an area of China, ended the monetary expansion and thereby cured the inflation. Is it any wonder that Chiang lost China?

U.S. Experiences during World War II

Virtually all of the Allied countries practiced wage and price controls during World War II. Great Britain and the United States, in particular, experienced widespread government intervention in their economies. Britain went so far as to standardize production and to take over the importation and distribution of meat.

The U.S. program was not as far-reaching, but it was

nevertheless far more extensive than that of World War I. First of all, it is interesting to point out that the controls office was established by the president *prior* to our entry into World War II. The presidential decree came in April, 1941, and the Emergency Price Control Act (Public Law 421, 77th Congress) was presented to Congress in August, 1941. It passed the House a few days before Pearl Harbor, and it passed the Senate in January, 1942.

The Office of Price Administration, established under the Emergency Price Control Act of January, 1942, was first headed by Chester Bowles, a former advertising executive. The act set a goal of "stabilizing" prices. Basically the act sought to keep prices and rents from rising so fast as to be "inconsistent" with national policy. The act also called for subsidies to particular industries, "if necessary." Controls were not to be put on agricultural products unless prices reached a "parity" of 110 or more. Wages were specifically exempt. Only selected commodities were regulated.

The Emergency Price Control Act was largely voluntary in nature, and it proved to be ineffective in holding down prices. As a result, in April, 1942, the OPA issued "General Max," or a general freeze on prices. Mandatory price ceilings were imposed, based on prices in March (the previous month). Despite this freeze, prices continued to rise. (The reasons for this will be explained in chapter 5.)

In October, 1942, wages and food prices, which had previously been excluded from controls legislation, were covered by the Economic Stabilization Act. For food and farm prices, parity was set at 100. Both wages and prices were to be stabilized at levels prevailing on September 15, 1942. Wages were regulated by the National War Labor Board.

The OPA used dozens of formulas for establishing maximum ceilings on goods and markets. These formulas failed to check inflation, however. As a result, President Roosevelt issued his "hold-the-line" order in April, 1943. This decreed an end to further price and wage concessions. Several new regulations were adopted by the OPA at this time. First, "dollars-and-cents" ceilings were placed on grocery store goods, including food items. Second, stores and retail outlets were required to post these price ceilings in conspicuous areas. Finally, due to shortages and long lines, rationing was imposed in twenty different categories.

Throughout the war, there were several federal agencies responsible for controlling inflation. The most important were the Office of Price Administration, the Office of Economic Stabilization, and the Office of War Mobilization. Oftentimes their duties overlapped.

Regulations were complex for many items. Chester Bowles said the OPA had a six-page regulation for the control of fruit-cake prices. Other regulations ran to twenty-five pages in small legal print. In total, the OPA issued over 600 price and rent regulations, covering prices of over 8 million articles and twenty categories of rationing.

Because of the detailed controls, the federal bureaucracy grew rapidly. Approximately 68,000 employees worked for the OPA and related agencies. In addition, there were about 400,000 voluntary "price-watchers" around the country.

Black markets developed in a number of commodities during the latter part of the war, especially in meat, tires, gasoline, and sugar. (This will be dealt with in more detail in chapter 12.)

Government statistics show that the controls program during World War II was relatively successful in holding down the cost of living, if government statistics are to be believed. Wholesale prices, for example, rose only 14 percent from November, 1941, to August, 1945. These prices, of course, do not take into account supralegal and black market prices. It is worth noting that wholesale prices rose substantially after controls ended. From August, 1945, to August, 1948, prices jumped 55 percent.

The government controls program broke down quickly after Japan's surrender in August, 1945. In June, 1946, Congress extended authority for controls, but the president vetoed the bill. For three weeks there were no controls, during which time prices and wages jumped to near market levels. Finally, another bill, which the president found acceptable, was signed into law, but by then it was too late. In November, 1946, fourteen months after the war ended, virtually all controls (except on rents) were removed by President Truman.

The Korean Controls

Sticking to their belief that controls are necessary during war-time, even when the fighting is thousands of miles away, government leaders imposed controls during the Korean conflict. With a rapidly growing demand for war supplies, prices began to increase in 1950. A freeze was finally instituted on January 26, 1951. Maximum price ceilings were established for most prices at the highest point they had reached during the previous five-week period. This was a stopgap measure used to give the government more time to set up government commissions, rules and regulations, and so forth. The Office of Price Stabilization was established to handle most of the program.

After the freeze ended, various methods were employed to hold down prices. There was greater emphasis on a firm-by-firm examination. An earnings standard was set up, based on the average net dollar profits before taxes during the 1946–49 period. Businesses were expected to voluntarily hold earnings down to that level. But the system broke down, so OPS returned to general price regulations similar to World War II.

Dozens of black or "gray" markets developed during the Korean War. The gray market in steel was subject to intense investigation by Congress, and I will look at that situation in chapter 12.

The bureaucracy set up for regulating business and prices was not as large as that of World War II, although the government employed about 17,000 workers in this field.

Other Western Experiences with National Incomes Policies

Western European countries have experimented with incomes policies of various kinds during the past three decades. Their programs have been the subject of several major studies, and interestingly enough, they were examined by the Nixon administration before the 1971 freeze was announced.

Generally, European countries have tried to regulate prices

and wages when inflation was coupled with high unemployment. In a number of countries, a severe balance-of-payments deficit has triggered the freeze.

Studies have generally concluded that these incomes policies were successful in the short run but failures in the long run (the usual result of these government programs). Labor support was considered essential, and without it, the programs collapsed, even in the short run.

United Kingdom

In 1948, the new Labor government placed a freeze on wages and dividends. It was, however, a voluntary program. Prices were not covered. The program broke down in 1950, as both wages and prices rose faster and faster.

In 1957, the Council on Prices, Productivity, and Incomes was created, but little action was taken until 1962, when guideposts on wages were set up. In 1962, the National Incomes Commission was created, but its influence was negligible. In 1964, the National Incomes Commission was replaced by the National Board for Prices and Income. This commission engaged in "jawboning," but its task was purely advisory, and again prices and wages rose.

In the summer of 1966, Britain faced a balance-of-payments crisis. To combat the ill effects of this deficit, the British government, with labor and business support, introduced a six-month "standstill" of wages, salaries, prices, and dividends. According to government records, the freeze worked; prices and wages were virtually stable after having risen 8 percent or more prior to the "standstill." This freeze was followed by six more months of "severe restraint." The whole program ended when the Labor government lost the election of July, 1970.

After prices surged another 10 percent in 1972 and labor settlements averaged 17 percent, the Conservative government imposed a ninety-day freeze on prices and wages. The freeze was later extended to April, 1973 (in late October, 1972, fresh foods were exempted).

After this, the British government instituted Phase I (governments tend to copy one another), which allowed the pass-through of costs of raw materials. Phase II lasted from April to November, 1973, during which time 8 percent wage increases and general base period pricing were permitted.

Phase III lasted from November, 1973, to November, 1974. Prices remained under tight control, except for firms with less than 8 percent return on investment.

Since this time, Britain's situation has deteriorated badly, with prices and wages rising up to 30 percent a year. (A look at the incredible growth in the nation's money supply tells the story.)

France, West Germany, and Italy

In 1952, French leaders set up price controls. They again froze the prices of manufactured goods in late 1963 and forced a rollback on the prices of cigarettes, beef, and gasoline. The freeze was followed by guidelines and gradual decontrol.

The German experience with controls from 1936 to 1948 taught the West Germans several unforgettable lessons. One of them was that tough controls were counterproductive. Consequently, West Germany engaged only briefly (during the 1960s) in wage guidelines.

Italy announced an "emergency freeze" of prices in 1946–47. Afterward, there was no Italian incomes policy until 1963, when the government sought to restrict wage gains.

The Netherlands and the Scandanavian Countries

In the Netherlands, international trade and its impact on domestic prices were emphasized. Strict controls were established on prices in the early 1950s, and when a balance-of-payments crisis occurred in 1957, the government forced restraint on union demands. From 1959 to 1963, the Dutch government set up productivity guidelines and wage targets. Then in 1967, following another balance-of-payments crisis, the government froze prices for several months. After 1968, all guidelines were dropped.

Denmark's attitude was also heavily influenced by imports. It set up an Economic Council in 1962 to deal with a balance-of-payments deficit. In February, 1963, the council instigated a two-year (!) freeze on wages with, naturally, some exceptions. It was regarded as effective in holding down wage demands, but by 1965 wages were increasing even more rapidly than before. In 1968, a "partial" freeze was imposed by a "conservative" government. In 1970, another "temporary" freeze was instituted.

Norway and Sweden both froze prices in 1971–72. The programs in these countries were considered failures, largely because of the strength of unions and their refusal to go along. Many exceptions were permitted, and prices continued to rise. Wages were held back for a while, but then they exploded.

Finland announced a five-month price freeze on all goods except food in early 1976. Wages, which rose about 23 percent in 1975, were to be limited to a 6 or 7 percent increase by a nationwide agreement with labor.

Canada, New Zealand, and Others

In 1975, *when inflation was moderating,* Canada decided to try slowing it down more quickly through an incomes policy. As part of the package, which was being set up on a piecemeal basis, the Ottawa government has set up guidelines on wages as well as tight profit-margin controls. Over 6000 companies have been required to file with the Anti-Inflation Board numerous reports on prices, profits, dividends, and wages. Companies found to have "excess revenues" have been required to either reduce prices or absorb costs. (This of course is a great opportunity for businesses to increase "fictitious" costs.) Canadian Prime Minister Pierre Trudeau has warned that if the controls are ineffective, "the government may be forced to impose mandatory, comprehensive, all-embracing price and incomes controls upon every man and woman in Canada."

New Zealand's new National Party government, which in 1975 cancelled a three-year-old selective price freeze, announced in 1976 that wage increases will be restricted to 3.2 percent. New Zealand is suffering from double-digit inflation.

In Belgium, the government imposed a nine-month price freeze in 1975. It was considered only moderately successful. Under a new program, firms must submit an application to the Ministry of Economic Affairs in order to raise prices.

Latin America

Argentina, under President Isabel Perón, arranged a labor settlement raising wages more than 10 percent in 1976, and then immediately announced a wage and price freeze. Argentina has been suffering from such rapid inflation in the past five or six years (now in the triple-digit range) that such a freeze is totally absurd. No wonder Mrs. Peron was ousted.

Under Marxist Salvador Allende, Chile experienced the ravages of an extreme program of price-fixing below market rates. When Allende took office, he raised wages dramatically and at the same time froze prices. As a result, Chileans practically emptied appliance stores almost overnight. They had plenty of money with their increased incomes, but still were unable to buy bread and other necessities without waiting in long lines. The economic debacle that Chile encountered under their first Marxist regime was a bitter one and led ultimately to Allende's overthrow.

Nixon's Stabilization Program, 1971–74

Through the years the United States has had numerous programs of intervention into the economy. Examples include price ceilings (fixed interest rates on savings accounts and time deposits, natural gas prices), price supports (farm products, minimum-wage laws), price-fixing (interstate airlines, gold), and so forth. However, the imposition of wage and price controls during peacetime was a clear break from tradition.

The case for a thorough-going incomes policy became popular largely due to the existence of an "inflationary recession" in 1969–71, during which rising prices and growing unemployment occurred simultaneously. Many economists and government officials, chief amongst whom was Arthur F. Burns, argued that the traditional tools of government economic policy were no longer working. Such a view fails to explain the real situation, however. Monetary and fiscal policy *never* have worked. Rather, as I explained in chapter 2, these government policies have been the culprits in creating both inflation and unemployment.

At any rate, government planners and Congress began searching for alternative interventionist programs to take the place of monetary and fiscal policy. Rather than accepting the more difficult (and economically sound) choice of dismantling the inflationary apparatus, they chose wage and price controls. On August 15, 1970, the president signed the Economic Stabilization Act (Public Law 91-379). The act did not impose specific controls, but rather authorized the president to "issue such orders and regulations as he may deem appropriate to stabilize prices, rents, wages and salaries at levels not less than those prevailing on May 25, 1970." Exactly one year later, President Nixon, under increasing pressure from the Democrats and some businessmen, announced the start of a ninety-day freeze. Let us examine the individual phases of the Nixon program.

Phase I: August 15, 1971, to November 14, 1971

According to the White House, the immediate reason for the ninety-day freeze was the "deteriorating international monetary situation"—the depreciating, continuing balance-of-payments deficits. At the end of the Nixon controls program, a Cost of Living Council official more honestly admitted, "The program was a cover for highly expansionary fiscal and monetary policies."

Nixon's plan called for a ninety-day freeze on wages, prices, and rent. He also requested that corporations voluntarily "extend the wage-price freeze to all dividends." He appointed the Cost of Living Council. In his executive order he elaborated on the meaning of the freeze. Prices, rents, and wages were not to exceed maximum levels prevailing during the thirty-day period prior to August 15, 1971. "Raw agricultural products" were exempt. Fines for violations were $5000 or less.

For a number of reasons, the freeze created only a few real hardship cases during the ninety-day period. Not many shortages occurred during these three months.

Phase II: November 14, 1971, to January 11, 1973

There was an attempt to extend the freeze, but Phase II won out. The overall goal established by the president was to reduce

82

the rate of inflation to 2 or 3 percent. A Price Commission, headed by C. Jackson Grayson, was set up to monitor prices and rents. A Pay Board was set up to monitor wages and salaries. Numerous advisory committees were established to make recommendations on dividends, interest, rent, and so forth.

In compliance with the 2-to-3 percent national goal, the Price Commission established 2.5 percent as the overall limit on annual price increases for private firms. Even with the 2.5 percent allowance, price increases had to be cost-justified. In addition, there were limits set on profit margins. Companies were divided up according to size, with the larger corporations being required to obtain approval for price increases. Smaller firms were expected to comply with the goals, but were basically "self-administered."

A 3 percent a year automatic increase was allowed on rents, plus a pass-through of documented state and local government taxes. Wage increases were limited to 5.5 percent, based on an inflation goal of 2.5 percent and traditional productivity gains of approximately 3 percent. "Wages" included almost all types of fringe benefits. During Phase II, dividends were limited to a 4 percent increase each year.

Congress amended (Public Law 92-210) the Stabilization Act in December, 1971, setting standards for exemptions and exclusions from the controls program. Due to various exemptions, the government had no control over 20 percent of the economy.

Phase II was regarded by many economists and government officials as very successful in reducing the rate of inflation. It was not without problems, however. These included black markets in lumber, false job upgrading, and shortages in some markets (fertilizer and others).

Phase III: January 11, 1973, to June 13, 1973

Phase II ended with the dissolution of the Price Commission and Pay Board. The organization of controls was left in the hands of the Cost of Living Council. A less restrictive policy was adopted by the Nixon administration. Wage limits were dropped. The same general Phase II price standards were continued, but except for the food, health, and construction sectors, they were self-administered. The restrictions on dividends were liberalized and changed to base-period limitations based on the preceding four-year period.

It was during Phase III that strong inflationary pressures built up. Prices rose rapidly in many areas, especially food and meat. The press blamed the lax controls for the accelerated inflation, and political pressure mounted for a return to a freeze or at least Phase II standards.

The blame was wrongly placed and extremely shortsighted. It is more logical to blame the controls, rather than their removal, for the surge in prices. In addition, an expansive fiscal and monetary policy created a strong inflationary climate (deficits ran into the $20 billion area, and the money supply was increasing at double-digit rates).

At any rate, no matter what the cause of renewed price escalation, extreme pressure was put on President Nixon to reimpose a strong interventionist policy.

Phase III½: The Second Freeze—June 13, 1973, to August 12, 1973

Nixon imposed a second freeze, this time to last sixty days in preparation for Phase IV. It covered only prices. This time it included food prices (only the *first sale* of food products was exempt). Wages were not controlled because they were not considered a major cause of inflation in 1973. Rents were also exempt, as were interest and dividends, which were under voluntary agreements by the Committee on Interest and Dividends. Price ceilings were based on the base period June 1–8. In addition, during this period a "new system of export controls" began.

The freeze also applied to "those raw agricultural products sold for ultimate consumption in their original unprocessed form, after the first sale." Eggs, lettuce, meat, and other similar items were controlled. It was during this second freeze that some farmers found it less costly to kill baby chicks than to raise them. There were also many processors, wholesalers, and retailers who were forced to sell at extremely low profit margins or even below cost. This was because their ceiling prices, set according to prices during the first week in June, generally

84

reflected the previous year's seasonal prices. Meat simply disappeared from the counters for several weeks. The market disruptions of Nixon's program were probably most severe during this second freeze. Public support was strong at the beginning of the second freeze, but it quickly waned as shortages appeared. Phase III½, more than any other phase, broke the back of idealistic support for a price freeze.

Phase IV: August 12, 1973, to April 30, 1974

Under Phase IV, the Cost of Living Council reestablished base-period pricing in general, although it was more flexible than base-period pricing under Phase II. Much of Phase IV was an attempt to decontrol the economy on a sector-by-sector basis. Regulations were phased out when certain commitments were made by industry leaders. Dollar-for-dollar increases were allowed for food prices (meaning that if, for example, the cost of tomatoes to retailers went up twenty cents a pound, retailers could increase the selling price of tomatoes by twenty cents). This helped relieve much of the demand pressure on grocery items. By April 30, 1974, when authority for controls lapsed, only 12 percent of the consumer price index was subject to controls.

The Nixon administration pushed for the continuation of authority to implement regulation of wages and prices, but by April, 1974, congressional support for controls had waned considerably. All efforts to pass some kind of new controls program ended in defeat.

Near the end of Phase IV, the National Association of Manufacturers—a supporter of the Nixon controls when they were first put on—conducted a survey on the effects of controls on large firms (over $50 million in annual sales) and small firms. According to the survey, 31 percent of the small firms and 46 percent of the large firms had been forced to eliminate or reduce certain lines of goods and services. Interruptions and curtailments affected over 240 product lines, including paper, steel, animal feeds, and mayonnaise.

Many shortages in finished or semifinished goods were in evidence. About 89 percent of small firms and 97 percent of large

85

firms experienced unusual difficulties in obtaining supplies. Most of these shortages were considered to be caused by price controls, although other related factors were mentioned, including international price differentials, environmental programs, insufficient foreign production, and other federal programs. Controls also caused problems with production schedules, marketing programs, personnel programs, and so forth.

Looking at the cost of compliance, small firms reported that their average cost to comply was $27,000 a year. For larger firms it was $175,000. One firm estimated costs of $6 million a year! Interestingly enough, utilities and most companies with less than sixty employees—which were exempt from controls—said that they were in favor of continuing controls.

Chapter Four

What Kind of Controls Are Coming?

What kind of controls are coming? This is a both vital and difficult question to answer. History is not always a sure guide, but fortunately it can be helpful. Government controllers have had a habit of drawing on past controls programs in their efforts to administer a more effective program themselves. This is especially true of the last experience we had.

This question is also paramount to anyone seeking to avoid the ill effects of wage and price controls. The businessman will want to know whether his particular business will be monitored or not, whether controls will be tight or loose, what kind of administrative costs will be involved in complying with the national scheme, and so forth. He will no doubt also want to plan ahead and perhaps diversify into areas that will probably be exempt from controls the next time around.

The investor will be interested in which markets will be under restrictions and which will still be "free markets." He may want to consider shifting funds into foreign investments, free from government manipulation. He will no doubt want to avoid or get out of certain stocks that will fare poorly under the restrictions.

The consumer will want to be aware of and have easy access to retail markets that will be able to avoid shortages and deliver goods on time. He will want to become familiar with the used-goods market, which under the tightest measures will still be uncontrollable.

The wage- or salary-earner will want to know if his income will be low enough to exempt him from controls. He will want to know what industries to stay away from in order to remain safely employed.

The landlord will need to know whether his rental property will be tightly regulated or not. And he will also need to know under what circumstances he will be allowed to raise his rents.

The Overall Program: Freeze, Rollback, or Formula Pricing?

Before one can effectively prepare for controls, one needs to know what kind of overall program will be initiated. As I showed in the previous chapter, there have been several methods used in the past, each with its benefits and costs.

The Freeze

Clearly, the freeze is the most popular measure (although the rollback of prices is a close second). In the past thirty years, a great many controls programs have begun with a freeze, including those in the U.S., Europe, and even Latin America.

Freeze is not exactly an appropriate term to describe this controls approach. All a freeze does is put a *maximum ceiling* on prices and wages. It only freezes prices in one direction. It does not establish a *minimum* support level. Prices are not allowed to rise, but they can fall.

Which brings me to another important characteristic of this method of control. Under a freeze, only *shortages* are created, not surpluses. This is shown in the following graph.

As you can see, the supply of the example good has been reduced for some reason. Under a free market, the price would naturally rise above the freeze price to P_m, rationing out the smaller supply. But, because of the freeze, the price must stay at the enforced maximum. As a result, there is a shortage. At the freeze price, people keep demanding the same amount they demanded before the shortfall. Unfortunately, the supply has dropped. The seller is forced to somehow ration out the smaller amount without raising his prices. He resorts to (1) limiting the size of purchases per customer, thus making customers wait in long lines, or (2) selling at illegal prices.

EFFECTS OF A FREEZE

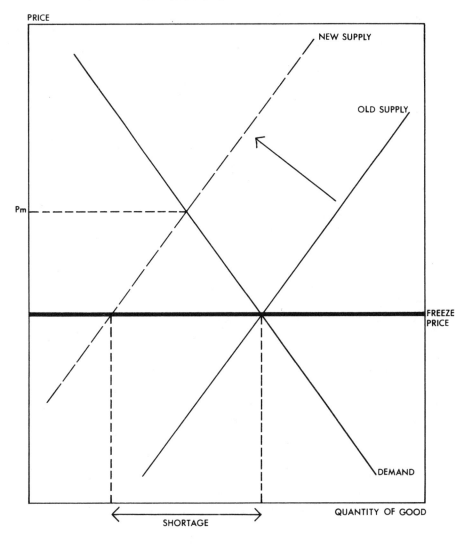

The same results occur if the demand for the example good suddenly increases. Since prices are not allowed to rise and more people are demanding the same quantity, a shortage results.

What would happen if the supply increased? In order to sell all the increased supply, suppliers would have to reduce prices. Under the freeze, there are no restrictions on falling prices, so

89

there is no unsold supply, or surplus. The price adjusts freely to the market.

In the next chapter, I will further examine the consequences of a freeze and will show how this popular measure creates immense distortions over time.

A freeze serves many purposes. First, it is regarded as a stopgap measure by government to give the bureaucrats time to set up a long-range program. It is, then, emergency pricing. That is why a freeze is seldom used for more than three months. Second, it is easy to enforce. The public generally knows what prices, rents, and wages have been recently, and they can serve as voluntary price-watchers.

Based on a study of European experiences with incomes policies, William M. Tongue concluded in his *How We Can Halt Inflation and Still Keep Our Jobs* that "the best-accepted and most widely observed control is the general freeze. It is simple to understand and can be readily seen to be a clear interruption to any wage-price spiral. . . ." A general freeze was used during both the Korean War and the Nixon "stabilization" period.

Government officials are generally familiar with some of the more flagrant shortcomings of the freeze approach. Almost overnight, a freeze creates shortages of products that vary substantially in supply from month to month. For this reason, farm products are invariably exempt from a freeze. Other problems include seasonal factors, variations in ceiling prices from firm to firm, failure to account for shifts in demand, et cetera.

In the U.S., our experience with the 1971 freeze is often looked upon favorably. Another freeze is especially likely if inflation suddenly flares up again. You should definitely act on the assumption that another freeze will be part of the government's controls package the next time around.

Rollbacks

A rollback, a government-imposed reduction in the price of a good, is generally only popular for "necessities." For example, during the 1960s in France, the prices of beef, gasoline, and cigarettes were rolled back. During the Nixon controls program and the energy crisis, several bills were introduced in Congress calling for the rollback of gasoline prices. Surprisingly, even at the height of the energy crisis, these bills never became law, though they might have had it not been for opposition from the Nixon administration. But Congress did pass the 1971 amendment to the Economic Stabilization Act to give the president power to force a rollback in prices and rents in cases of lowered costs, labor shortages, and "other pertinent factors." In early 1976, Congress voted to roll back the price of "new" oil, and the president signed the legislation.

These necessities are likely targets for future price rollbacks: food, gasoline, fuel oil, natural gas, clothing, shoes, medicine, and similar products. Of course, a rollback of prices, especially among these essential goods, is likely to create shortages and rationing.

Dollars-and-Cents Ceilings

For all practical purposes, price ceilings are similar to freezes. Dollars-and-cents pricing was being used extensively by the Office of Price Administration by the end of World War II. A specific price was set for individual products, and the prices had to be displayed publicly in a conspicuous place. Naturally, these ceilings were very popular during the war because they allowed Americans to ascertain legal prices without much trouble. This made enforcement a relatively easy task. It worked best for standardized products. Part of the dollars-and-cents method's success was due to the rationing of grocery items. Rationing is sine qua non once ceilings are imposed on necessities, to prevent hoarding by consumers taking advantage of the below-market prices.

This controls approach, though popular in the past, will probably not be initiated again unless widespread rationing is envisioned by the government.

Formula, or Cost, Pricing

Formula pricing incorporates various schemes to control profits and prices through costs of production. Prices are determined by the seller but are limited according to costs, profits, and the like. During World War II, formula pricing was adopted for machinery, tools, packaged goods, cosmetics, paper, construction materials, furniture, hardware, and building equipment. Base-period pricing was used to determine allowable profit margins. There were also margin controls on retail prices, allowing retailers to make their usual markup on goods.

Pricing formulas were more sophisticated during the Nixon program. After the first freeze, the Price Commission and the Cost of Living Council adopted several measures. In order to keep administrative costs down, the Cost of Living Council chose three tools to control prices: base pricing, allowable cost increases, and profit-margin constraints. In his *Confessions,* Jackson Grayson discusses six different methods considered by the Price Commission: cost reimbursement (dollars-and-cents pass-through), margin requirements and maintenance, fixed percentage (flat rate) formula, unit price control formula, net profit formula, and return on investment formula.

In the *Historical Working Papers,* John Flory has an important article entitled "Price Control Mechanisms." In this article, Flory analyzes the pros and cons of various schemes available to government controllers. In his critique of the "profit-margin constraint," he argues at one point that controls on a profit-to-sales ratio could be favorable for a firm. He states that in reducing profits and prices, a company's volume of business could actually increase, and thus total profits could rise! There are a number of shortcomings to this view, however. First, Flory assumes the company faces an elastic demand curve (i.e., as the price falls, consumers buy more dollar-volume of goods), a questionable assumption. Second, higher volume does not guarantee higher profits. Many businesses have gone bankrupt even though they were selling at a high volume. At any rate, it is interesting to note a case in which a government economist supports to some degree a profit-margin constraint.

For other reasons, however, Flory generally finds the profit-margin test an inadequate tool. It tends to penalize increasing productivity, causes increases in discretionary costs, distorts the capital structure (favoring short-term borrowing over long-term), and tends to eliminate low-profit lines. "The profit margin rule," Flory concludes, "would tend to *cause* inflation. . . . It ties a firm to its own past performance." He suggests several alternatives, none of which is without disadvantages. Other disadvantages of the profit-margin rule have been pointed out during World War II and the Korean War. They include loss of incentive to produce cheaply and efficiently, encouraging higher pricing; violations are difficult to detect; and finally, it means submitting detailed statements about the business' past performance in terms of income, taxes, and costs, which is both costly and an invasion of privacy.

Despite these disadvantages, formula pricing is the only form of control that the government is likely to administer if it wishes to repress inflation over the long term. This pricing method is likely to be coupled with the public display of prices and a prenotification requirement for large companies wishing to make price increases. Businesses should be prepared for an increase in administrative costs due to this scheme.

Rationing

Rationing of goods is likely to occur in areas where prices have been rolled back, where tight below-market ceilings are maintained, or when a freeze lasts for a year or longer. Rationing will only cover necessities in very short supply.

What is the best formula for rationing? During World War II, there were essentially two forms of rationing. The *certificate type* permitted a one-time authorization to buy a particular product. During the war, this form was for tires, automobiles, typewriters, bicycles, rubber footwear, and stoves.

The *coupon type* was used for food, fuel oil, gasoline, and shoes. Coupons valued in "points" were used toward the purchase of food, gasoline, and other products. The coupon idea was also used in Nazi Germany through 1942 for clothing.

In Great Britain during World War II, the government imposed *value rationing*. The British were permitted to spend a specific sum of money per week for meat. The sum varied weekly, depending upon the availability of meat. The consumer could buy one expensive cut of meat or several pounds of a cheaper meat.

It seems most probable that the coupon form of rationing will be used in the future. Indeed, this was the type chosen by the Nixon administration for gasoline rationing.

In reference to the point system of coupon rationing, researchers at Mansfield and Associates concluded: "The breakdown in 1944 is attributable, not to inherent difficulties in 'pointing,' but to the over-issuance of points and to the fact that the operating principles of the system, not being understood by those then in charge, were too often ignored. . . ."

To avoid the problem of overissuance (and the possibility of long lines of people waiting for food), a major consideration by government officials has been whether or not to legally permit the selling and buying of ration tickets (often called a "white market"). Under a white market, the price of ration tickets would fluctuate according to supply and demand. This obviously makes sense from an economic point of view and if the government wishes to avoid customer anger over bureaucratic mismanagement of rationing. There is no certainty, however, that the government will permit a white market in ration tickets once rationing is imposed.

The United States is heading inexorably toward another energy crisis. Why? A major factor is price controls. Decontrol of oil prices is expected over the next three or four years, but by then it will probably be too late. No longer is "new" oil free from controls. The artificially low price for "old" and new oil can only mean a continuing drop in domestic output. At the same time, price controls have resulted in artificially low prices for gasoline at the pump. (Witness the drop in gasoline prices in 1976.) This can only mean higher consumption of gasoline by the public. It is no wonder that oil imports have tripled since the oil embargo in 1973! In 1976, for the first time, the U.S. imported more oil than it produced.

Such vulnerability to the power of the oil cartel governments can only spell disaster. Another oil embargo will make our situation far graver than it was in 1973. The pressures then were almost unbearable. Another month of waiting in lines for gasoline would surely have meant gasoline rationing.

Interestingly enough, the ration tickets printed up during the height of the embargo in early 1974 are still with us. Will they ever be used? When Secretary of the Treasury William E. Simon was asked "What happened to your great blunder, gas ration coupons?" he replied in *Family Weekly,*

> No blunder—just preparing for the worst (and we've still got the stamps if rationing, heaven forbid, should ever come). Think back to the oil embargo, those long lines at gas pumps and all the demands for rationing. I was against rationing then and I still am. It's inequitable and costly. *Still, if the embargo had continued, we might have been forced to impose rationing, like it or not.* We were prepared. A three-month supply of coupons was printed under the authority of the Defense Production Act with funds appropriated by Congress. The cost, never a secret, was $10 million. (Emphasis added.)

Production: Free from Controls?

One area that will probably be left alone under general controls is the actual production of goods and services. The government may require the businessman to keep prices below a certain level, but it will generally not tell him how much he can produce or what he must produce. Americans may acquiesce to wage and price controls, but they are not very agreeable to permitting the government to tell them precisely what they can and what they cannot produce.

There have been exceptions to this rule. In Nazi Germany, the Third Reich took over the production of some goods and standardized them in an effort to reduce severe shortages. It also banned the production of "luxury" items. Britain also standardized the manufacture of certain articles to avoid quality deterioration. During World War II, the U.S. government influenced production, but only indirectly. The production of war materiel and food were two areas that were closely controlled. The OPA spent millions of dollars on farm-goods subsidies in an effort to contain shortages. At other times, the federal government has restricted output of certain farm products that were overproduced due to price controls. In socialist countries, including the Soviet Union, governments have sought to control both prices and production.

But in "democratic" Western countries, governments have a hard enough time just administering prices and wages. Serious consideration may be given to controlling production directly if controls are kept on for a lengthy period of time, but fortunately there are other less extreme alternatives, such as providing subsidies in markets that suffer from shortages.

Freedom to produce should be a great relief to the businessman. This means that controls will not necessarily destroy his whole business. Even under price regulations, a businessman can shift resources into areas that are not tightly controlled or into "free-market" areas. He can drop unprofitable lines in favor of higher-margin, more profitable endeavors.

Trade Restrictions: A Different Story

Restrictions on foreign trade are a different story. Traditionally, of course, foreign trade has always been limited by import duties, quotas, and export controls on certain items. Import quotas were imposed on crude oil imports during the 1957–73 period. Quotas were temporarily put on soybean exports in the summer of 1973.

Domestic price controls lead to further controls on trade. Businessmen and speculators naturally have a strong incentive to export goods, since international prices are uncontrolled and become more favorable over time. When consumers feel the pinch at home and see wheat and other products being shipped abroad, they tend to support export controls.

Imports are not always exempt (they were subject to regulation in World War II), but they are less likely to be controlled than exports. The exemption of imports is an important factor for consumers who wish to avoid shortages at home. Once shortages become alarming and rationing is imposed, import controls are just another step away.

General export controls were considered during the Nixon controls program. George P. Shultz, formerly secretary of the treasury and secretary of labor as well as chairman of the Cost of Living Council, stated that "as the program progressed, the implications of our having domestic prices that were lower than world prices for internationally traded commodities became more and more apparent . . . . international controls will as surely lead to domestic controls as domestic controls were leading to international controls."

A Test for Exemptions and Exclusions

The Economic Stabilization Act of 1970 did not specify any single market that should be exempt or excluded from the program. Nor did the 1971 and 1973 amendments to the act. Congress left this question completely up to the executive branch. The president was to "provide for the making of such general exceptions and variations as are necessary to foster orderly economic growth and to prevent gross inequities, hardships, serious market disruptions, domestic shortages of raw materials, localized shortages of labor, and windfall profits." (According to this definition, *no* price controls should be imposed!)

The government developed several measures to test "gross inequities, hardships, and serious market disruptions," but they seemed extremely provincial. Even though the Stabilization Act called for exceptions based on "gross inequities," no private firm ever met the test—even when bankruptcy was threatening. No firm should depend on concessions of this type to avoid the effects of controls.

During the entire Nixon program, 1971–74, there were 8100 general requests for exceptions and 600 for reconsideration. In all, only a small portion were approved. During the Phase I freeze, only five were approved, while 3230 were denied. During other phases, many requests were withdrawn under pressure from the Price Commission and the Cost of Living Council. Of those ruled upon, only 10 percent were approved.

Price Exemptions

Numerous goods and services were exempt from controls during the Nixon program and other controls periods.

(1) *Raw agricultural products.* Farm products have not always been exempt. Except for fresh fruits and vegetables, all food prices were subject to dollars-and-cents ceilings during

97

World War II. Recently, government officials have come to realize that unless they are willing to impose rationing, farm goods should be exempt from controls.

From a political point of view, this is a difficult decision to make. Rising food prices are utmost in the minds of the voting public when it comes to inflation. The Price Commission under Nixon felt the public's anxiety over double-digit increases in the price of food. During Phase II, food was the biggest factor in the rapid increases of the consumer price index. Under public pressure, the Price Commission recommended to the Cost of Living Council that it "place raw agricultural products under control." Despite his support for a free market after Phase II ended, Jackson Grayson felt that food and health controls should be continued. And while he first opposed food controls, he later felt that they were necessary. The Cost of Living Council did not follow his recommendation at the time. But during Phase III½, the second freeze (June-August, 1973), raw agricultural products were put under controls after their first sale.

Meat has always been an important food product. According to Marshall Clinard, who worked for the OPA during World War II, "experience during the past war indicated that the success not only of a wartime food program but of the entire system of price and rationing controls centers on the effective control of the distribution and price of meat." During World War II, meat was rationed, prices were set for livestock, slaughtering quotas and grading standards were established, and subsidies were granted to slaughterers. Under growing public pressure, Nixon clamped price ceilings on meat in early 1973. Fortunately, he waited to do so until the price of meat had already risen to historically high levels. Nevertheless, shortages did appear in the latter part of the summer of 1973. Since that time the price of meat has generally fallen, but we can expect rising prices in the future. This will no doubt be a major topic of controversy in the years ahead.

Another important fact to remember is that processed foods were under control in the recent past. While *raw* agricultural products were exempt, *processed* foods were not. Sometimes it was a hard decision for the Price Commission to decide what constituted a "raw" product and what was "processed." For example, honey remained a raw commodity, even when "drained or strained." On the other hand, fish and other seafoods were considered processed when "shelled, shucked, skinned, or scaled." The issue is complicated even more by the existence of other conflicting federal laws. For example, shelled peanuts were categorized as a raw agricultural commodity because the federal support price for peanuts at the time of the 1971 freeze was above the ceiling price. Thus, under strict controls, the federal government would have had to purchase over $50 million worth of peanuts! So shelled peanuts were made exempt.

(2) *Raw seafood products*.

(3) *Certain custom-made products and services.* This is a difficult area because in a sense all goods and services can be considered "customized." Heavy machinery, for example, which is made to order every so many years to meet the particular needs of a company, is in a sense customized, but the Price Commission under Nixon ruled otherwise. Custom-products industries also included aerospace, construction, advertising, publishing, and broadcasting. These are large sectors of the economy, and under a strict program, they simply will not be ignored. They are difficult to monitor, however, due to the nature of their products.

(4) *Exports, imports, and international shipping rates.* Exports and imports were generally exempt from controls throughout the Nixon program. *Only the first sale* of goods imported into the U.S. was exempt, not any sales thereafter. Foreign crude oil, for instance, was not exempt after it was refined. During the 1973 freeze, higher costs of imported refined oil products could be passed on to consumers on a dollar-for-dollar basis, but if oil had to be processed by a U.S. refinery, they could not. A 1973 staff memo to John Dunlop, director of the Cost of Living Council, stated, "The higher cost of imported crude oil will have to be borne by refiners because under Freeze regulations, the higher cost of an imported material can be passed through the distribution chain on a dollar-for-dollar basis only so long as the imported material is not transformed or becomes part of another product. Clearly, the refining process results in a major transformation of crude oil."

Another interesting fact is that any product originating in the

U.S., even if it had been exported and then imported back into the U.S., was still subject to price controls (live cattle exported to Mexico and Canada is one example).

(5) *Damaged and used goods*. Damaged and used products are virtually impossible to regulate. Prices vary extensively according to individual tastes, the age of used goods, or the extent of damage.

Damaged products are a part of nearly every business. "Irregulars" or "seconds" in pants, dresses, and bedsheets would be exempt from controls. Refrigerators, stoves, and washers and dryers with dents and other defects would not fall under price regulations. And so forth.

(6) *Tuition and other charges by public and private nonprofit organizations*. Tuitions were exempt during the 1971 freeze due to political pressure. Tuition was called a "transaction fee" rather than a "price." Sales of religious goods and services were and would be excluded from regulation.

(7) *The sale of government property*. (It figures!)

(8) *The sale of securities, commercial paper, commodity futures, and certain brokerage fees*. This makes sense. The prices of stocks and commodities fluctuate by the minute. Ceiling prices on these things would certainly create a dramatic sell-off and a bear market. However, the government has in the past tried indirectly to regulate stocks and commodities by limiting dividends and controlling companies. In World War II, the commodity futures market was relatively dormant because the federal government had such extensive control over the marketplace. With few exceptions, supply and demand simply were not allowed to operate.

Interestingly, under Nixon the government tried to force the commodity futures market to conform to price controls on certain traded commodities. During the June-August, 1973, freeze, iced broilers, frozen pork bellies, platinum, palladium, silver, copper, and silver-coin futures were all put under new price-freeze orders. The ruling closed out all July and August contracts. Except for liquidations and previously made positions, trading was terminated. And there was some concern that other markets would be affected. The freeze was extended to these commodity futures markets because the spread was widening between cash prices, which were controlled, and the futures markets, which were not. In addition, ceilings were placed on platinum and silver-coin contracts and July, 1973, lumber futures.

(9) *Retailers and restaurants with annual sales of less than $100,000.* Smaller firms were exempt from price controls during Phases II through IV of the Nixon program. This was largely because Nixon wished to minimize the federal bureaucracy in charge of the controls program. The $100,000 cut-off point was simply an economy move by the Price Commission. Actually, Price Commissioner Grayson felt that a higher cut-off would have been better from an administrative point of view. He said that the commission considered a cut-off point of $250,000 instead of $100,000. After choosing the lower figure, the commission found its workload *tripled!*

There is another reason for the small business exemption. Many economists, including Galbraith, Walter Heller, and Arthur F. Burns, argue that smaller firms do not exert much pressure on rising prices, as compared to the larger, more concentrated industries. Therefore, there is little need to regulate them. This attitude may very well prevail in the next round of wage and price controls. It pays to be small.

(10) *Various life insurance policies.*

(11) *Specific industries: The case of petroleum.* Petroleum-product prices have been subject to controls off and on since the 1971 freeze. On March 6, 1973, mandatory controls were placed on crude oil and petroleum products. Base-period pricing was used. Prices were limited to a one percent average increase per year. Due to the nature of the regulations, however, little control was exerted during this period. For one reason, there existed important exemptions. Many state and local governments—particularly the states of Texas, California, and Louisiana—had authority to lease land for oil and natural gas. They were exempt. In addition, there was the "stripper-well" exemption. Oil wells producing ten barrels or less a day were exempt from regulation. This was largely for the same reason that exempted small business retailers and restaurants. The stripper-well exemption turned out to be a significant exclusion, however. Although the average stripper well in the U.S. produced only

three or four barrels of crude a day in 1973, together these wells accounted for 13 percent of domestic oil production. Incredibly, about two-thirds of U.S. wells produce less than ten barrels a day.

Another interesting development resulted in less control of the oil market. Special Rule #1, which reimposed controls on petroleum, covered 95 percent of industry gross sales, but the controls were not universally applied. The twenty-four major companies subject to controls were not the ones that ultimately set prices! Most sales were made by independently franchised dealers over whom the majors had little influence. At the retail level, only 10 percent of gasoline stations were direct company operations. The rest were run by independents. So the effect of Special Rule #1 was to set up two independent sellers—one controlled and the other uncontrolled—at nearly every level of the industry. This naturally led to brokers buying at controlled prices and selling at uncontrolled prices. The consequence was rising oil prices.

A situation like this one can easily be imitated elsewhere in the economy when some businesses are controlled and others are free.

(12) *Antiques, art objects, coins and stamps, precious stones, rock and stone specimens, handicraft objects, and other miscellaneous items*. The reason for exempting these sectors is fairly obvious. There is simply no standard of comparison by which to control prices. In this sense, these commodities are similar to damaged or used goods.

Despite this, the government can be obtuse. During the 1971 freeze, controls bureaucrats at first sought to administer the freeze comprehensively. So they included within the scope of the freeze commodities sold at auction or those subject to competitive bids! The ceiling price for a work of art was the price for the most "competitive work" sold in the base period. The controllers also told the American Philatelic Society that prices of used stamps bought and sold by collectors were subject to freeze! During Phase II, these regulations were relaxed and forgotten.

As in the case of damaged or used goods, antiques, coins, and similar products are very unlikely to be controlled, and even if they are, there is simply no objective way to enforce such arbitrary legislation.

(13) *Prices charged by federal, state, and local governments for services, except health and utility services.* This kind of exemption demonstrates the self-serving nature of government. Government knows it must have the power to control prices so that it will never be the victim of a shortage. You and I may have to wait in line, but the government sells and gets what it wants, whatever the price.

(14) *Sale of certain real estate.*

(15) *Prices of U.S. companies abroad.* Obviously, this area is exempt simply because the U.S. government has no way of enforcing its controls regulations abroad.

It is worth noting that there are literally hundreds of exemptions during any controls period. Most of them have been covered above. Where can you find a complete listing of exemptions and exceptions? The best source is the *Federal Registry,* which in previous periods has detailed all federal controls regulations.

Rent Controls and Exemptions

The motivation for rent controls is largely political, not economic. Rent controls have existed from time to time in nearly every Western country. Because residential and apartment rent is the largest single budget item for most Americans (25 to 30 percent of take-home pay), rent controls are bound to be politically popular both locally and federally. Even the realty industry is acutely aware of what's coming, especially in large Eastern metropolitan areas such as Washington, Baltimore, and Philadelphia. Recently, New York City took its first steps toward phasing out rent controls, but I very much doubt they will be able to free themselves from them. The political clout of tenant groups is growing. In times past, renters have been so transient that they have not registered to vote in significant numbers. Now that registration is becoming easier in state after state, the largest voting block will soon be the tenants. As a result, local, state, and federal politicians will undoubtedly woo

103

these voters and will favor tenant-landlord commissions and rent controls. With an expected housing shortage coming up, the influence of apartment dwellers will have an even greater impact.

Fortunately, as in past programs, certain rental properties will be exempt from rent controls. In the past, these have included:

(1) *Industrial, farm, nonresidential, and commercial property.* These were exempt from controls during World War II, the Korean Conflict, and the Nixon program.

(2) *New construction offered for rent for the first time.* Usually, this pertains to construction after the date that the controls start. During the 1971 Nixon freeze, new rental buildings were exempt if offered for rent for the first time after August 15, 1971.

(3) *Rehabilitated dwellings* (where the cost of rehabilitation is more than one-third of the total value of the rehabilitated property). These were exempt during both the Korean War and the Nixon program.

(4) *Single family dwellings rented on a greater than month-to-month lease where the owner owns no more than four such dwellings.* This was an economy move on the part of the Price Commission during Nixon's Phase II program. It favored the "small landlord."

(5) *Owner-occupied rental dwellings of four units or less on a longer than month-to-month basis.* This "small landlord" exemption along with (4) above covered two-thirds of all rental units.

(6) *Units renting for $500 a month or more.* This Phase II exemption affected only 5 percent of the residential rental units in the U.S., but it becomes an important exclusion in terms of profitable opportunities when rent controls are established again. It is likely that this "luxury rental exemption" will be made again.

(7) *Units covered by local rent control programs.*

(8) *HUD-FHA housing.* (Again, it figures!)

Because rent controls are politically motivated, the government may choose to avoid a stringent program, as it did during Nixon's Phase II. A strict rent-control plan would be costly to monitor and enforce. There are over 25 million housing units that would be covered by controls. Based on the New York City experience, the government would need 20,000 to 25,000 people to administer the program.

Wage Exemptions

Important exclusions have been made in past controls programs for wages and salaries.

(1) *"Substandard" or "working poor" wages*. Congress specifically exempted this class of wage-earners in its 1971 amendment to the Economic Stabilization Act. "Substandard" wages were defined as $3.50 an hour or below. This would have exempted roughly half of the nation's work force! The Cost of Living Council felt it could not accept such a high cut-off level, and at first it adopted a wage exemption level of only $1.90, the minimum wage. It was increased to $2.75 in July, 1972.

(2) *Small business exemption*. Once again, we see how Congress has recently "favored" the small businessman and his employees as compared with the big corporations. The Cost of Living Council ruled that employment of sixty or less workers constituted a small business. This exempted about 19 million employees under the Nixon program. Another quasi exemption existed under Phase II. All wage increases by employee units of 5000 or less were not required to seek Pay Board approval of wage hikes prior to implementation.

(3) *U.S. citizens abroad, civilian and military employees of the federal government, professional athletes, members of the entertainment industry, and many self-employed persons (e.g., freelance writers)*. These groups were largely exempted by executive order rather than by Congress. The Pay Board argued over whether athletes and actors should not be subject to wage restrictions due to their public exposure, but the exemption was finally allowed because it was thought that such action had little influence on general wage trends.

(4) *Fringe benefits*. In past controls programs, fringe benefits have been regulated, but usually on a small scale. Due to World War II wage controls, many companies shifted wage increases to "fringe benefits"—two-week vacations with pay, various forms of insurance, pension plans, et cetera. The Wage Stabili-

zation Board began to monitor this trend closely. It set the amount of time for vacation and limited holiday pay and overtime. The controllers realized that it would be too difficult to ban these benefits. During the 1971 Nixon freeze, however, fringe benefits were regarded as part of wages and therefore could not be increased during the ninety-day period. This rule was relaxed in Phase II and later. In fact, in the 1971 amendment to the controls act, Congress specifically exempted certain forms of fringe benefits: "reasonable contributions" to pensions, profit sharing, annuity or savings plans, group insurance plans, and any disability and health plans. Overtime premiums, paid leave, holidays, paid vacations, and such things were not exempt.

(5) *Promotions, merit increases, and step increases.* During the Nixon program, a promotion was not considered a wage increase and was thus exempt (except during the 1971 freeze). A "merit" increase was ruled "discretionary" and allowed. "Step" increases were not permitted if they were based solely on the time of service.

Profit Controls

Controls on profits are usually established as an indirect means of holding down price increases. During Nixon's Phase II and at later stages, the Cost of Living Council developed a number of ways to restrict profits. They are listed above under the discussion of "formula pricing" in this chapter. This method of formula pricing based on costs has recently been adopted by Canadian authorities. From an economic point of view, strict controls on profits can be devastating in terms of efficiency and allocation of resources. Politically, it is often carried out to please organized labor, which may support wage and price controls with the stipulation that "obscene" profits be limited.

In the 1971 amendment to the Economic Stabilization Act, profit controls are not specifically mentioned. They were not exempted, however. A section of the act included the declaration that one of the purposes of the act was to prevent "windfall profits." Of course, defining windfall profits in a meaningful way can be an arduous task.

Restrictions on Interest and Dividends

Credit and interest rates have been limited by government decree since the time of the Law of Moses (which outlawed "usury"—except in dealings with strangers and foreigners). During the medieval period, usury laws were enforced among countries under strong ecclesiastical influence. Even today many states in the U.S. have statutory limits on interest for certain kinds of consumer loans. Studies have shown that finance companies, credit card companies, and banks have been reluctant to operate in these areas.

Under the 1971 extension of the Economic Stabilization Program, the president was given permanent authority to initiate a program of "voluntary credit controls" among private lenders.

Interest rates of all kinds—for certificates of deposit, prime interest rates for large corporations, first and second mortgages—have reached high levels in recent years. In 1974 the prime interest rate reached 12 percent. During this time, the United States was experiencing an inflationary recession. The call for wage and price controls during this period as well as that a few years earlier included the demand that controls should also cover interest and dividends. George Meany and other labor leaders strongly supported this measure. They argued that white- and blue-collar workers suffered from high interest rates on consumer loans.

No direct restrictions were placed on interest rates during the Nixon program, however. Under the 1971 freeze, there was some discussion about whether or not "points" on loans were prices or part of interest. Obviously, they can only be considered part of interest, a view accepted by the Cost of Living Council. Interest rates are unlikely to be controlled directly by a government ceiling because the Federal Reserve and other agencies regulate credit with other indirect methods.

Dividends were voluntarily controlled during the Nixon program. Dividends were permitted to increase 4 percent a year during Phase II. Afterward, they were allowed to increase according to a five-year base period, 1968-72. Under labor pressure, dividends are very likely to be regulated in some fashion in future government schemes (labor sees controls on dividends as a way to control management).

Grayson's Recommendations for Future Controllers

Former Price Commissioner Grayson believes so strongly that another round of wage and price controls is coming that in the last chapter of *Confessions* he directs some suggestions to future controllers. Based on his own experiences, he makes the following recommendations:

(1) *Planning*. Act quickly.

(2) *Policies*. A *brief* complete freeze should be used, but only brief, so as to avoid "severe distortions."

(3) *After the freeze*. Manufacturers and service industries should be required to justify prices on the basis of costs. This policy should be pursued only under conditions of "cost-push inflation." Grayson warns that it will not work under "demand-pull inflation." Of all the "formula policies," Grayson favors "term limit pricing," based on the average aggregate percentage increase in all products. Eight percent should be the limit to increases for any one product.

(4) *Exemptions*. All retailers and wholesalers should be exempt from controls.

(5) *Rents*. The only feasible form of control on rents is a flat percentage cap, or a freeze.

Chapter Five

The Consequences of Price Controls

The consequences of controls depend entirely on the severity of the government program. In one case, a plan may be so weak as to be just a waste of taxpayers' money. After over a year of Phase II controls under the Nixon program, for example, economist Marvin H. Kosters commented that he could find not a single clear-cut case of distortion. "I'll tell you, the controls are so flexible that we have what amounts to a free market situation now," he said.

On the other hand, the price controls in postwar Germany under the Allies probably constitute the best example of how artificial ceilings on wages and prices can destroy the legal foundation of a society and force practically everyone into participating in the black market. .

In *Incomes Policy and Inflation,* economist Gottfried Haberler has pointed out a number of the consequences of controls:

> They include gradual distortion of the wage and price structure; creation of the nucleus of a new bureaucracy with a tremendous growth potential; wholesale diversion of entrepreneur and managerial talent and energies from productive work to unproductive but time-consuming and tiring attempts to comply with, or evade and circumvent, the controls; and growing uncertainty, reflected in lagging investment and the slump of the stock market, about the future course of the policy and its implications for the vitally important recovery of profits from present low levels.

Before we examine in depth some of the consequences referred to by Haberler, let us look at some of the general results of wage and price controls.

Why Controls Cannot Stop Inflation

Price controls do not and cannot stop rising prices. Even if prices for *all* products were frozen and rigidly enforced the general price level could still rise!

The general price level is usually measured by some kind of index, such as the consumer price index. A price index that took into account only a simple average of the prices of all goods and services would be extremely biased and practically useless. Some goods are more important than others. We purchase a lot of some products and less of others. We are more concerned with an increase in the price of sugar, for example, than we are with the price of sealskin coats. A good price index must take this into account. The consumer price index, for example, considers prices weighted according to demand and production.

The general price level is not only based on prices but on the amount of each good that is produced and consumed by the public. Under price controls, prices of goods and services may stay constant, but the amount of each good produced may change radically. This would in turn cause the general price level to change. Herein lies the reason why price controls do not keep average prices from rising. Most government programs seek to control prices, not production.

What kind of production changes can take place that might result in rising prices? In the past, industries have cut back production of lower-priced items (where the profit margins are lower due to bigger volume and greater competition on "essential" goods) and increased production of higher-priced items (where profit margins are greater). With a shortage of the lower-priced, essential goods, consumers start buying more expensive goods (e.g., they buy higher-priced shirts because the cheaper brands are unavailable). So the general price level rises as more and more people purchase more expensive goods and services.

A few examples from history should explain what I mean. During both World War II and the Korean War, price controls on machinery tended to shift production from loss-lines or less profitable items to more profitable items, even though it often was the less profitable items that were most urgently needed.

The low-markup, high-volume goods were always the popular "necessities"—shoes, shirts, et cetera.

One of the best examples of this trend is the apparel industry during World War II. In 1942, shortages were evident in lower-priced essential items: men's shirts, underwear, and working clothes. While the dollar volume for inexpensive dresses declined sharply, volume for expensive dresses climbed. The reason for this is evident. The bigger markup on expensive dresses led businessmen to expand production of them, while cutting back on the production of cheaper clothes. Price controls effectively kept the prices of inexpensive clothes low, but due to the shortage of these cheaper clothes, people had to buy more and more of the expensive brands. The *average* price for clothes therefore went up!

A similar dramatic shift occurred in men's apparel. Sports jackets and slacks became more available than regular business suits. The production of men's separate coats increased more than seven times during the war period, while production of standard men's suits was off by half.

The paper industry during Nixon's Phase IV program is another good example. During the controls-induced paper shortage of 1974, printers had difficulty obtaining such lower-quality papers as 45-pound, 50-pound, and newsprint. At the same time, however, the paper companies were more than eager to sell the more profitable, and consequently more abundant, 60-, 70-, and 80-pound papers. Why? Because there was hardly any savings in producing lower-grade paper.

What is it that allows this to happen? What allows companies to drop less profitable lines in favor of more profitable lines? Why does this distortion take place under controls and not in the free market? The answer, I believe, lies in an understanding of how the market works. The fundamental error of advocates of wage and price controls is the belief that *equilibrium* exists in the marketplace, especially at the time that controls are imposed. This is particularly true of a freeze. Prices are supposedly frozen where supply and demand meet, at equilibrium. The following graph shows this concept of equilibrium.

Because it is believed that market prices are stable and at equilibrium, it is also believed that a freeze on prices will not

PRICE

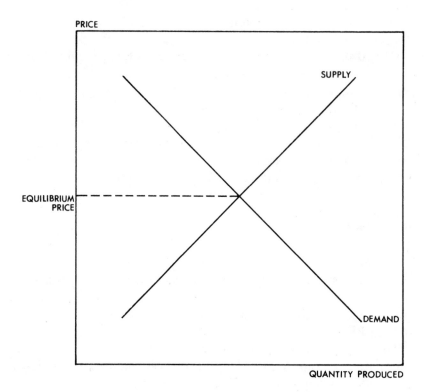

EQUILIBRIUM
PRICE

SUPPLY

DEMAND

QUANTITY PRODUCED

result in any distortions or shortages. The trouble is there is no such thing as market equilibrium! Equilibrium *never* exists in the marketplace. Prices are merely estimates of market conditions. They change only when there is a perceived shift in supply or demand. Yet at the time a freeze is imposed, shifts might have taken place without immediate price responses.

For example, suppose a grocer sells oatmeal at fifty-nine cents a box and he keeps 200 boxes in inventory. He regards this inventory as an adequate amount to take care of present customer demands for oatmeal. (In other words, he believes that fifty-nine cents a box approximates the equilibrium price of oatmeal.) Then consumers in the area increase their demand for oatmeal due to a boost in income. The grocer is at first unaware of this increase in demand. All he sees is that more boxes of oatmeal are being taken off the shelves and his inventory is being depleted more rapidly than expected. His first reaction is *not* to raise prices (after all, the increased sales might only be tempo-

112

rary, and raising prices might lose him customers to other stores), but rather to order more boxes of oatmeal from his wholesaler. Only after weeks of sustained increase in demand can he safely raise his prices.

Prices are always tending toward equilibrium, but never actually reaching it. Supplies are always shifting and demand is always changing as the needs and wants of individuals change. Sometimes the changes are slow, other times they occur daily. (This fact determines whether the effects of controls are felt immediately or over a lengthy period of time.)

The key to production distortions under controls is the fact that the market is always in *disequilibrium*. When price controls are imposed, companies are faced with price ceilings even though shifts in demand and supply have *already* occurred. When the companies finally become aware of the shifts, they cannot adjust prices upward accordingly. Therefore, they are "locked" into low-profit margins. Because they have only limited resources to produce, they shift away from lower-margin, high-volume products into higher-margin, low-volume products, and shortages appear. The effects snowball when certain key factors of production are in short supply, causing high-volume production to slow.

Getting back to why prices continue to rise even under controls, another important factor is the elimination of discounts. During World War II, due to the existence of shortages and a "seller's market," manufacturers gave preference to those who were willing to receive smaller discounts or none at all. So prices continued to rise in real terms, even though, superficially, prices and discounts remained the same on the books.

Problems with a Freeze

As I have mentioned above, the freeze approach has in the past had tremendous popular support and is likely to in the future. The basis for this popularity is the concept of cost-push inflation. Workers demand and get higher wages; companies in turn raise their prices in order to maintain profits (as the media say, companies pass on their costs to the consumer);

113

workers demand higher wages to maintain the purchasing power of their money; companies increase prices; and so goes the wage-price spiral.

This popular mythology is really unbelievable to anyone who understands the basic workings of the economy. The wage-price spiral concept completely fails to explain why companies often "absorb" increases in costs, or why companies may raise prices by more, less, or by the same amount of the increase in costs.

If cost-push inflation is a reality, why should companies wait for wage increases before they raise their prices? Why not raise prices higher and higher overnight? Businessmen do not deliberately keep prices at the lowest selling level they can find. If the market permits higher prices, firms will take advantage of this fact long before workers demand a pay increase.

The cost-push theory of inflation also wholly ignores the demand side of the market. Supply and demand are both essential ingredients in any realistic explanation of a rise in prices. Alfred Marshall often compared supply and demand to a pair of scissors: both blades are required to cut paper.

The importance of demand cannot be ignored in any discussion of inflation. Here is just one instance supporting this assertion. During Nixon's Phase II, Dow Chemical asked for a 2.5 percent increase on *average* prices of all lines of products. Why? Because, according to former Price Commissioner Grayson, "they get the flexibility to put their price increase where the market dictates instead of where their costs are."

A shift in the demand side of inflation can aggravate the situation under price controls. As Paul W. McCracken observed, "Since it is inherent in controls that they tend to create bottleneck shortages, these controls may have aggravated the rate of inflation by limiting the ability of the economy to respond to strong demands with increased supplies."

Nevertheless, advocates of the cost-push inflation idea combine it with the equilibrium idea discussed above to give theoretical support for wage and price controls. As they see it, equilibrium can be established at any number of places without harming or distorting the economy. This is shown in the graph below.

According to the graph, the wage-price spiral has caused prices to rise (inflation) without any change in production or

COST-PUSH INFLATION

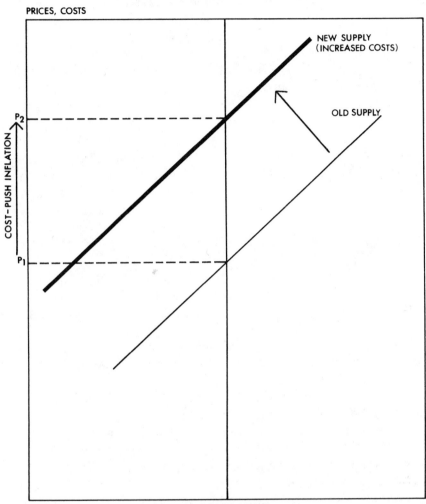

PRICES, COSTS

COST-PUSH INFLATION

NEW SUPPLY
(INCREASED COSTS)

OLD SUPPLY

P_2

P_1

SAME OUTPUT (GNP)

output. So, theoretically, there should be no problem in freezing *both* prices and wages. Nor should there be any problem in reducing wages and prices by an equal amount (a rollback). As the graph shows, it makes no difference whether the price level is at P_1 or P_2. Obviously, the output is the same in either case, and so from a social point of view, it would be better to have lower prices. Freeze advocates strongly support a freeze on *both* wages and prices.

Actually, a freeze can amount to a rollback in prices rather than just a ceiling. Take for example the case of wage increases negotiated prior to a freeze, but which become effective after the freeze is imposed. These contracts may be outlawed or delayed from taking effect during a freeze (as they were under Nixon's 1971 freeze). Implementation of rent increases can also be delayed even though contracted for.

A freeze can create a number of problems that often go unnoticed at first. Take for example products that are made only periodically, say, every three or four years. Special types of machinery are made at infrequent intervals, sometimes years apart. A freeze, if comprehensive, would require that such machinery sell at the prices of years past, even if costs had exceeded these prices in the meantime. No one can deny this would have deleterious effects. The same problem occurs with seasonal ticket sales (such as football tickets during the 1971 freeze).

Timing is a major problem with a freeze. In 1971, for example, major steel firms raised prices just prior to the freeze. As was the custom, smaller steel firms, who bought from the majors, would have raised their prices sometime after the majors did. But with the unexpected freeze, these smaller companies were caught in a squeeze and ended up producing at a loss or a low profit because their costs rose.

The same problem exists in wage negotiations. Traditionally, wage increases are negotiated by the larger unions and followed by similar demands by the unions in smaller firms. A freeze creates differentials in wage levels for the same tasks, even in the same industries. As a result, smaller firms can lose their best employees to larger firms.

Landlords often buy new rental property with the idea of raising rents immediately after purchase, and this is reflected in the price and interest paid. With a freeze, such costs often cannot be covered, as was the case in 1971.

Seasonal problems are created by a freeze. Companies with seasonal sales are forced to set prices based on the previous year's prices. In 1971, this included Christmas items, resort operations, school bus operations, home-heating-fuel supplies, et cetera. The base period upon which the 1971 freeze determined legal ceiling prices resulted in using the prices of a year before rather than the usual month-before-the-freeze method.

Here is another example where a freeze created shortages and the risk of an energy crisis in home-heating oil. When oil price controls were imposed on August 15, 1971, under the ninety-day freeze, distillate prices were near their usual seasonal low. Gasoline prices, on the other hand, were near their seasonal high. Traditionally, it is just the opposite in winter. But the freeze locked prices in place when the price structure favored gasoline over distillates and home-heating fuel oil. Thus, the controls gave added incentive to produce more gasoline than usual and less distillate than usual. This resulted in the production of less home-heating oil than should have been available for the winter.

A freeze on prices without a freeze on costs can be especially pernicious. This was true during Nixon's second sixty-day freeze of June, 1973, in which even food was subject to controls. Costs in general were exempt, however, and stories were told about how baby chicks, for example, had to be killed to avoid a cost squeeze and daily losses.

Loss of investment opportunities is another major drawback under a freeze. Economist Yale Brozen reported these results under the Nixon freeze:

> Right now we face the problem, for instance, that under the freeze prices for paper and aluminum the return on new capacity, if it were to be put up, would run on the order of three or four percent. Well, if you've got to pay eight to 10 percent for money, you're not going to put it into three- or four-percent uses. So, in effect, all the plans for adding to capacity in paper and aluminum industries have been at least temporarily set aside.

In June, 1973, during Nixon's second freeze, the *Wall Street Journal* reported:

> Because suppliers didn't receive high enough prices to provide an adequate return on investment, they didn't build new pulp and paper mills, chemical plants, or steel mills, and they delayed purchasing production machinery. Even in some industries where shortages are developing, producers say they're still holding off on major expansion until prices go higher because present price levels wouldn't provide an adequate return on new plant equipment.

117

The price freeze of 1971 did not create widespread shortages and distortions, however. As economist Roger Leroy Miller states, "Because of this already existing inventory of labor and of substantial unemployed men and machines, no noticeable widespread shortages occurred within Nixon's 90 days, but if the all-inclusive wage-price freeze had continued far into 1972, shortages undoubtedly would occur."

As has been stated before, a price freeze relies on a base period, usually directly prior to when the controls are imposed. The effects of an ill-timed base period can also cause undesirable consequences. For instance, the base period may have been a cyclical low for a new firm with no established customs. Or the base period may be poor because of bad management at the time. How is it possible to rectify these situations? Under strict regulations, base-period pricing could in these instances drastically reduce the efficiency of a firm. In some cases, base-period pricing has stimulated concentration of industries because smaller firms had to sell out to bigger firms.

A price freeze also tends to create "dual markets." Because knowledge of market conditions is imperfect, prices for similar products are not always the same. As shortages develop under a controls program, the differential between prices, even in the same locality, becomes evident. Middlemen spring up to take advantage of this disparity. They buy lower-priced goods and then sell them at the higher prices. The difference is their profit. A similar situation occurs with domestic and international prices.

The Effects of Below-Market Ceilings

Traditionally, price ceilings have been placed at prices below prevailing market rates. The following graph shows the results of this policy.

At a ceiling price below the market price, more consumers demand the product. At the same time, however, suppliers are less willing to supply the product because their return is reduced. Moreover, this artificial ceiling eliminates the *marginal* producers, who previously were just making enough profit to stay in business. During World War II, the Senate Subcommit-

PRICE CONTROLS CAUSE SHORTAGES

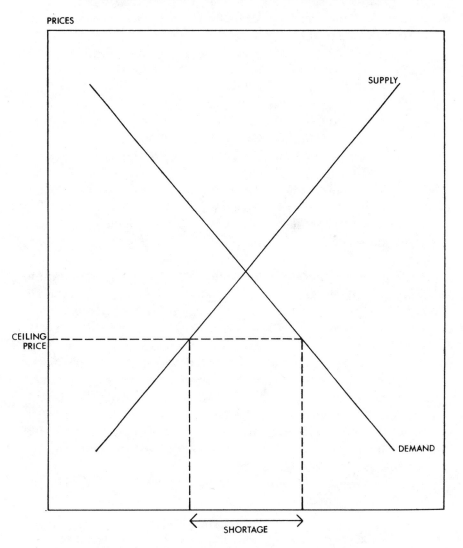

tee on Small Business repoited that price ceilings "drove 16 percent of small manufacturing companies in America out of business."

The gap between supply and demand becomes a shortage. The shortage results in long lines of consumers waiting to buy a product at bargain prices. The sellers are forced to somehow ration the shortfall the best way they possibly can. They resort

119

to favoring certain customers (such as established customers), taking bribes, bartering, or dealing in the black market. The more severe the shortages and the more vital the product, the more widespread these methods become.

Distortions are also created to avoid controls. Firms may try to create as many "new" products as possible that will not be subject to the regulations. Extra processing, different packaging, and minor changes in products—all things the consumer does not want but gets under controls—are tried. This kind of distortion occurred frequently during World War II. For example, Price Administrator Leon Henderson told of the case of a manufacturer of oak flooring who "stopped making desperately needed oak flooring and is cutting his good oak wood into round seats for baby strollers. He was making a normal profit on oak flooring, but he can make more money by supplying seats to the manufacturers of baby buggies. The OPA cannot touch him. . . ."

The postwar German experience was most enlightening on this score. A flood of "new" products was continually being manufactured in an effort to escape the stringent regulations. Nicholas Balabkim, in *Germany Under Direct Controls,* reports that "ash trays, fancy lamps, dolls, chandeliers, and other low utility items poured forth while the production of cups, pails, pots, plates, and other daily necessities stagnated. For example, a firm that formerly produced 75,000 electrical switches a month began manufacturing previously non-existent bakelite ash trays for which it had obtained a profitable price from the price-fixing authorities." One Swiss economist called postwar Germany "a hair oil, ash tray, herb tea economy."

In *The Vampire Economy,* a history of controls under Hitler, Guenter Reimann wrote:

> Rubber, for example, is extremely scarce, and it is consequently very difficult to buy a new rubber tire. It has become an officially decreed rule that no new tires may be sold unless the old tire is returned completely worn out. But this system does not work out in practice. Reserve tires are needed so badly that firms have resorted to buying entire new trucks just to obtain new tires. These tires were then removed and the new trucks sold without the tires as scrap iron. Business ingenuity in circumventing the State bureaucracy thus results in fantastic waste of materials, all in the name of preventing waste.

During this same period, certain trades flourished, such as companies specializing in the demolition of old buildings. Materials salvaged were valued near levels of new products. Secondhand automobiles were in tremendous demand, and were broken up and sold part by part.

Another case of distortion: During World War II, a nine-man gang of tire thieves stole automobiles in Washington, D.C., drove them out to the suburbs, removed hard-to-get gasoline and tires, and abandoned the cars.

A lumber producer said that his customers desperately needed one-inch boards, but due to OPA ceilings, they were not profitable to produce. So he sold them three-inch boards, on which he could make a small profit. His customers bought and recut them.

Other consequences of below-ceiling controls are a deterioration in the quality of products, the artificial expansion of exports, and distortions in grading methods.

Price Controls Lead to Socialism

Government has never been inclined to sit idly by and watch the unwelcome effects of its policies take hold. Instead, it seeks to deal with shortages, black markets, quality deterioration, distortions, and queues of angry consumers by extending even further its arm of authority. It imposes rationing, restricts exports, institutes strong penalties against quality reductions and other hidden evasion methods, reduces shortages by generously subsidizing specific markets, and so forth. All of these additional measures have been taken from time to time to plug the gaps created by price controls. Eventually, the controls program becomes so pervasive that a democratic country finds itself under complete socialist rule.

During World War II, the hand of government was present everywhere. In the U.S. alone, sugar rationing required the registration of every citizen in America, as well as half a million retailers, another half-million institutional and industrial users of sugar, and all wholesalers and refiners!

Ludwig von Mises was one of the first economists to recognize this universal tendency of gradual government expansion of

121

its powers under economic controls. He witnessed firsthand the socialist take-over in Europe. In *Planning for Freedom* (Libertarian Press, P.O. Box 218, South Holland, IL 60473), he lucidly outlines step-by-step how "Middle of the Road Policies Lead to Socialism." He begins with a simple example of government wanting to control the "high" price of milk:

The government believes that the price of a definite commodity, e.g., milk, is too high. It wants to make it possible for the poor to give their children more milk. Thus it resorts to a price ceiling and fixes the price of milk at a lower rate than that prevailing on the free market. The result is that the marginal producers of milk, those producing at the highest cost, now incur losses. As no individual farmer or businessman can go on producing at a loss, these marginal producers stop producing and selling milk on the market. They will use their cows and their skill for other more profitable purposes. They will, for example, produce butter, cheese or meat. There will be less milk available for the consumers, not more. This, of course, is contrary to the intentions of the government. It wanted to make it easier for some people to buy more milk. But, as an outcome of its interference, the supply available drops. The measure proves abortive from the very point of view of the government and the groups it was eager to favor. It brings about a state of affairs, which—again from the point of view of the government—is even less desirable than the previous state of affairs which it was designed to improve.

Now, the government is faced with an alternative. It can abrogate its decree and refrain from any further endeavors to control the price of milk. But if it insists upon its intention to keep the price of milk below the rate the unhampered market would have determined and wants nonetheless to avoid a drop in the supply of milk, it must try to eliminate the causes that render the marginal producers' business unremunerative. It must add to the first decree concerning only the price of milk a second decree fixing the prices of the factors of production necessary for the production of milk at such a low rate that the marginal producers of milk will no longer suffer losses and will therefore abstain from restricting output. But then the same story repeats itself on a remoter plane. The supply of the factors of production required for the production of milk drops, and again the government is back where it started. If it does not want to admit defeat and to abstain from any meddling with prices, it must push further and fix the prices of those factors of production which are needed for the production of the factors necessary for the production of milk. Thus the government is forced to go further and further, fixing step by step the prices of all consumers' goods and of all factors of production—both human, i.e., labor, and material—and to order every entrepreneur and every worker

122

to continue work at these prices and wages. No branch of industry can be omitted from this all-round fixing of prices and wages and from this obligation to produce those quantities which the government wants to see produced. If some branches were to be left free out of regard for the fact that they produce only goods qualified as non-vital or even as luxuries, capital and labor would tend to flow into them and the result would be a drop in the supply of those goods, the prices of which government has fixed precisely because it considers them as indispensable for the satisfaction of the needs of the masses.

But when this state of all-round control of business is attained, there can no longer be any question of a market economy. No longer do citizens by their buying and abstention from buying determine what should be produced and how. The power to decide these matters has devolved upon the government. This is no longer capitalism; it is all-round planning by the government, it is socialism.

Under Hitler's controls program, the centralization of economic power seemed to come almost by accident. As German economist Walter Eucken wrote, "After 1936, the German economy came more and more under central direction and administration. This was not the result of a conscious effort of policy to create a new form of economic organization. It was rather a result produced accidentally. It was the full-employment policy which started the movement, and it was the implementation of this policy which led step by step towards a centrally administered economy."

The government has at its disposal many tools to deal with the ill effects of controls. Mises points out only one such method—placing additional controls on the factors of production. Today such a method is generally considered futile in attaining the desired goal (as Mises aptly showed). So government resorts to more effective methods: direct subsidies to producers or consumers, rationing, standardization of production, and sometimes nationalization. In *Planning for Freedom,* Mises notes how this happened to England during World War II:

Then Great Britain again resorted to price ceilings for a few vital commodities and had to run the whole gamut proceeding further and further until it had substituted all-round planning of the country's whole economy for economic freedom. When the war came to an end, Great Britain was a socialist commonwealth.

It is noteworthy to remember that the British socialism was not an achievement of Mr. Atlee's Labor Government, but of the war cabinet

123

of Mr. Winston Churchill. What the Labor Party did was not the establishment of socialism in a free country, but retaining socialism as it had developed during the war in the post-war period. . . . Great Britain is to be called a socialist country not because certain enterprises have been formally expropriated and nationalized, but because all of the economic activities of all citizens are subject to full control of the government and its agencies.

In the United States, the expansion of government powers spread in all directions during World War II and in later programs. Controls were imposed on imports and exports, rationing was imposed, and so on. Concerning export controls, for example, the research firm Mansfield & Associates wrote: "Once comprehensive price controls were imposed on domestic commodities, it became necessary to subject sellers on foreign markets to control, or in response to inflated prices excessive diversions to foreign-markets would follow."

Joseph A. Schumpeter recognized this universal tendency of the expansion of controls in his *Capitalism, Socialism, and Democracy:* "In other words, price control may result in a surrender of private enterprise to public authority; that is, in a big stride toward the perfectly planned economy."

Other Forms of Controls

Profit Controls

Various methods have been developed by government to limit company profits as an indirect way of suppressing price increases. (I discussed these in chapter 4.) Profit controls, however conceived, are extremely difficult to enforce and can easily lead to distortions and waste. For example, under the profit-margin test of the Nixon controls, one firm deliberately encouraged larger expense accounts among executives. For the first time, it scheduled its annual stockholders meeting in the Bahamas. One of the company's executives said, "If we have to be inefficient, we may as well enjoy ourselves."

Rent Controls

New York City provides a clear example of the detrimental results of a long-standing rent-control program. New York City fell under a nationwide rent-control program in 1941 at the beginning of World War II. After the war, cities were given the option of continuing the controls. New York decided to keep its rent-control program, and it is still in effect. The city has finally adopted a "decontrol" program, but frankly, I think it is unlikely to ever reach its final stage.

A 1971 *Wall Street Journal* article by Richard Stone described the damage and distortions that resulted from decades of rent controls:

> The dimensions of the New York shortage are vast. The rental vacancy rate is below one percent. . . . Private building is at near-paralysis. . . . Increasing numbers of landlords simply give up, abandoning buildings they can neither afford to maintain nor sell at any price. Tenants, left with no heat, water, or electricity vacate such buildings in a matter of days. When that happens, blight swallows up whole neighborhoods, almost overnight.
>
> Every day there are fewer housing units available in New York City than the day before.
>
> New York's archaic rent-control law keeps the marginally poor whose fortune is improving from moving out of slum neighborhoods.
>
> Partly because of rent control, rent on private housing built since 1947—housing that doesn't come under the law—skyrocketed over the past decade. . . . After fierce public outcry, the city last summer passed a law holding annual increases to five percent. To no one's surprise, several major builders responded by withdrawing from the city.

In 1946, Milton Friedman and George Stigler wrote a pamphlet entitled *Roofs or Ceilings?,* which called attention to the consequences of rent controls in New York City and elsewhere. They wrote:

> Rent ceilings cause haphazard and arbitrary allocation of space, inefficient use of space, retardation of new construction. The legal ceilings on rents are the reason there are so few places to rent. Because of the excess of demand over supply, rental property is now rationed by various forms of chance and favoritism. As long as the shortage created by rent ceilings remains, there will be a clamor for continued rent controls. This is perhaps the strongest indictment of ceilings on rent. They, and the accompanying shortage of dwellings to rent, perpetuate themselves, and the progeny are even less attractive than the parents.

125

Paul Samuelson refers to the plight of French landlords and tenants as well as the New York City case in his textbook, *Economics:*

> To protect the poor from being gouged by landlords, maximum rentals are often fixed by law. These fiats may do short-run good; but they may also do long-run harm. Thus, France had practically no residential construction from 1914 to 1948 because of rent controls. If new construction had been subjected to such controls after World War II, the vigorous boom in French residential building since 1950 would never have taken place. New York City rent controls do favor those lucky enough to find a cheap apartment; but they inhibit new private building in low-cost housing, and they discourage economies of space utilization that high rents tend to induce.

Chapter Six

The Government as Regulator

The government's attitude toward its incomes policy has varied widely over the years. In some cases, particularly during war, the government's program has been a huge undertaking, affecting nearly every citizen. At other times, the plans have been so weak as to be entirely enforceable without additional expansion of the government bureaucracy.

The Bureaucracy

In order to carry out its grandiose plans to control prices, wages, exports, imports, and rents, implement rationing, and subsidize farm products during World War II, the Roosevelt administration ended up using over 68,000 federal employees. In addition, the government had about 400,000 volunteer "price-watchers." And even that number was far from sufficient to enforce the regulations.

Since World War II, the U.S. government has tried to minimize the bureaucratic setup of its controls programs. The Korean War controls staff amounted to about 19,000 workers. However, the Korean program was not as comprehensive as that of World War II. The Nixon staff was even smaller. Only about 4000 federal employees were involved during the 1971–74 period. Nixon emphasized from the beginning that he did not want a large bureaucracy created. To do that, and still have a strict program, the Cost of Living Council relied heavily on assistance from other government departments, such as the IRS and the Justice Department.

Costs of Controls Programs

There are no exact figures on the cost of federal wage and price programs. One Republican congressman estimated that a controls program similar to what took place during World War II would cost in 1970 $1–1.5 billion annually! According to government figures, the cost of two and a half years of Nixon controls amounted to nearly $200 million, not counting the costs incurred by business and other economic groups. Costs to industry were estimated to run anywhere from $721 million to $2 billion. Price Commissioner Grayson once said, "I guess that if we had gone with a rigid, highly enforceable program, we would have needed a hundred thousand people as a minimum. And that figure is probably low."

The Folly of Government Bureaucracy

Because the decision to begin an incomes policy is largely political in nature, the hard decisions on organization, compliance, and the kinds of controls to be used are usually made *after* controls are announced. President Nixon provides the most recent example of this. Nixon's decision to freeze prices for ninety days was made on an August weekend with only a superficial study made of economic controls of the past. Then, after the program was announced nationwide, the administration got around to setting up the bureaucracy to run the program. And it was two months later, in October, 1971, when the administration got around to planning Phase II and its organization. On top of that, when high officials finally chose a man to head the Price Commission, they chose someone without any experience with such a program. C. Jackson Grayson himself admitted, "My knowledge of controls and past control programs was abysmal."

Needless to say, the controls program was put together on a

piecemeal basis. The same has been true of virtually all other such programs, and drastic changes have been made from time to time according to the whims of government leaders. Philip D. Coleman, an official of Nixon's Cost of Living Council, made the following analogy to the Economic Stabilization Program:

Let us assume for a moment that a very rich and influential man desires to have a house built and he hires a group of very competent and very senior carpenters to build his house. He knows these workers to be of the highest caliber, and therefore he calls them together and says, "Please build me a house. Since I recognize that it's going to cost money to build my house here is my bank account—spend out of it what you need, but by all means get my house built quickly." With this, he turns and walks away expecting to come back and find his house built correctly.

Initially the carpenters squabble a little among themselves, because each had within his own mind the "best understanding" of what our friend's housing requirements are. Hence, each knows best how the house should be built. Eventually the carpenters resolve what differences of opinion they may have had and commence building the house.

Just as our workers are putting the finishing touches on our friend's house, he returns and the carpenters say to him, "Look, don't you have a beautiful house?" To this our friend replies, "Yes, it is a beautiful house. But it is not exactly what I had in mind—what I would like you to do is make a slight change here—move that wall over about two feet, shorten this room just a little bit, and make some other modifications. When this is done, I'll come back again to review your work."

Again the carpenters go to work, after a few discussions among themselves with a few "I told you so's" tossed in, and begin to modify and rebuild the house in accordance with their latest instructions.

And again, just as they are putting the finishing touches on the house our friend comes by. The carpenters say to him, "Isn't this a beautiful house?" Again our friend replies, "Yes, it is a beautiful house but it is still not just exactly what I had in mind." And here he gives further instructions that ask for new changes like raising the roof just a little bit, enlarging this room slightly, or changing the dimensions of another room. And again our friend walks away and says, "I'll be back to check your modifications to my house when you have finished."

This process iterates a number of times and still our friend is never exactly satisfied with the way that the carpenters have built his house. He is always wanting to make an additional modification, another deletion, a change here, or just a small change there, to make sure that as the house grows it fits his desires. All this confusion arises because he continues to evolve his own requirements over time.

It is obvious to see that when the house is "finally constructed" it is no more than one big patchwork of building and rebuilding, and at each of its stages, it less and less resembles that which had been originally in the minds of all at the start of the construction.

The Nixon program was always in a state of flux, and many businessmen in particular complained that they couldn't follow all the regulations (especially during Phase IV). There was one instance in March, 1973, when the administration changed positions practically overnight. Just two weeks before the Cost of Living Council imposed ceilings on beef, lamb, and pork, the Nixon administration announced that price controls on food products would be "counterproductive." Only two weeks! (Another case, unrelated to price controls, involved the about-face by President Ford in late 1974 when he went from favoring a *tax increase* to favoring a *tax cut* within a couple of months.)

Characteristics of Government Controllers

Whatever the type of incomes policy implemented, federal employees are likely to be overzealous in their pursuit of "social justice." The young workers during Nixon's controls program were described as "gifted tigers," who had "almost fanatical commitment to solving problems." They were known to have put in "exorbitant amounts of overtime and weekend work." This is the type of people that will be developing the nuts and bolts of future controls programs.

Can You Rely on Government Predictions?

In addition to being aware of the capricious nature of government wage and price policies, you should be very suspicious of predictions made by government economists. This is especially true of predictions about food prices, where supply and demand conditions change so rapidly. The following table shows a comparison of the predictions made by the Department of Agriculture and the actual results of food prices during 1972–73.

As the table shows, the government consistently severely underestimated food-price escalation. The lesson is clear: do not

Price Projections by the Department of Agriculture versus Actual Results

Month	Government Price Projections	Actual Changes (seasonally adjusted)
	(Percentage Changes)	
Nov., 1972	7.2	8.4
Dec., 1972	2.9	-1.2
Jan., 1973	5.8	25.2
Feb., 1973	7.6	22.8
Mar., 1973	4.7	28.8
Apr., 1973	2.9	16.8
Jun., 1973	1.9	10.8

rely on the government to correctly predict the rate of inflation, especially in food.

Are Controls Constitutional?

Earlier I asked "Are controls constitutional?" In my introduction I pointed out that, despite real doubts about the infringement of civil and property rights under controls, the federal courts have consistently ruled in favor of the government's arguments, in time of war and peace. The primary decision concerning the constitutionality of the World War II price-control authority was made in 1944 in *Yakus* v. *United States,* in which the Supreme Court upheld wide authority by the legislative branch to regulate prices and wages in general. Moreover, the *Yakus* decision permitted Congress to delegate to the executive branch legislative power to decide what prices, wages, and rents would be regulated. This would seem to fly in the face of Article 1, Section 1 of the Constitution, which clearly states, "All legislative Powers herein granted shall be vested in a Congress of the United States." Federal courts have been largely ignoring the separation-of-powers issue, however. Using the

Yakus case as precedent, the Supreme Court upheld the constitutionality of the 1970 Economic Stabilization Act. (It is worth noting, though, that the court did say that "blank check" authority to the president would be unconstitutional if provisions were not made for "gross inequities." The 1970 act and amendments did contain such provisions, and it is likely they will be included in future acts.)

Due Process and Equal Protection

Due process of the law and equal protection under the law, as contained in the Fifth and Fourteenth amendments, are potentially serious drawbacks to any price-controls program. Discrimination is clearly evident whenever the government permits exemptions to the general rules or tries to enforce a single rule on a particular industry. Such was the case with petroleum products, and a number of court battles insued during the Nixon controls. In one case regarding special rules for retail gasoline dealers, a district judge granted a preliminary injunction against the federal government's program, stating that the regulations "are arbitrary and discriminatory and bear no rational relationship to the ends sought to be achieved by the Act . . . and therefore violate the due process clause. . . ." The ruling was only temporary, however. A higher court reversed the district court, ruling that the retail dealers had not exhausted all the administrative remedies available under the regulations.

The sectoral approach, under which one sector of the economy had certain rules while another had different rules (e.g., rent rules were different from those for prices), was also challenged as a violation of the equal protection clause. The courts did not agree, however.

Taking Property without Just Compensation

The Fifth Amendment states, in connection with cases involving eminent domain, ". . . nor shall private property be taken for a public use without just compensation." This clause was used on occasion by litigants against wage and price controls. If we define *just* to mean that which the buyer and seller agree upon voluntarily without force or fraud involved, then clearly "just compensation" has not been accomplished when the buyer and seller are *forced* to accept a different price. However, the courts have questioned whether any property is actually "taken for a public use" in the case of wage and price controls. The courts have ruled that "if regulation goes too far it will be recognized as a taking," but no specific case has been tried using this interpretation, nor have the courts determined when a regulation has gone "too far."

A similar constitutional criticism involves the breaking or impairment of contracts. Contracts involving wages and delivery are often made in the future. These contracts are often voided by government decree under a controls program, especially under a general freeze. Is this not unconstitutional? The courts have generally dismissed this contention on the basis that federal laws can override private contracts as "social needs" dictate.

Jury Trials: A Loophole?

Based on past court decisions, an effort on the part of a citizen to get a controls program dismissed by taking the government to federal court appears to be largely futile. Similarly, if you are held in violation of the government's regulations, you are unlikely to win your case on constitutional grounds. But there is a "loophole" in the judicial system through which more and more citizens are trying to escape what they regard as unconstitutional acts of government. They are insisting on a jury trial whenever they are found to be in violation of a civil law involving wage and price controls.

In a jury trial, the accused is tried by a jury, not a judge. It is the jury that decides guilt or innocence. Now the judge in such a case will no doubt tell the jury that it is its duty to determine only the "facts"; if the jury finds that the defendant has broken the law, then the jury must find him guilty.

A jury does have another alternative, though these days judges never mention it. A jury has the power to rule on the constitutionality of the law itself! If a jury is convinced that to be forced to sell goods at a certain legally fixed price is unconstitutional and immoral, they can dismiss the charges even though the defendant clearly broke the law.

In legal circles, this is commonly known as "ignoring the law." But it is more than that. According to ancient common law, juries have always had the power to rule on not only the facts but the law itself. However, if a jury dismisses charges because it believes the law under which they were brought is unjust, the result does not apply universally. It only applies to the case at hand. The law is *not* regarded as unconstitutional solely on the basis of a jury's opinion. A jury's decision does not set a precedent; the Supreme Court's decision does.

The following article from the *Freedom Fighter* (4045 E. Palm Lane, Phoenix, AZ 85008) deals with this important concept:

A truth quite concealed from the general public is that the jury under the common law has the right, and is told that it has the right, to decide the law as well as the facts in a criminal case, even though the jurors must listen to the judge tell them what in his opinion the law should be.

You can scarcely find one case in the first 40 years of the history of this country, either on a federal or state level, where the jury did not decide the law as well as the facts of a criminal case.

In fact, in 1805 Supreme Court Justice Samuel Chase was impeached by the House of Representatives and tried by the U.S. Senate for trying to interfere with the jury's right to decide law in a prosecution for treason. Another charge Chase was tried for was that of trying to limit the defense's right to argue the law, quoting cases, to the jury.

Today the government's position is 180 degrees reversed from its position in the Chase impeachment. The judge tries to make the jurors swear to be bound by the "law" as it is given to them by the judge. This effectively invites tyranny and slavery, and degrades the juror.

Our founding fathers never even bothered to define "jury" in the Constitution and the Bill of Rights because every one knew that a jury decided law and fact in a criminal case.

Even in the first civil case held before the Supreme Court, *Georgia v. Brailsford,* 3 Dall 1 (1794) the five justices of the Supreme Court, three of whom had been delegates to the Constitutional Convention, charged the jury that there was no dispute of the facts and that it was the right and duty of the jury to decide the "law of the land" arising from those nondisputed facts in that case.

The change in the charge to the jury amounts to amending the Constitution, destroying fundamental rights of an accused, by redefining the word "jury" rather than by going through the difficult amendment process.

The reason the truth that the jury can decide the law as well as the fact in a criminal case is now concealed from the jury, the reason that a juror is told just the opposite and made to believe that he would be "taking the law into his own hands" and almost be in contempt of court if he used his conscience and brain to exercise his true duty to consider the justness of the law, is that this is the way socialism is poked down the throats of an otherwise unwilling public.

Socialism is unconstitutional under our limited government, but if you can make a jury swear to uphold it and to punish resistance to it, you can make the people think the country is accepting it, "democratically" because juries uphold it.

Of course, from a practical point of view, the biggest problem is convincing jury members that they have this right. To convince a jury that it should rule on the law itself because it is unconstitutional is no doubt an uphill battle, but it can be won under certain circumstances. One of the handicaps in convincing a jury is the accused's status in the community. If, for example, he is the president of one of the largest retail stores in the area, the jury may see him as part of "big business" and responsible for inflation. So use of this idea is for all practical purposes limited to small businessmen and individual citizens who appear wronged by "big government."

How Government Regulates

Government regulations under a controls program are not known for their clarity and simple understanding. This is largely due to two major factors. First, there are wide differences in market conditions, forcing the government to issue separate rules for different sectors of the economy. Second, evasive action on the part of businessmen, landlords, workers, and consumers requires the government to update with more detailed regulations. Differences in market conditions require allowances for exemptions, exceptions, varied methods of cost-pricing, and so on. Evasive actions require detailed listing of specific violations, what is allowed and what is not.

The complexity of controls regulations has at times completely baffled citizens. During World War II, for example, regulations for each commodity sometimes ran to twenty-five pages of fine print! The complex wording was often difficult to understand. Stories were told of visiting local OPA offices for an interpretation of a specific regulation, only to find the controllers could not understand the regulation either. Faced with a similar situation during Phase II of Nixon's program, Price Commissioner Grayson commented, "And the final regulations were often so complex (the rent regulations, for example) that even our Philadelphia lawyer (Bill Coleman) said he couldn't understand them."

Regulations involving "customary business practices" demonstrate the bureaucratic complexity that existed under Nixon's Phase II program. Grayson notes,

> For instance, one of the regulations stated that a firm could apply its "customary initial percentage markup" on invoice costs to determine selling price. If a grocery store customarily "marked up" peas by 20 percent in the past, then they must mark up peas by 20 percent under controls.
>
> Simple?
>
> It wasn't.
>
> Does the regulation apply on a firm-wide basis (such as, for all Kroger stores or for individual stores)? Does it apply to departments or to individual items within departments (the entire meat section or sirloins, rib eyes, T-bones, and so on)? Does it apply to all products by general categories or by brand (all peas sold, or Del Monte peas, Libby's peas, and others)?

"Use your customary business practice," was the answer. But that was not easy either. The practice might have changed since the base period. Also, what about a mixed-price system? Here, the prices of some items were based on an aggregate markup where items are grouped together. In other cases, prices were marked on an item-per-item basis. Consequently, as Grayson noted, "unless the firm was on a detailed item-by-item pricing system, it was difficult to pinpoint an exact violation." By the same token, using a mixed-price system, even the retailer may have a difficult time complying with the law.

In regulating business, the government was involved in the following considerations: defining sales, costs, product lines, or a transaction; FIFO or LIFO inventory system; seasonal variations; mergers and acquisitions; divestitures; export sales; promotional allowances; productivity and volume; long-term interest; by-product costs; transfer pricing; base-period determination; cost reach-back date; systems changing in a firm; joint ventures; treatment of variances; class of purchaser; foreign subsidiaries; customer products. Under this kind of comprehensive regulation, one wonders if it is proper to call American business "private" enterprise.

Government Biases

The *Historical Working Papers* describe at least four fundamental attitudes the government had regarding business during the Nixon controls.

First, antipathy toward big firms. The government tended to be tougher on larger companies, especially the automobile and steel industries. This was encouraged by policy-level officials. The huge corporations were in the public spotlight and had to be monitored closely.

Second, sympathy for smaller companies. Generally, this meant companies with less than one or two million dollars in revenue and fewer than 100 employees.

Third, antipathy toward multi-product/conglomerate firms. These companies were almost universally *not* granted relief.

Fourth, a shift to a sectoral approach. Rather than establishing regulations that applied to all areas of the economy, controllers found it more effective to issue individual regulations for each sector—industries, rents, unions, et cetera.

How Government Enforces Controls

In times past, governments have gone so far as to impose the death penalty for breaking laws placing ceilings on prices and wages. Seldom was this penalty, which hardly fit the crime, actually carried out. Punishment for these "economic crimes" has now been largely confined to fines, imprisonment, or civil sanctions.

During World War II, violators were subject to up to one year imprisonment or fined not more than $5000, or both, for *each* violation. Violators of ration orders were liable for fines of up to $10,000.

It sounds harsh. In practice it was not. Only "willful violators" could be prosecuted during the war. And this was difficult to prove, especially when regulations were hard to understand or were announced capriciously.

Violations by businessmen were more often punished by civil sanctions rather than fines or imprisonment. During the five years of war controls, 260,000 sanctions were issued against violators, but only 14,000 involved criminal prosecution. Other sanctions included: consumer's treble damages (68,000 cases), administrator's settlements (41,000), suspension orders (52,000), injunction suits (78,000), and 7000 miscellaneous actions.

Criminal proceedings amounted to less than 6 percent of total sanctions. The major reason for this was that it required much preparation by the Justice Department, which handled cases for the OPA. OPA enforcement officials were also reluctant to ask for criminal sanctions because controls were only temporary. In addition, the courts were months behind in civil and criminal suits. However, once the decision was made to file for criminal prosecution, the rate of conviction was 93 percent. But even then, the sentences were extremely mild. Only 25 percent of those convicted were imprisoned. Another 46 percent only received a fine. And 55 percent of prisoners were sentenced for six months or less.

Injunctions were issued, ordering that illegal activities be stopped. Interestingly enough, two of the most important considerations in such a court case were whether or not the businessmen knew the law and whether or not they had had meetings with OPA officials.

Treble damage suits only amounted to collections of $73 million during the war. Chester Bowles estimated that food overcharges alone were $1 billion a year.

One of the reasons the controls were not strictly enforced was because of cost considerations and the size of the controls staff. Clinard, in *The Black Market,* reports that "during the war there was a maximum OPA investigative staff of only 3,100 (with some supplemental assistance from other agencies and private citizens) which was expected to keep under surveillance the activities of millions of individuals and hundreds of thousands of business establishments, with millions of commodities and billions of transactions involved." The task of the government enforcer can never be easy under such circumstances.

138

Dealing with Evasive Acts

During World War II, government controllers were in many cases helpless in the face of the surprising ingenuity of businessmen and others in evading the controls. Clinard notes,

> Many violators indicated such great ingenuity that they undoubtedly represented the assistance given by lawyers and others who helped work out a method of getting around or violating the regulations. Reports from informed persons indicated that advisers were hired by business concerns, or legal advice was sought, in order to discover just how close one could come to breaking a regulation without being subject to prosecution. Numerous amendments to the various regulations, which were often the subject of ridicule by the press and various business interests, became necessary when ways and means of getting around them were devised.

Clinard also points out that some attorneys were hired away from the OPA for the very purpose of finding legal ways to circumvent the regulations!

Actually, direct price violations *without* evasion did not constitute the most common violation found during the war. The bulk of OPA violations involved "evasive price violations." The *Basic Manual* of OPA investigators lists dozens of evasive ways to get around the price ceilings. They include concealed violations, false invoices, billing for fictitious goods and services, false computations, cash-on-the-side, withholding sales records, back-dating sales, upgrading (falsely grading merchandise on invoices), and tying agreements (selling a product on condition of another sale), and quality reductions. Clinard outlines all these violations in his *Black Market*. It is obvious from these reports that the government sought to close every conceivable gap in the controls regulations in order to make them work.

In some cases, the OPA was able to obtain assistance from other agencies of the government. For example, quality deterioration in food could be prosecuted under the Pure Food and Drug Act. Adulteration and misbranding violations could be prosecuted under other laws. Upgrading was in violation of Department of Agriculture standards, particularly in meat, poultry, and eggs. In addition, a few states and municipal governments passed laws against evasion, including New York, Wisconsin, Rhode Island, and Arizona. In general, however, the states preferred not to get involved. Some seventy-five cities passed laws making it illegal to sell products above ceiling prices. Based on the World War II experience, Clinard recommends that enforcement be concentrated at the producing, manufacturing, and wholesaling levels—not the retail level.

Nixon's Economic Stabilization Program

Enforcement under Nixon's new economic policy of controls is worth examining. Of peculiar interest is a statement by the Nixon administration in the beginning that it would depend on the "voluntary compliance" of the American people to control prices, not a bureaucratic establishment. Interestingly, the same kind of double talk is used by the IRS, which continues to promote the idea that somehow the American people pay their taxes "voluntarily." And then they remind all Americans that they hold a "stick in the closet," ready to come down on anyone who does not "voluntarily" pay up.

It was the same way with the Nixon administration. Grayson stated that "heavy reliance on voluntary cooperation and customary business practice did *not* mean, however, that we did not monitor and audit firms, nor that there were no mandatory compliance checks and no follow-through." This was all part of the phoney claim that somehow the controls program was a democratic move.

Under the Economic Stabilization Act, violators were subject to a fine of not more than $5000 for *each* violation. "Each violation" was once proposed to mean every single sale above the legal price, but such an extreme interpretation was never seriously followed, nor would it likely stand up in court. Imprisonment as a sanction was not included in the law this time, as it was in previous controls periods. Injunctions and treble damage suits continued, however. And violators had to be "willful violators."

During Phase I, the government relied heavily on public support, which it generally received. "Phase I worked," government officials said. The complexity of the regulations grew substantially under Phase II, requiring public announcements,

140

publications, and posting of prices in stores. Enforcement of controls was lifted to a large degree in Phase III. And Phase IV, with numerous and often vague regulations, proved confusing to the public, and fewer complaints were registered as a result.

Under strict guidelines to hold down the controls bureaucracy, the controllers were extremely cautious and limited in enforcing the rules. A backlog of cases grew rapidly. The Justice Department and local assistant U.S. attorneys refused to prosecute unless large sums of money or big firms were involved. This was a "thorny problem" throughout the 1971–74 period. During Phase II, the Price Commission tried to place a 3 percent ceiling on price increases in the service industries, but it found it could not because there were "millions" of service firms in the U.S.; the IRS could not possibly enforce the ruling. Besides, there was no way to judge the data. Enforcement was so meager during the Nixon controls that the controllers at one point tacitly approved of black market operations in the domestic oil industry. A staff memo of June 13, 1973, concerning the effects of the second freeze on the domestic oil market, said the government should "indicate tacit acceptance of pre-Freeze black market prices for products and tacit acceptance of bonuses and premiums paid above posted prices for crude oil." Even officially the government has never been above breaking its own regulations!

The Role of the IRS

In keeping with the low-bureaucracy profile, the Nixon administration chose not to establish its own enforcement arm and compliance agency, but rather decided to work "within the system." The IRS was the most logical agency to take on the responsibility of enforcing the regulations because it had field offices throughout the U.S. and was familiar with all sectors of the economy. The IRS assigned 2000 agents to the task. That number proved to be far below what was necessary, even with public support. At first, during the 1971 freeze, the IRS was inundated with complaints from the public. Almost half of the inquiries to the IRS concerned rent regulations during the freeze. Naturally, the IRS was glad to see rent controls relaxed after the freeze and later eliminated completely. Even when rent controls were still on, though, the IRS had great difficulty in determining allowable rent increases. And the Justice Department was extremely reluctant to litigate any but the largest and most flagrant violations. In dealing with newly discovered rent and other violations, the tendency was for the IRS to *request* compliance rather than go to court.

The difficulties with retail gasoline outlets were particularly bothersome to the IRS. In a few cities, the IRS was overtaxed (!) by attempts to enforce Phase IV regulations on gasoline—octane levels, posting of legal prices, et cetera—and agents ended up simply reporting the types of violations. (In 1973 there were over 15,000 retailers and 250,000 retail outlets.) Without public support, the IRS was handcuffed. Many senior IRS officials objected to Phase IV regulations. They did not like the image problems presented by the mounting of a massive investigation against one particular industry—in this case, the oil industry.

Part II

The Citizen versus Price Controls: A Practical Guide

Chapter Seven

The Consumer Faces
Price Controls

Under price controls, shortages and related effects are the most important problems facing consumers. Prices certainly are no problem—they are at bargain levels, below what the market would set naturally. At the same time, however, the utility of money is reduced. A portion of the purchasing power of money is destroyed by price controls. No longer is the dollar almighty in the marketplace. Other factors are important in determining whether you can obtain the goods and services you desire. The most important factor is *time*—time enough to stand in line for hours to get a loaf of bread or spark plugs for your car. Time, then, becomes a good even more scarce than before controls were imposed.

How to Deal with Shortages

In previous chapters, I explained in detail why shortages arise as a result of controls. I also examined areas that are most likely to have shortages. In particular, I noted that mass-produced, price-competitive essential goods and services will become scarcer as controls continue. These necessities are characterized by high-volume sales, but low markup levels. They are the first to be subject to production cutbacks, while companies begin favoring low-volume, high-markup "luxury" goods. Gary North writes:

145

Since it is more difficult to make a profit in controlled industry, labor, capital, and raw materials tend to go into the uncontrolled industries where greater profits are likely. So the market for industrial goods begins to dry up. You cannot buy a home appliance easily, and new automobiles get scarce, and electrical goods disappear. And the available goods get shoddier as manufacturers are forced to cut costs to make ends meet. We are already seeing this to some extent, as inflation takes its toll; with price controls, these effects on workmanship are amplified. . . . One thing which we can expect to see is that new household electrical appliances and similar manufactured goods will become more difficult to obtain. Governments always place price and wage controls over those industries that are large enough and "vital" enough to be worth the effort to control. All industries are not equally subject to controls. Controls are put on such things as mining, steel manufacture, metals of all sorts, electronics, and automobiles.

Making Preparations in Advance

Preparations should be made now, during a period of slack in the economy and relatively low inflation rates. What kind of preparations should you make in expectation of coming shortages?

Stocking up is one of the most important steps you can take. This includes all basic consumer items, anything that you regard as essential. Tools, equipment, clothing, furniture, culinary items, and home materials are just a few examples. Make up a list of these items and make purchases over the next few years at a leisurely and comfortable pace until price and wage controls are announced. This will mean, of course, setting aside a substantial amount of money for this purpose (some have suggested at least $1000).

Your automobile is an important consideration. We are heavily dependent on our automobiles for transportation to work and for most of our leisure activities. The energy crisis in early 1974 demonstrated just how vulnerable we are to shortages. In his extremely useful article, "Auto Maintenance and Price Controls," auto mechanic Edward Powell writes:

With the imposition of controls, new parts for foreign and older domestic vehicles (pre-1967) will, because of limited demand, stop being manufactured, while quality of auto parts for the later models will deteriorate, possibly to the point of being dangerous.

146

The proper time to prepare for any event is *before* it happens. Since controls are coming, it is necessary that automotive parts and supplies be purchased and stored ahead of time. But mere storage of these items is a waste of time, energy, and money unless your vehicle is in proper condition. A car properly cared for is the assurance that you will be able to ride out the controls in safety and comfort. Proper maintenance, quality parts, and familiarity with your car are the keys to long life and minimum trouble.

Powell's article covers the following areas regarding car maintenance: lubrication and periodic inspection, tune-ups and repairs, additives and add-ons, dealer-specialty shops, tools, "minimum auto kit," foreign car kit, parts, storage, manuals, and a maintenance check list. His two-part article was published in the September 17, 1975, and October 1, 1975, issues of Gary North's *Remnant Review* (P.O. Box 1580, Springfield, VA 22151). The two-part series is available for $4.

Repair manuals for your automobiles and other forms of transportation will be very important during controls. One of the best catalogs for automobile parts is the Warshawsky & Co. (J. C. Whitney) automotive catalog (1900–24 State St., Chicago, IL 60616). In addition, Autobooks (2900 W. Magnolia Blvd., Burbank, CA 91505) offers easy-to-read manuals on practically every American and foreign car on the road today. Write for their free catalog or check their ads in most car magazines.

You should also consider purchasing extra oil and good oil filters (one of the best is the astounding Frantz Oil Filter, c/o Sky Corp., P. O. Box 6188, Stockton, CA 95206). You might also buy new tires. Finally, for tune-ups, you should have extra spark plugs, points, and condensers.

Preparations for the Next Energy Crisis

While on the subject of automobiles, I want to mention what you will need to be adequately prepared for the next energy crisis. Above, I mentioned the likelihood of price controls on gasoline and rationing. The government is simply not going to allow gasoline prices to rise to their market levels, which could easily be between $1 and $2 a gallon. There will be too much public outcry against it. At the same time, government leaders

147

will not be allowed to tolerate a situation in which Americans wait in long lines for gasoline as occurred in the early 1974 energy crisis. The ration tickets that are now sitting idle will be fully used.

On what basis will ration tickets be distributed? During World War II, gasoline rationing depended on the driver's needs. Coupons were graded A, B, or C. Most people received the "A" ration for "essential driving." "B" coupons were reserved for businesses and others who required additional driving. The "C" coupons were available to medical doctors and other "essential" persons. The "C" ration permitted almost unlimited driving, while the "A" ration was the most restrictive, aimed at curbing the "Sunday driver." Applications were required for basic rations and supplemental uses. In a single war year, rationing boards processed an estimated 30 million basic gasoline applications and 68 million supplemental applications. The type of ration coupons a person received depended on his driving needs, his occupation, and the number of cars he owned.

The next rationing distribution scheme may be similar, with one exception. In order to avoid the problems of black markets in gasoline, the government may permit a "white market," allowing users to buy and sell their ration coupons.

The following suggestions should help you obtain the most flexibility under gasoline rationing. First, hold on to any used cars you presently have. The more cars you use, the greater chance you will have of getting additional rationing tickets. Second, the more drivers you have in your family, the greater the chance for more coupons. And third, if you have a second, part-time job that requires automobile transportation, the better chance you have of getting more ration coupons.

Another very important consideration is the type of automobile or truck you own. In his excellent article, "How to Prepare for the Next Energy Crisis" (available from *Inflation Survival Letter,* 901 N. Washington St., Alexandria, VA 22314, $1.50), Roy A. Johnson writes:

> Small automobiles, six-cylinder cars with manual transmissions, pick-up trucks or vans manufactured from as early as 1960 to as late as 1968 by Ford, Chevrolet or Dodge are very utilitarian. Such vehicles (in good condition) get better gas mileage and are more easily maintained than

148

newer models. Repair and maintenance are more easily accomplished by purchasing identical models as spare parts. Further, they are not indicative of affluence.

Older models, however, are not as practical if you are not familiar with tools and machinery. Your best choices then are smaller, newer units, even though they are a serious compromise. Avoid larger units, especially four-wheel drive off-road types, unless their need is really justified. You'll spend a lot of money on fuel and maintenance.

Johnson also discusses the uses of motorcycles, bicycles, and even "exotic-powered vehicles" such as electric, fuel-celled, and steam turbine automobiles (which he does not recommend at this time).

Gasoline consumption will be particularly important when we are faced with another energy crisis, even with rationing and price controls. Unfortunately, you cannot rely on mileage figures released by the Environmental Protection Agency. Experts estimate that EPA mileage figures *overestimate* gas mileage by 20 to 30 percent. It is best to depend on independent consumer guides and car magazine reports for more precise mileage figures. The EPA figures *are* helpful in making comparisons, since all cars are tested under identical conditions.

During the next energy crisis, storage of oil and gasoline products will be an important consideration. You should have no problem in stocking up on gallons of motor oil. But what about gasoline storage? Is it safe? Gasoline storage is a complicated matter. The simplest thing to do is to fill a fifty-gallon steel drum absolutely full, add the proper amount of fuel-stabilizing additive and store it in a safe place. There is always a serious fire hazard, however, and there are many local laws against storing large amounts of gasoline.

Gasoline additives are absolutely necessary to maintain a proper gasoline mixture over time. Without these additives, gasoline will become useless in a matter of months. Such additives are relatively inexpensive and are available from Survival, Inc., P.O. Box 2246, Culver City, CA 90230.

The Need for Food Storage

While in the past agricultural products have largely been exempt from price controls, it is quite possible that controls *and* rationing will be placed on food products in the future. There are two reasons for this. First, during the controls period under Nixon, government controllers came closer and closer to placing full-scale limitations on food items. *Processed* foods were always under control. Only "raw" agricultural products were exempt, and in 1973, only the *first sale* of these was excluded from controls.

Second, price controls may be placed on agricultural products as a result of a crop failure in the United States. In the last couple of years, grain stocks have fallen to alarmingly low levels. The *Mead & Co. Newsletter* (630 Dorchester Blvd., W. Montreal, Canada) reports:

> The International Federation of Institutes for Advanced Study reached a consensus that the present climatic trend would continue the rest of the century, the climate would be more unstable, and that a climatically-related disaster was likely within the decade. Since 1972, a series of climatically-induced crop reductions occurred worldwide. In 1972, the Indian monsoon and the West African monsoon failed and there was a drought in Russia. In 1974, a disastrous drought hit the U.S., and the monsoons failed in India. 1975 saw drought hitting Russia again, causing crop failures of catastrophic proportions. As of today world grain reserves shrank to less than 30 days supply, compared to global stockpiles of 91 days in 1965, while world population followed the exponential growth curve.

Commenting on the possibility of famine, Howard Ruff has observed:

> We now produce surpluses in America. We sell a lot, we give some away. It has prevented worldwide catastrophe. There were 22 net food exporting nations four years ago. Now there are three, the U.S., Canada, and Australia. Due to temperature changes in the far north and far south temperate zones, and new patterns of drought, Canada and Australia will soon contribute little. In the third world, where population growth is by far the greatest, food production has dropped sharply due to drought and floods, on an unprecedented scale. Most have embraced socialism, which always lowers food production. Laos, Cambodia, and Vietnam will never again be exporters of rice. Even if the U.S. continued with bumper crops, and gave away all our surpluses, famine would overwhelm the world by 1980.

These quotes paint a gruesome picture. Whether famine conditions occur or not, though, it pays to be prepared just in case. The federal government will simply never allow prices to rise to their free market level under famine conditions. Controls will be put into effect and rationing will be imposed.

What will rationing of food be like? What needs to be done to prepare for it? During World War II, food in the U.S. was rationed about like gasoline was rationed. A "point" system was used. The Office of Price Administration validated stamps in each consumer's ration booklet, which was worth a total of forty-eight points per month. Each booklet had twelve stamps denominated in points—eight, five, two, or one each. Consumers could spend these points on any combination of items. By changing the point values among items, the government could discourage consumption of one item or encourage consumption of another. Processed foods were denoted by "blue" ration-point tickets, and meat had "red" point tickets.

There were a number of problems with this system. Shortages still appeared at times; counterfeiting, falsifying of applications, and stealing of coupons were widespread. The economic incentive for these violations could largely be eliminated in the next round of rationing by permitting the selling and buying of ration tickets.

One important problem facing those who store food during times of rationing will be whether or not issuance of ration tickets will depend on the amount of food stored. Will you get fewer ration tickets if you have a lot of canned goods in storage at home? In World War II, the number of coupons received depended on the amount of supplies Americans had on hand. Extra allowances were supposed to be made for home-canning, but this question was never resolved during the war. This naturally penalized those who had made preparations in advance by canning fruits and vegetables and making extra purchases before shortages appeared. It also led to widespread falsifying of supplies stored at home when Americans first applied for ration coupons. Could this happen again? It is definitely a possibility. Government controllers may even want to inventory home food stocks. I have heard it reported that some individuals have tried to circumvent this possibility by storing food away from their residences and in commercial storage compartments.

One class of food products that might escape government inspection is long-term, dehydrated and freeze-dried food. This

is food that has been sealed in cans (packed in an inert atmosphere, free of oxygen) to last for fifteen years and longer. The
reason it might be exempt from consideration for ration tickets is
that it is not usually stored for immediate consumption. It is
stored to be used in extreme cases, when no other food is
available.

When purchasing this kind of food, you need to be careful. In
the past few years, a dozen new dehydrated food companies have
sprung up. Prices, quality, and nutritional value vary substantially from company to company. A list of eleven different companies with addresses and phone numbers can be obtained from
the *Inflation Survival Letter* (901 N. Washington St., Alexandria, VA 22314, $1.50; ask for the July 16, 1975, issue). One
well-known, large, and long-standing company is Sam Andy
Foods (525 S. Rancho, Colton, CA 92324).

You should plan on spending at least $1000 per person for a
year's supply of food that will really support an adult. One of the
best books on the whole subject is Howard Ruff's *Famine and
Survival in America* (P.O. Box 172, Alamo, CA 94507; $4.95),
which discusses at length what you need to store.

Joining a Food Co-op

Another avenue to consider in preparation of coming controls
on food is joining a food co-operative. This is a system that is
increasing in popularity. Under controls, members of food
co-ops may fare better in obtaining the food they need, since
they compete directly with the large retail merchants.

A food co-op is composed of citizens who are primarily interested in reducing grocery expenses. Some co-ops have
realized savings of $80 to $100 per month on high-markup items.
The co-op is run by a committee. Usually there are committees
for order-taking, buying, filling orders, cleanup, and maintenance. Most co-ops are incorporated as nonprofit businesses.
Credit is established with wholesalers at major food distribution
centers. A co-op generally requires a building to store and dis-
tribute its food.

For more information on how to set up a food co-op yourself, or to join an existing one, write to the Cooperative League of the USA (Suite 1100, 1828 L St., N.W., Washington, DC 20036). Their literature includes: "How to Organize a Consumer Co-op" (free), "Moving Ahead with Group Action: the Buying Club" (85 cents), and "A Manual on Co-op Depots" ($3.25).

Food Terminals

You do not necessarily have to join a food co-op in order to take advantage of wholesale purchases. It is possible to make purchases as an individual at food terminals across the nation. Usually, though, you are required to buy in bulk. A food terminal list covering twenty-three major cities and fifty smaller towns is available from the U.S. Department of Agriculture, Consumer and Marketing Service, Fruit and Vegetable Division (12th St. & Independence Ave., S.W. Washington, D.C. 20250).

Purchases at food terminals, either by a co-op or an individual, only involve those items that have a high markup in the supermarkets—fresh fruits and vegetables, meat, eggs, and so on. Canned goods, sugar, and other items generally have a low markup at supermarkets and can be purchased there. These products can also be stored at home in large quantities and rotated for use.

The Role of Churches

Gary North writes in *Remnant Review* that "local churches, with their face-to-face contacts, their family atmosphere, and the strong element of self-help that should be present, will become important centers for establishing lines of supply."

North observes, though, that most churches today are not prepared to take on that responsibility. "The problem, of course, is that today's churches are seldom fit to exercise leadership. The social gospel denominations have generally forfeited the support of the laity. . . . They are in deep trouble, both financially and in terms of the confidence of the members. . . . The pastors are not used to the kind of responsibility that serious

153

economic breakdown would place on them. . . . The last people who seem to know what is happening are the members of the local conservative or fundamentalist denominations. They have a kind of gut-level conservative reaction to the drift of modern society, but they have done nothing, or next to nothing, to begin to work out alternatives for a time of crisis.''

One of the few major churches to play a significant role in preparing its members for future economic disasters is the Church of Jesus Christ of Latter-day Saints (Mormons). Since 1936, the Mormons have been exhorted by their leaders to store at least one year's supply of food, clothing, water, and fuel. Many of the dehydrated-food companies were started by Mormon businessmen.

The Latter-day Saints also have numerous practical programs to deal with the economic problems of today. Since 1936, they have operated a welfare program for members, a program separate from government efforts. In fact, members are discouraged from participating in federal or state welfare programs. "Our primary purpose," the church states, "was to set up, insofar as it might be possible, a system under which the curse of idleness would be done away with, the evil of a dole abolished, and independence, industry, thrift and self-respect be once more established amongst our people. The aim of the Church is to help the people to help themselves. Work is to be re-enthroned as the ruling principle of the lives of our Church membership.''

The foundation of the Mormon welfare system is the welfare farm. Each stake (local membership) has access to its own welfare farm, where there is always plenty of worthwhile employment for members temporarily out of work (interestingly enough, *nonmembers* can also participate in this program).

In addition to the welfare farm, the church receives donations from members for taking care of immediate needs of members in distress. The church prides itself in providing immediate assistance in times of natural disasters. When an earthquake hit Guatemala in February, 1976, the church flew in supplies and medical assistance within hours.

Funds are specifically set aside for assistance to those in need and for future hardships. Mormon bishops have access to a "bishop's storehouse," used for storing commodities for welfare workers.

The Relief Society, composed of the female members of the church, is the bishop's chief help in administering to the needs of those in distress. Through a monthly "home visit," the Relief Society president determines the welfare needs of a family—a food budget, clothing, shoes, household supplies, housing and utilities, household equipment, health and medical requirements, fuel, and household management—as well as attending to the spiritual needs of the members. In addition, the Relief Society holds meetings once a week to teach homemaking skills.

The fact is that the Mormon Church, insofar as its members heed the counsel of their leaders, is well prepared for any future economic debacle or widespread shortages. For further information on the church's welfare plan and related programs write to Church Office Building, 50 E. North Temple St., Salt Lake City, UT 84150, or contact a local church authority.

Of course, I am not suggesting that you join a church solely for the purpose of buying insurance for hard times. In becoming a member of any church, one must take on certain religious obligations not directly related to welfare assistance. If you already attend a church and little has been done to prepare for future shortages, consider developing a program with the assistance of your pastor and other members.

Personal Contacts and Barter Arrangements

Gary North characterizes establishment of controls on the economy as the "feudalization of the economy." "The medieval economy," writes North,

> like any preponderantly rural economy, was highly personal. Each man knew his supplier. The extent of the market was limited. Personal contacts were of great importance. This is one very important reason why Jews had a competitive advantage in international trade: family and religious contacts within this ostracized segment of the population were elevated in importance. But there really was not much trade, given the high costs of transportation. Bulky goods did not move very far from major waterways. Barter was basic to the economy, and face-to-face contact between producer and consumer was the standard operating procedure of that era.

Personal contacts with local merchants will again be extremely useful in obtaining needed supplies. Now is the time to get to know store managers. How? By making suggestions on the kinds of products sold in the store, seeking to resolve complaints, or complimenting—in all of these cases, you should have no problem meeting personally with the manager.

My wife had an experience that demonstrates the importance of knowing whom to contact for getting the supplies one needs. In the summer of 1975, there was an extreme canning-lid shortage. The lid companies operated at full capacity, yet they simply were not able to keep up with the overwhelming demand. Consequently, retail outlets in many parts of the country instituted various methods of rationing canning lids. Some limited the number of lids allowed each customer; others did not advertise that they had them, and so on. My wife went to one store and looked everywhere for canning lids. They were nowhere to be found. Finally, in desperation, she went to the store manager and asked him where the canning lids were. He explained that the store had only a small inventory and they were storing them in the back, giving them out only to people who asked. You had to ask or you were out of luck. Similar circumstances could occur again under rationing and price controls.

Another aspect of the "feudalization of the economy" will be the wider use of barter arrangements between buyers and sellers. Since money loses some of its utility under price controls, some people may find it advantageous to deal with sellers on barter terms. As mentioned in chapter 3, barter with cigarettes and other goods became widespread in postwar Germany when the reichsmark became worthless and price controls were continued. When goods and services become scarce, it often pays to exchange directly, scarce good for scarce good, especially if when sold alone they would fetch a price higher than the legal ceiling.

Barter was far more common a few decades back, even in the United States. In a delightful book called *Let's Try Barter*, Charles Wilson recounts how an average country store in the Arkansas Ozarks from 1890 to 1912 would clear at least two-thirds of its annual trade in barter. In the same place and time, most rural families effected at least half of their living by way of direct barter. Fresh meats were among the most-bartered items.

156

During the Great Depression of the thirties, many department stores offered barter exchanges (washing machines for stamps, for example).

Today much barter is carried on to avoid the tax man. Real estate is exchanged to avoid capital gains, for example. Wilson writes:

> Barter never was and by its very nature can never be the tax collector's friend. If you should doubt this, inquire of the U.S. Internal Revenue Service, which lifts more money from purses, wallets, socks, mattresses, lock boxes, safety vaults, and bank accounts of the U.S. public than all conquered nations or empires have paid in tribute throughout history. Barter stops sales taxes the way hanging stops the horse thief. Legitimate barter is enormously difficult to "declare" or compute on routine tax forms, and it stops capital gains. . . . Many of the tax-escaping barter practices have long since become so workable that they are rarely mentioned as barter. The trade-in of used autos for new autos is a most-practiced example. It is a modified and, alas, too often an abused barter.

Barter deals on a one-to-one basis usually involve a lot of time and trouble. I remember one good friend who sold pool tables for a living. In making his own purchases, whether for his business or for personal use, he tried as often as he could to swap a pool table for what he wanted. He was surprisingly successful.

Swapping pool tables has its limitations, however, especially when buying small items. This is where the trading posts, the home exchange for clearing duplicated or unwanted gifts (e.g., wedding gifts), the homemaker's swap shop, the collector's swap shop, the traveling trading post, the overseas barter center, and the traditional country store, all become useful. These kinds of barter shops will undoubtedly proliferate under controls. Wilson notes: "In fundamentals the best barter tends to stay at the levels of the playpen, the back porch, the kitchen or other work shops, the community center or local store, or the church benefit or public market." Wilson says that barter can even include food items. "Barter shelves in stores also offer possibilities for many types of home-produced foodstuffs, including canned fruits, vegetables, berries, jams and jellies, and dried fruits. All may be displayed for open offers or swapped directly for similar edibles required to fill out and diversify home food shelves."

In conclusion, Gary North writes:

157

It must be understood that barter represents a collapse of productivity and the reduction of everyone's income. It is not an efficient system. But it is more efficient than the repressed economy under price controls. This is why it would pay people to become familiar with swap meets, auctions, local bazaars, "flea markets," and all other similar institutions. There will be a day when knowledge of "junk" may mean survival. The proverbial horse trader may be seen again in some parts of America. It would be wise to start making contacts now if you are already in a rural area.

For further information on barter exchanges, write any of the following companies: Business Exchange, Inc., 871 Melrose Ave., Los Angeles, CA 90046; Business Exchange East, Inc., 745 Fifth Ave., New York, NY 10022; Hilton Exchange Plan, 5032 Lankershim Blvd., Room 6, North Hollywood, CA 91601; and Barter Charge, 6725 Sunset Blvd., Los Angeles, CA 90028.

Use of Gold and Silver Coins

Gold and silver coins are no longer legal tender in the United States (except for pre-1965 silver coins), and therefore can be considered barter items. Under price controls, gold and silver coins may well serve as the medium of exchange in barter transactions due to their universal acceptance and versatility. Gold and silver will return to prominence and once again become "money."

The coins of today vary considerably in value and should facilitate the purchase or trade of nearly all goods and services. Small gold coins include the Mexican two, two and a half, and five peso, the Austrian one ducat, the Colombian five peso, and the British sovereign. Larger coins include the South African krugerrand, the U.S. double eagle, the Mexican 50 peso, and the Hungarian and Austrian 100 corona. Silver coins include dimes, quarters, half-dollars, and silver dollars. Gold and silver coins can probably be used to purchase products selling today for anywhere from thirty cents to hundreds of dollars.

Gold and silver coins can be purchased at any coin dealer or at some foreign-exchange dealers. The best coins to purchase for barter purposes are those that are well-recognized in the United States—particularly U.S. coins (double eagles, silver dollars, and the like) and perhaps the Mexican fifty peso and the kruger-rand. Bullion coins (those with little or no numismatic value) are the cheapest to buy in terms of low premiums over their metal content. Numismatic coins sell far above their gold or silver value and may not serve as well as bullion coins for barter purposes. Pre-1965 silver dimes and quarters are likely to be the most universally accepted coins for trade. You can purchase these coins in lots of ten or by the bag ($1000 face value).

Repairs during Controls

I mentioned above how products such as new household products and manufactured goods will become scarce under controls. And the new products that are sold will likely be shoddy and in need of repair. Gary North writes: "If manufactured goods, especially home appliances, get scarce, then the home repair expert experiences a bonanza. People have to make-do with the old washing machine or refrigerator."

The consumer will have to learn how to do basic repairs on his essential home appliances and products if he is to avoid exorbitant charges by repairmen. (Some would say that exorbitant fees are already being charged by repairmen, but in any case, under controls they would be worse.) Moreover, if wage controls are imposed on repairmen (a likely situation), then consumers must know how to repair their own appliances if they want to keep them running. North elaborates: "The demand for repair manuals and how-to-do-it books will increase, and so will prices for such publications. The smart individual will buy his 10-year subscription to a home repair magazine the day following the announcement of price controls." (Problem: the publishing firm may go bankrupt under controls. Risk, thy name is bureaucratic meddling!)

There are numerous books on the market to help you repair your own home appliances and products. *Know-How (A Fix-it Book for the Clumsy But Pure in Heart)* by Guy Alland, Miron Waskiw, and Tony Hiss is probably one of the best of recent releases on helping the uninitiated. If you are interested in really knowing how appliances, televisions, radios, stereos, and the like work, you should investigate do-it-yourself kits. In any case, a full supply of repair tools should be purchased over time.

Taking Advantage of Exempt Markets

In chapter 4, "What Kind of Controls Are Coming," I discussed numerous areas that have previously been exempt from controls. Many of these exempt areas will serve as relatively unlimited sources of supply. Demand for exempt products will increase when shortages arise elsewhere. Moreover, with the increased demand, these exempt producers will not be deterred from increasing output. Let us look at the exempt areas of specific interest to the consumer.

Foreign Products

Imports have been exempt in the past, though they have been restricted at times (World War II). You would be amazed at how many different consumer items you can purchase from foreign lands. You can buy almost any basic household item from importers. I recently received in the mail a brochure from a "foreign buying club." The company described in detail how it was possible to obtain practically anything one could want from its foreign suppliers at prices even below what *wholesalers* pay for U.S. products here. And these were not cheap, breakable products either; they were such items as Nikon cameras, Swiss watches, Peruvian wool blankets, Canadian appliances, and so on.

Here's a quote from a recent brochure describing a publication called the *American Directory of Importers* (Printing Unlimited, 1013 South Kansas, El Paso, TX 79901; $3.50):

> Lists hundreds of U.S. importers and products handled. Many offer free catalogs and sales aids. Buy direct from the importer at less than wholesale prices! All products are warehoused in the USA and ready for delivery to you in small or large lots. All regular importing chores, duty, taxes, customs, etc., have been paid. Now you can skip the "middle man" and deal directly with these importers. Buy oriental products from the bazaars of Hong Kong . . . miniature radios and electronic gadgets from Japan . . . linens and curios from Ireland . . .

wood carvings, music boxes and beer steins from Germany . . . watches from Switzerland . . . figurines from Africa . . . and much, much more from hundreds of importers representing dozens of countries.

Importers are also listed in the Yellow Pages, especially in such large coastal cities as New York City, San Francisco, and Los Angeles. Contact large suppliers and ask for sales literature and "foreign buying clubs." When shortages in home items become widespread, it pays to be a regular, established customer with importers.

Damaged and Used Goods

There is simply no way that federal controllers can control the prices of damaged and used goods because prices vary so widely. They are therefore invariably exempt from controls. Learning to make purchases in used or damaged goods will be extremely helpful in the future. Where should you look for these exempt goods?

The classified ads section of your newspaper is a good starting place. If you have never read the classifieds extensively, you will be surprised by what is sold there. Besides cars and homes, the classifieds offer building equipment and supplies, all kinds of merchandise, and legal notices of bankruptcy and other sales of real estate and other property.

Garage and yard sales can be a source of supply. Here are some tips that might help you make wiser purchases. Check first in the classified section of your newspaper. Many garage sales are advertised there, listing many of the items for sale. By calling first, you can find out much about the items for sale. Go to the sale early, or better yet, go before the sale begins if the sellers will allow it. Have something specific in mind before you go to a garage sale. This will keep you from buying a lot of unnecessary goods. Go to bargain. *Refuse to pay listed prices.*

Flea markets and used-furniture stores offer some good buys on occasion. Remember, though, that as with garage sales, there is little uniformity in quality or pricing. Nor are there guarantees that enable a dissatisfied customer to return a purchase. Nevertheless, used furniture in good shape is about 50 percent

161

cheaper than new furniture of comparable quality. Under controls, of course, discounts like that may disappear, but at least used furniture will always be available.

Auction markets constitute one of the best opportunities to obtain high-quality products at reasonable prices. And because auctions are, in a sense, restricted to expert bidders, they are likely to remain good sources of supply in times of widespread shortages. Every item you use in your home or business can be purchased at auctions.

John Kamin, in his excellent *How to Make Money Fast Speculating in Distressed Property,* distinguishes between two types of auctions, retail and wholesale. (Unfortunately, the distinction is never made in auction advertising.) Essentially, the retail auction is characterized by close-to-retail prices for common merchandise, high-pressure auctioneering, and the absence of professional dealers. At retail auctions, it is even possible to end up paying more than retail prices. You should avoid these kinds of auctions if you are interested in buying at below retail.

Wholesale auctions are characterized as follows: (1) the goods *must* be sold, no matter what the price, (2) a lot of dealers are present, (3) there are plenty of good products, and (4) prices are low.

Some of the best wholesale auctions are:

IRS auctions. The IRS has the power to seize property of delinquent taxpayers, individuals and businesses. Usually there are no minimum bids in these auctions and dealers bid low. Everything *must* be sold.

Bankruptcy auctions. This type of auction provides one of the best ways to buy *brand new* equipment, merchandise, and products of all kinds at low prices. These are distress sales. During price and wage controls, there will be an increasing number of personal and business failures resulting in liquidation of property at auction. This should be an extremely lucrative area of supply during shortages.

Probate and estate auctions. These types of auctions may be conducted by a probate court, a bank trust department, or the relatives of a deceased property owner. You should check out the kind of merchandise offered for bidding *before* the auction, since in many cases all that is available is "left-overs" and "junk."

162

Creditor's auctions. These auctions sell property that was used as collateral in loans that went bad. This can involve automobiles, real estate, furniture, trucks, and so forth.

Lost property auctions. The police auction is the most common example of this method of selling items that have been lost or abandoned. The police auction is a good place to pick up a bicycle for your children, for example.

According to John Kamin, it is best to attend auctions during bad weather, when competitors tend to stay away, and during the months of April (after taxes are paid), June (when families need money for vacations), September (when kids go off to college), and during December (Christmas).

The rules vary on the best ways to bid during an auction. Kamin recommends the "quantum jump" technique of waiting until most of the bidding has ended and then entering the bidding for the first time with a big advance. Kamin writes, "Your goal is to put that other bidder in a state of *shock.* . . . You want to make him so disappointed that he won't even have the heart to bid. You want to catch him by *surprise.* . . ." René Baxter suggests a different approach. In *Financial Survival in the Seventies,* he writes, "Start bidding at once when the item comes up. . . . Never hesitate a second to raise the bid when called by the auctioneer. Remember your ceiling price. That's what it's worth to you, so calmly and confidently raise the bid each time someone else bids above you. The effect is devastating. The other bidders have no idea how high you will go and will often drop out early, leaving you with a *real* bargain. If you hesitate, you will give the other bidders the idea that you are about to drop out and might not meet just one more raise. . . . When your ceiling is exceeded stop bidding at once. . . . Don't get excited and pay too much. It's surprisingly easy when you really want the item. Just keep in mind that there are *plenty* of other auctions." Baxter also suggests that you go early and look over what is being offered at the auction. Also, you should limit yourself to what you want and nothing more.

Where can you look for news of auctions? There are several places—the Yellow Pages, the Sunday papers, legal newspapers, notices of sheriff's sales at local court houses and post offices, to name a few.

Chapter Eight

The Worker Faces Wage Controls

This chapter is devoted to the most important area of employee-employer relationships. Price and wage controls tend to make labor-management problems worse than they would otherwise be. And even in cases of harmonious relationships, discord and divisiveness can occur between the worker and his boss as a result of controls.

An inflationary climate creates an unfortunate situation in which employees are given raises wholly unrelated to any increase in productivity. The "increases" in income are offered to offset a general rise in the workers' cost of living. During an inflation, this is a natural consequence, and "cost-of-living increases" are largely a result of new supply and demand relationships. Under wage controls, these natural relationships are severed by government edict. An employer may want to give his workers a raise, but he cannot. Is there a solution? Are there legal ways to circumvent capricious government edicts that artificially hold down wages and salaries? How can *you* get a raise during wage controls?

Exemptions from Wage Controls

It is first of all important to recognize the existence of loopholes under wage controls (just as there are numerous loopholes under price controls). I examined these wage exemptions in chapter 4. They include the "working poor," employees of small businesses (employing sixty workers or less), U.S. citizens abroad, civilian and military employees of the federal government, and professional athletes, actors, and other similar classes of "freelance" workers. These labor sectors were exempt from controls during the Nixon program and are likely to be excluded again in the future. If the government institutes a stricter controls program, small businesses might not be exempt as before. Without this exemption, however, a huge bureaucratic controls organization will be required.

Employees of small businesses do not always fare well under controls, however. A freeze can be devastating, as some small businesses learned in 1971. The "Basic Steel Agreement," which was concluded right before the August 15, 1971, freeze, gave a 13 percent raise to employees of seven major steel companies. But employees of other, smaller companies, which traditionally have caught up six months or so later, ended up with wages frozen below their counterparts. This kind of situation puts a strain on the management of smaller corporations, which must offer some form of nonpecuniary benefits to keep their employees from going to work for larger companies.

From the worker's point of view, the best way to circumvent or avoid wage controls is to be exempt, either by working for a small company or outside the U.S. Or you could become an athlete or an actor!

Another area that could be tried is the service sector, especially those jobs involving consultation. The service area is simply too vast to control, and the government may choose to tacitly exempt it by failing to enforce the regulations. It *may* be possible to change the *name* of your current occupation to take advantage of these exemptions, without actually looking for a new job.

A serious dilemma continues to face those working for large corporations or the federal government. Wages and salaries will be closely monitored and artificially restricted by the government. Federal wages will probably keep up with private workers. How is it possible to obtain higher income under these circumstances?

Circumventing Wage Controls

Wages and salaries are not the only pecuniary benefits attached to working for a particular company. Every major company offers fringe benefits, working conditions, office equipment, and various sorts of promotions. Is it possible to improve any of these categories without breaking federal controls laws?

Fringe Benefits

Of course, the government is well aware of some of these methods. Wage controls were so severe during World War II in the U.S. that all major private companies began offering all kinds of fringe benefits—pension programs, life and casualty insurance, vacation and holiday pay, and on and on. The Wage Stabilization Board carefully monitored and ruled on these fringe benefits. It set the amount of time for vacations and limited holiday pay and overtime. Due to increasing fringe benefits as well as the extensive use of overtime, workers were able to increase their earnings during the war. Dexter M. Keezer notes that "it is largely because of working longer hours and on better paying jobs that during the war period the average weekly earnings of workers in industry increased about four times as much as the average rate of pay for doing the same job."

The Wage Stabilization Board did not have the facilities to check up on company methods of increasing the income of their workers. Near the end of World War II, the Wage Board actually promoted the use of fringe benefits.

The Nixon administration was not as lenient with fringe benefits, however. Under the 1971 freeze, fringe benefits were not allowed to be increased. They were considered to be the same as wages. Under Phase II, wages and fringe benefits continued to be considered "perfect substitutes," and so the two together could not exceed the 5.5 percent limits. Congress, however, sought to make exceptions to this hard-and-fast rule. The 1971 amendment to the Economic Stabilization Act excluded certain fringe benefits from the controls program. This exemption was contingent upon the condition that they could not be "unreasonably inconsistent" with the goals of the Economic Stabilization

Program. (Congress decided that if they exceeded a 0.7 percent increase annually, they were "unreasonably inconsistent.")

The exemptions were: group insurance plans, disability and health plans, certain pension programs, and profit-sharing or savings plans. Those areas not mentioned (and therefore not exempt) were overtime premiums, paid leave, holidays, paid vacations, and similar "extras."

Of course, the government was not always organized sufficiently to determine what was and what was not allowed during the Nixon controls. During Phase IV, in September, 1973, for example, the *New York Times* asked the IRS, "Suppose an employer wants to reward an employee. He can't give him a wage increase or a bonus during the freeze, but could he grant an extra week's vacation?" The *Times* reported that "the question about whether an employee could be given an extra week's vacation as a reward for good work produced slightly more no's than yes's. But one official, who said the extra vacation was prohibited by the freeze, volunteered the suggestion that the company go ahead and do it anyway. 'It would be considered a bonus,' the official said. 'But who would know. Just don't say anything about it.' "

Employee Stock Ownership Plans

A relatively new form of profit-sharing that will probably fall into the exempt fringe benefit category is the Employee Stock Ownership Plan (ESOP). ESOP is a trust set up by a corporation for the benefit of its employees. But it actually benefits both the employer and the employees because all contributions to the ESOP are tax-deductible to the employer and tax-free to the employee. ESOP funds may be invested anywhere, unlike ordinary profit-sharing and pension programs. The most well-known advocate of the ESOP, Louis Kelso, a San Francisco attorney and author of *The Two-Factor Theory,* sees the ESOP as a way of giving employees equity in their companies. This should tend to promote productivity. It is uncertain how ESOPs would be affected by wage controls, but they appear to bear investigation. For an explanation of how ESOPs work, write for the January 28, 1976, issue of *Inflation Survival Letter* (901 N. Washington St., Alexandria, VA 22314, $1.50).

167

New Promotions and Titles

One of the easiest ways to get a raise is to be promoted. Under the 1971 freeze, "bona fide" promotions were allowed. What was a "bona fide" promotion? The government approved all promotions based on completion of a college degree, apprenticeship, and genuine demonstration of superior work. Actually, the promotion of an employee is subjectively determined by his superiors, and consequently it is quite difficult to prove that promotions are "undeserved."

An indirect way of giving a promotion is to assign a new title to an employee. Sometimes such practices can get out of hand. During World War II, waitresses working for government contractors in Alaska were classified as "journeymen carpenters." Workers in a steward's department were given the title and pay of "crane and bulldozer operators." These were blatant violations of war wage controls, but the Wage Board simply lacked the facilities to check up. Cases like this will not be tolerated in the future. Employers better count on being more elusive than that.

Gary North provides an example:

A truly competent secretary should be made an executive secretary, preferably before controls are imposed, certainly immediately after they are imposed, and absolutely once labor shortages appear. People are status seekers as well as income seekers. They want others to understand their value to a firm, and a title is one means of insuring such recognition. With a promotion in title, the promoted worker should have more responsibility—true responsibility. If possible, the promoted secretary-clerk should have a full-time or part-time assistant. Again, the principle of division of labor must be recognized and honored in the price control breach. It is absolutely imperative that people be paid in direct proportion to their economic contribution to production. Price controls make this wage-production relationship very difficult to ascertain with accuracy, but managers must try to discover it. *Every* worker must be paid in terms of the *cost of replacing* him or her.

Merit, Bonus, and Step Increases

Over the years, private companies have developed various methods of rewarding employees for accomplishing specific tasks. Merit, bonus, and step increases have been used in this manner. Would these practices be allowed under controls?

This is debatable. During the 1971 freeze, step increases were not permitted if they were based on longevity of service only. During Phase II, on the other hand, wage increases due to longevity and automatic progression were excluded from controls. Also during Phase II, the Pay Board ruled that if a "merit" increase was "discretionary," it would be allowed. A merit increase was defined as a wage increase based on an employee's performance rather than the cost of living or length of service. The Pay Board permitted increases of up to 7 percent in "formal merit compensation plans."

Many of the price and wage regulations that came out of the Nixon controls program were based on "customary business practices." Consequently, it may be to the benefit of a company to establish a tradition of offering various forms of bonuses. Gary North elaborates in *Remnant Review:*

> Prior to the imposition of controls, businessmen would be wise to use some form of the *bonus* system of compensation. I think that bonuses are superior to flat salary increases. It stimulates people to greater output. Bonuses, not being "owed" directly and regularly, are not mentally classified in the category of "minimum expected payment," which then serves as a launching pad for even more wage demands, whether actual or mental (i.e., resentment against management for not offering a raise). When raises are given, household budgets are expanded and even over-extended (thereby requiring another wage increase). Bonuses, on the other hand, are seen as special rewards for specific efficiencies. Furthermore, a tradition of bonuses established prior to controls might give a manager some leverage in the future. Obviously, price and wage regulators will regard bonuses as disguised raises. The firm that has a long tradition of bonuses may escape the controllers for a time. (Frankly, I doubt it. No one pays bureaucrats to compromise, except directly, and that is called bribery, and people go to jail for it. But a tradition of bonuses might help, and it pays off now anyway.)

Payments in Kind

Another ingenious method of eluding wage controls is through payments in kind. Because wage restrictions were so severe in

169

postwar Germany, German businessmen began paying workers in kind as well as in money. They would retain some output for distribution to workers at legal prices. This was especially effective when the company produced consumer products. If the workers could not directly use the products, they were still willing to take them. They would then use them to swap for other goods or sell them in the black market. Surprisingly, this practice was condoned by the Allies.

The system, known as a "truck wage system," was quite extensive. The workers in a cutlery plant received pocket knives, a shoe manufacturer gave out shoes, a clothing producer paid in textiles, electrical manufacturers gave out electric bulbs, cigarette producers distributed 800 cigarettes a month as part of wages, and so on. Some industries had a difficult time of it. The steel and building industries, for example, had practically nothing to offer and consequently had extreme difficulty in keeping their workers.

Another example is the practice of improving the office in which an employee works. Gary North writes: "An extremely effective means of non-wage competition is to drop a thousand dollars in a secretary's lap and tell her to go out and spend it on the office. Tell her she can do anything she wants with it: new furniture, tape recorded music, new filing cabinets, a new IBM self-erase typewriter, or whatever. Make it clear that it is for her benefit. What will make the office more pleasant for her? Your competitor who may want her services has not designed an office around her needs."

Gifts also serve as an excellent alternative to wage increases. These could include extra tickets to a football game, gold or silver medallions, paintings, calculators, and gifts for special times of the year (Christmas, Fourth of July, Secretary Week). There is simply no way the government can interfere with this kind of nonsalary payment.

Other Novel Methods

Ways to get around wage controls can be found under any circumstances. During the 1971 freeze, one university decided to circumvent the freeze on salaries for its faculty members by offering them interest-free loans! The government found out about it. The only way the Cost of Living Council could block this novel idea was to call the interest-free loans "wages." And that is what it did! I wonder what the government would have done if the university then decided to offer loans at the going rate of interest and then month after month fail to collect the principal.

There's always a way if there's a will. Other methods used in the past include sending a worker on a "business" trip to his home town or to the Bahamas, permitting increased overtime, from time to time letting workers off early with pay, longer coffee breaks, and so on. Deceptive practices never end under government wage-fixing.

Changing Jobs as a Way of Increasing Income under Controls

One of the quickest ways of increasing your income under controls is to be hired by another firm that pays higher wages for the same job. Differentials in wage levels exist in practically every industry for the same tasks, whether for waitresses, secretaries, or junior executives. This technique is limited to some extent, but it is possible to raise your annual income sometimes by $1000 or more. Differentials in wage levels may even be more glaring during wage controls. Remember the example of the 13 percent raise by steelworkers in the seven largest steel plants? Employees of the smaller companies were not allowed to catch up during the 1971 freeze. But there was nothing keeping them from being hired by one of the seven major steel companies.

When wage controls are reimposed, employees should always keep their eyes open for new job opportunities with other firms. As labor shortages begin appearing in competitive, vital industries, large corporations will offer additional incentives to potential employees in the form of free first-class travel to and from corporate headquarters, full reimbursement of moving expenses plus per diem allowances, et cetera. They will also no doubt offer new responsibilities at higher rates of pay. You may even be

171

offered a new title even though your tasks may be almost the same as in your previous job.

Another important thing to remember is that wage and price controls will force major shifts in the spending habits of the public. This means the creation of additional job opportunities in these areas of increased demand. Workers will flee from the tightly controlled sectors of the economy into the uncontrolled sectors (as will capital and management), and the first ones to do so will profit the most. What kind of uncontrolled areas am I talking about?

Repair and Trade Vocations

We previously mentioned the fact that controls will result in the reduction in quality of goods and services, especially in the "vital" consumer goods. Major appliances—refrigerators, washers and dryers, televisions, stereos, stoves, sewing machines, trash compactors—will be more and more in need of repair. This will increase the demand for good repairmen. Consumers will not be able to replace their old appliances with new ones. The new ones will be either in short supply and unavailable or they will not last long. Major companies will be forced to reduce or even eliminate their warranties.

How will this affect the repairman? Gary North writes:

> If manufactured goods, especially home appliances, get scarce, then the home repair expert experiences a bonanza. People have to make-do with the old washing machine or refrigerator. The day that price controls are declared, the intelligent buyer will go down and buy every $25-$50 used refrigerator he can store. He will buy old broken motors from junk stores. The junk store man, if he is smart, will try to increase his supplies, holding inventories for as long as possible, waiting for the economic boom. It will not be long in coming. When price controls are in effect, a startling effect is produced: the price differential between new and old goods begins to narrow. In some cases the differential may even shift in favor of the used goods: The used good is not under price controls, while the new good is. People can bid up the prices of used goods in a way that they cannot with the new goods. They can buy what they are willing to pay for—but only in the used goods market. If the price controls were imposed in 1975 [North was writing in January, 1971] by 1980 a man might be able to triple his original investment. He could do far better if he were a repairman who had bought junk discards

172

to begin with. That is a good return on one's money; the stock market will never match it, for controls invariably spell the death of blue chip capital stocks; it is these industries that are placed under the controls first. Controls, by definition, are intended to reduce profits.

North also points out how the increased demand for repairs will stimulate sales of home repair magazines. "The repair journals and the collectors' journals will reap the harvest of these subscriptions, for it will be through information in these hobby publications that men will find the answers to critical problems. The man with specialized knowledge of these markets and these skills will be in the driver's seat."

How will all this affect unionized workers in professional trades—plumbers, carpenters, electricians, TV repairmen? They will be the first to be subject to stiff controls, since they belong to guilds. North elaborates: "The result will be a fantastic increase in labor's black market, or as it will be called (as it is called today), 'moonlighting.' A professional will spend as little time as possible on his official job, saving his skills and energy for his 'underground' occupation. Even if the unions escape controls, the market for the amateur repairman will expand as people refuse to pay the going unionized wages."

The increase in repairs will also stimulate the learning of trade vocations. As North writes,

This may turn out to be one of the major benefits of price controls. Repairs will be the staff of life. If you are unable to buy new manufactured goods at the artificially low prices, then you will have to shell out the money to keep what you have operating. This is where the incentive factor enters the picture. Young men will see the advantages to learning complex skills. They will have to seek out older men to learn some of these skills, since the schools seldom provide craft training, and certainly not in local communities that are too far from a junior college to commute easily (especially under gasoline rationing). . . . The feudalization of the economy will impel men to exercise their talents to meet local needs. They will be forced to learn who their neighbors are and what they need and can produce. What we lose in efficiency we hopefully will compensate for in increased neighborliness and co-operation in the community. The wealth of urban life brought with it isolation, anonymity, and loneliness. Perhaps the loss of wealth will help us to regain what we lost long ago. . . .

The young man who has skills mechanically would be wise to stay out of college. He would be far wiser to get into a trade school,

173

especially if he should have a skill that would not require highly specialized machinery. With some 8,000,000 young men and women on the college campuses today, there will be a glut of people holding college degrees. In fact, the glut is already quite visible. The automatic job for the man with the bachelor's degree is not automatic any longer, at least not at the older higher wage. The skilled craftsman is about to have his day. The man who can produce a thing of beauty or of use through his own genius, with simple tools and common materials, should find the coming decade exceptionally profitable. If he must sacrifice the false prestige of a college diploma in order to get such skills, the sacrifice ought to pay off in the future—perhaps the very near future.

Hobby Industries and the Luxury Trades

One of the largest uncontrolled markets will involve the "luxury" collectables: art, numismatic coins, stamps, rare books, rare wines, antiques, and the like. All of these collectables appreciated in value during the recent Nixon controls. In fact, the 1971–74 period was a bonanza period for investors in "real goods." One of the chief reasons for this profitable opportunity is the shift in demand from controlled markets to uncontrolled markets.

Again, to quote North (who has done more than anyone else to probe this important area):

Here is where the hobbyist reaps his great monetary rewards. The hobby "industries" that deal with unique items that are no longer in production—antiques, coins, some kinds of stamps, vintage year wines—find that they are left relatively free from the controls. How can some bureau say what should be the true price of antiques or rare coins? How can it enforce its decision? Why should it bother with collectors? So those who have purchased coins beforehand now see the rush of the public to buy into the market. People who had ignored collectors' markets before now see that coins and other unique goods are excellent hedges against inflation (even in times when controls are absent) and the best possible investments when the controls are imposed elsewhere in the economy. The increase in the appreciation of the coins therefore matches the rate of inflation; later on, the increase will exceed the rate, as demand increases when people outside the market try to enter it. . . . The man who plans carefully at this stage stands to survive the price-wage squeeze, the shortages, and the defective workmanship that are on their way. The hobbyist has one item that will rise in value, will be marketable, and will be in heavy demand:

174

specialized knowledge. In some cases that knowledge will be so valuable that a hobby may become a new occupation for those men who
take advantage of new conditions. For white collar workers, or those
associated with heavy industries that will be hit hard by the economic
controls, their skills in the home shop may be more profitable than their
skills in the factory or office.

Other Areas for Job Opportunities

There are many other potential opportunities to find profitable
employment under controls. The key is always to look for the
uncontrolled markets. Will agricultural products be free to fluctuate in price? Then look into the possibility of producing farm
products. Buy a section of fertile farmland and become an agricultural expert.

Another potential area for employment may be the leisure
markets: travel, camping, entertainment, resorts, sports, and
hobbies. With more money available but fewer goods to spend
it on, consumers may turn more and more to various forms of
amusement and entertainment. Demand for jobs in this area
will increase.

Other uncontrolled markets that may provide job opportunities include foreign trade, brokerage houses (for investments
in uncontrolled areas only), luxury apartment rentals, and so on.

Moonlighting

In addition to the possibility of changing jobs, workers should
also consider a second income as an effective way of getting
around wage controls. I have already mentioned in passing the
possible moonlighting activities of union workers. Despite price
controls, it will still pay employers to increase their annual
income.

Of course there are a thousand and one ways to earn extra
income; dozens of books have been written on the subject. One
of the best paperbacks on the subject is *101 Businesses You Can
Start and Run with Less than $1,000* by H. S. Kahm (Dolphin,
1973, $2.50). Kahm covers everything from day-care centers to
beach concessions. Keep in mind, however, that some job op-

175

portunities will be better than others under price and wage controls. On this basis, you should carefully choose your moonlighting activities.

One of the most fascinating and easiest second income opportunities today is the mail order business (Joe Karbo calls it the "lazy man's way to riches"). The mail order business may prove to be one of the best sources of income during controls, assuming mail service does not deteriorate further (a dubious assumption). Since advertising is a "customized" product, the ads you write and the prices you charge for your products are not likely to be controlled. This is especially true if you are a small outfit that advertises almost completely in the classified ads. Publishing is also generally exempt from controls, since each publication is a unique product.

One of the biggest decisions in mail order is, of course, what to sell. From my own experience, only *very unique* products will sell. Every year, thousands of people try their hand at mail order and fail principally because they lack a unique product or are unable to develop a unique twist to an old product. My "unique product" was a simple technique for obtaining interest-free loans. With interest rates climbing to double-digit rates, my idea was extremely useful and almost unheard of. And, most important, it was something people wanted.

Where should you advertise? In my case, I advertised in a financial publication called *Free Enterprise*. I targeted my audience. But I did not waste a lot of money on a display ad *before* I knew whether or not my ad would pay or not (a big mistake that a lot of novices make). Instead, I ran a small $10 ad in the *classified* section of *Free Enterprise*. It said, "Borrow $2,000 Interest-free! Free details."

Notice that I did not ask for any money. Asking for money up-front is another fatal error made by newcomers in the mail order business. Few businessmen can make money off a ten-word ad in the classifieds. I learned this lesson the hard way; I ran the very same ad earlier in another publication, but I asked $2 for "full details." I didn't make enough money to pay for the ad!

When I received requests in the mail for "free details," I sent out a two-page ad explaining in detail what I was offering, asking $10 for the information. It worked! On a $10 ad, I cleared $1000! Then, and only then, did I go to display advertising.

This is just a short lesson in the mail order business. If you want to try it, I suggest you read the February, April, and June, 1976, issues of *Free Enterprise* (800 Second Ave., New York, NY 10017; $2.50 each), which contain a complete analysis of the mail order business as well as books to read on the subject. Joe Karbo's book, *Lazy Man's Way to Riches*, contains a lot of useful information—*if* you keep in mind that he is talking about investing thousands of dollars on display advertising. My own approach is quite different and safer: start with the classifieds, always offering "free details." Only after establishing the profitability of your product should you go to display advertising.

Chapter Nine

The Businessman Faces Price Controls

Wage and price controls will hurt businessmen more than any other group in the United States. They bear the brunt of price controls. Even before widespread shortages appear, some companies may face bankruptcy, as they did under Nixon's controls program. In any market there are always large and small firms, highly profitable firms and marginal producers. The marginal producers are the first casualties in any price-controls program. Since they are marginal producers, their loss is little felt by consumers; if one or two small steel companies out of fifty go out of business, there is still a lot of steel being produced and sold.

Depending on the severity of the government's incomes policies, both small and large corporations can be hurt badly by controls. As this chapter will demonstrate, businesses of all sizes will need to take steps to prepare themselves in advance. The shortages and distortions that accompany government schemes are always difficult to deal with. Those which have prepared in advance will do better for it. In addition, this chapter will provide some interesting examples taken from the past showing how businesses avoided the harmful effects of controls—and in some cases profited from them.

How to Prepare for Controls

There are several preparations that all businesses should make in expectation of controls. If they wait until controls are imposed, it may be impossible to prepare properly.

Stocking Up

Under the free market, where prices are allowed to fluctuate according to supply and demand, businesses try to build up inventories sufficient to meet the needs of their customers. At the same time, however, they do not want to be saddled with such a heavy inventory of goods that the cost of holding them becomes overburdensome.

Inventory accumulation is one of the most difficult decisions facing businessmen. A business cycle only aggravates the situation. During the boom period of the cycle, a business tends to produce at or near capacity in an effort to accumulate or replenish a deficient stock. But when the recession strikes, the business finds that it has overstocked and excess inventories become a costly problem.

In an earlier chapter, I established that price controls are most likely when inflationary pressures are building, or in other words, during the boom period of the cycle. The timing could never be worse for the businessman. For it is precisely during the inflationary boom that the businessman will be striving to keep up with demand and trying to build inventories. Yet price controls will make it more difficult for him to build up his inventories. Shortages will abound. So how does the businessman prepare? He must be willing to carry a larger inventory than he would ordinarily. This, of course, is a costly action in the short run, and business managers may have a difficult time convincing company leaders that this is the best policy in the long run. But when price controls come, those with higher than normal inventories will be able to keep their customers happy and are likely therefore to remain in business longer than their competitors.

One of the most universal problems facing all businesses during controls will be *paper shortages,* especially paper used for stationery, invoices, and other forms. Remember that during controls government will be increasing its demand for paper, and businesses will have to compete with it. There will be more government forms to fill out. Paper shortages will create havoc for secretarial and clerical workers. Faced with wage controls at the same time, they may simply quit. Businesses should immediately stock sufficient supplies of stationery and all necessary forms for at least a year in advance, perhaps longer.

179

Alternate Sources of Supply

Another suggestion for businessmen is to immediately establish contacts and even buying agreements with *small producers and foreign suppliers*. Small producers, remember, were largely exempt from controls during the Nixon program. And even if they are covered the next time around, it will be next to impossible to enforce the regulations. There are thousands of small business operations in this country. Establishing a number of sources of supply may be costly now, but well worth the effort when controls return. Small companies do not necessarily charge lower prices than larger companies. In fact, in many cases, just the opposite is true, due to "economies of scale." Be prepared to be charged high or exorbitant prices. That's all right. You can still use the lower-priced company as your major source of supply, while establishing a business relationship with many suppliers. Surely you would rather pay high prices than not be able to purchase that vital product at all. Remember the story of the computer-parts purchaser at the beginning of this book.

Pricing Policies

Changes in pricing policies can definitely affect a business' condition during controls. There are many alternatives in this area that can soften the impact of controls.

First, businesses should seriously consider raising their prices as soon as the market permits. Many industries lag far behind other industries when it comes to pricing. This is a serious mistake that ought to be avoided at all costs. Sometimes the reason for a lag in raising prices is the size of the firm. The company is simply too small to undertake the costs necessary to determine prices. They depend on larger companies for price leadership. Consequently, small firms may wait several weeks or months after the larger firms raise their prices. With controls coming, it pays these smaller firms to raise prices as soon as they learn the plans of their competitors.

Now, of course, even if companies spend more money to determine how soon they can safely raise their prices, competition still keeps them from raising prices beyond what the market dictates. Fortunately, there is a way around this dilemma.

Businessmen can offer specials or discounts to keep their true prices competitive, while their prices on the books remain high. In 1975, car manufacturers offered "rebates" on new cars, an extremely wise maneuver, and to some extent, it was successful. If price controls had been imposed while the rebate program was going on, the car manufacturers could have dropped the rebates and still maintained prices at legal levels. Discounts, then, serve as an excellent way to elude price controls.

Not all companies can offer rebates on their products, however. And the government has become aware of this scheme, and to some extent it tried to discourage it during the Nixon controls program. Under Phase II base-period rules, "temporary special prices" were excluded from the regulations. That is, they could be dropped (allowing prices to rise) without any legal penalty. But the "special prices" had to last only "temporarily"—meaning less than ninety-three days. And in Phase IV, the allowable period was reduced to thirty-one days. The lesson of this story is: businessmen should offer specials or discounts only on a limited, temporary basis, never over a long period of time. By altering the discount slightly, say, offering 25 percent off one month and 23 percent the next, the net result is the same but the "temporary" requirement is met.

Sales and discounts are useful in anticipation of controls, but they should always be short-lived. This is particularly true if a freeze on prices is likely. The chairman of the executive committee of the Pillsbury Company, Terrance Hanold, told *U. S. News & World Report* that many grocers running long-term specials on Pillsbury products at the beginning of the 1971 freeze found these special prices frozen. As a result, the grocers were discouraged from reordering those items, and Pillsbury was hurt.

Another possibility in pricing policy is to start listing prices as "suggested retail," which is something car manufacturers have been doing for years. Usually this idea is only used with high-priced items for which customers are used to bargaining. But more and more manufacturers are going to this system, while at the same time allowing dealers to sell below the list price. Companies selling calculators, TV sets, appliances, and household goods are all starting to use this system. Even record albums have traditionally displayed a "suggested retail price," which no one ever pays.

A pitfall to avoid if at all possible is fixed pricing for delivery months in advance. During the second Nixon freeze in 1973, the custom of selling products at agreed-upon prices for delivery in advance really hurt. According to government regulations, prices could not exceed what they were during the week of June 1–8, even though under the system those prices might be months old. The solution is to reduce the time involved on agreed-upon prices. Many companies have been doing just that during highly inflationary periods. The new policy is "market price at delivery."

Many companies make numerous contracts for future delivery, and this can be a source of great consternation under controls. For example, during the Nixon freeze in 1971, contracts for future price or wage increases were generally disallowed. The Cost of Living Council adopted a "delivered" goods and services concept, meaning that transactions had not taken place unless workers had actually worked at higher rates, the rental unit had been occupied, or goods had been shipped by the seller. To prepare for future controls, one method used to circumvent this regulation was to send *partial* shipment (if at all possible) right away or have workers work for a short period of time at the higher wage. During the 1971 freeze, college tuitions were permitted to rise because supposedly deposits had been made prior to the school year, sufficient to make the "transaction" effective. Businesses with future contracts could do the same thing. For such a practice to be acceptable, however, the Cost of Living Council required during the 1971 freeze that at least 10 percent of the goods had to be shipped to qualify as "delivered" goods.

Another useful method to prepare for controls is related to "aggregate pricing." During Phase II and after, the government controllers developed a system of permitting a standard or customary "cost-plus" markup on goods. The easiest type of markup policy to enforce was one in which the company had a markup policy for each individual item. Price Commissioner Grayson stated, "Unless the firm was on a detailed item-by-item pricing system, it was difficult to pinpoint an exact violation."

182

Many grocers, for example, used a pricing system based on "aggregate" markup, under which items were grouped together by department, such as the "canned vegetables department."

Some food chains have a system whereby store managers are given gross margin targets and there is no control over individual products. This seems to be the best system and should be looked into. Whatever system you adopt, it should be done as soon as possible before controls are imposed, thus establishing a "customary business practice." The Price Commission often relied on the IRS to determine what constituted a "customary business practice."

Circumventing Controls

It is a whole new ball game once controls are imposed. Practices that were once completely legal and common suddenly become illegal and subject to fines and other sanctions. Just look at the "miscellaneous price violations" that the Office of Price Administration enforced during World War II: reductions in quantity without comparable reductions in price; reductions in quality or deterioration of grade without comparable reductions in price; upgrading; cash-on-the-side; false computations in establishing a maximum price; discontinuance of cash or trade discounts; improper loading, transportation, or other charges; improper commissions or brokerage fees; credit allowances to the seller as a form of additional payment; excessive payment for other goods or services, or for fictitious goods or services, or services given free or below cost; and tying agreements.

Almost all of these "economic crimes" are perfectly legal and ethical under normal business conditions. (The only exception that I can see is "upgrading," which involves falsifying grading standards.) Price controls have a harmful effect not only on the economy but on the moral attitude businessmen have toward law in society.

Tying Agreements

Tying agreements constitute one of the chief methods used to evade controls. Landlords have been notorious for them. Other businessmen have also used tying agreements. Guenter Reimann tells a story of such agreements under the Nazi controls:

A peasant was arrested and put on trial for having repeatedly sold his old dog together with a pig. When a private buyer of pigs came to him, a sale was staged according to the official rules. The buyer would ask the peasant: "How much is the pig?" The cunning peasant would answer: "I cannot ask you for more than the official price. But how much will you pay for my dog which I also want to sell?" Then the peasant and the buyer of the pig would no longer discuss the price of the pig, but only the price of the dog. They would come to an understanding about the price of the dog, and when an agreement was reached, the buyer got the pig too. The price for the pig was quite correct, strictly according to the rules, but the buyer had paid a high price for the dog. Afterward, the buyer, wanting to get rid of the useless dog, released him, and he ran back to his old master for whom he was indeed a treasure.

In the U.S. during the same period, there were many such arrangements. Some businessmen requested, in addition to the ceiling price, that payment be made on time at high interest rates. Others tied the sale of one product with another complementary product—like canning lids with rings. During 1945, a New York meat retailer purchased $4200 worth of stock in a corporation called the United Meat Co., Inc., in order to obtain some meat at ceiling prices. Apparently, the purchase of stock in this company was voluntary, but no doubt the meat company had discreet ways of letting purchasers know that buying stock in their company certainly would not hurt. As long as the purchase of stock was voluntary, the OPA could find no illegal activity. Unfortunately, the purchaser made one mistake. He tried to write off the $4200 stock purchase on his taxes as a cost of buying meat! Naturally, the IRS disallowed this write-off, and the discovery of the tying agreement, tacit as it was, was made.

A common tying agreement during the Korean War controls involved car "trade-ins." In many cases, a car dealer would not sell a new car until he received a used one at a price far below its resale value. These cases were reported to the Office of Price Stabilization, but the government was unable to do much about the practice.

Tying agreements cannot be simply ruled illegal because many businesses have had such agreements for years as a general business practice. F. M. Scherer, in *Industrial Market Structure and Economic Performance,* says that tying agreements by large firms have been outlawed by the Supreme Court and the Clayton and Sherman antitrust acts. According to this interpretation, tying agreements are generally considered a "restraint of trade." Tying agreements under controls, ironically enough, have just the opposite effect: they promote trade. For that reason alone, they should be legal. At any rate, Scherer points out that a "violation will not be found unless there is monopoly power in the tying market . . . . Small companies attempting to break into a new market also escape censure." Scherer also suggests that the law "does not reach tying arrangements which are purely voluntary and informal . . . ."

Nevertheless, tying agreements unrelated to general business practices were illegal under price controls during World War II. In *U.S.* v *Armour & Co. of Delaware* (May, 1943), a federal district court ruled on a case in which the defendant refused to sell butter without eggs. In this case, the court ruled that this was an "evasion within the meaning of the regulations." In a related World War II case, some butchers argued that certain unpopular cuts would not get sold without tying agreements with more popular cuts. Yet the regulations disallowed this practice.

Reductions in Quantity

If a business could somehow reduce the quantity of an item and still maintain the price, it could effectively get around controls. This method is only feasible in cases where the quantity is measured in sizes rather than numbers or weight. Bath towels could be shortened in size, for example. But the quantity of a dozen grade A eggs cannot be reduced. Needless to say, quantity reductions made without a comparable reduction in price were ruled illegal from the beginning in modern controls programs.

Some peculiar businesses have been able to elude such regulations, however. The Hershey Candy Company has a long tradition of maintaining the price of its candy bars at either five cents, ten cents, or fifteen cents a bar. In other words, it established a practice of raising its prices only every few years rather than

185

raising them by a penny or more whenever costs rose. Rather than raise prices on a frequent basis, Hershey would reduce or increase the size of its candy bars by one- or two-tenths of an ounce. Hershey has changed the size of its candy bars twenty-five times in the last twenty-five years! Only when the size of the bar had to be greatly reduced would the company raise the price of the bar five cents and change the size accordingly.

Hershey was able to continue this practice during the Nixon controls for several reasons. One, I believe, is that Hershey had set a precedent of frequent quantity changes in the size of its bars. Second, a major cost of manufacturing candy bars is the price of chocolate, or cocoa, and sugar, volatile products falling under "volatile pricing authorizations." Cocoa also needed to be imported, and companies were able to adjust prices according to import costs.

Reductions in Quality

Quality control is difficult to achieve. One of the reasons for this is that the quality of products may have deteriorated prior to the imposition of controls. A general inflationary climate, which usually provokes government incomes policies, induces strong financial pressure on companies to reduce costs, however possible. In many cases, this means developing new products made of cheaper materials. This process tends to continue even during controls. Here again the same incentives exist for reducing costs. In fact, they are often stronger because companies are restricted in raising prices. How can the government objectively tell whether an automobile manufacturer has reduced the quality of the parts in a car? There is no real way of knowing in the short run. So about all government can do in this area is issue regulations and hope that quality deterioration is not that noticeable. (During World War II, Great Britain forced the standardization of many products in an effort to eliminate quality reductions. Such an extreme measure could only be taken with basic products, however.)

The clothing industry has always been able to elude quality controls. During World War II, dollars-and-cents ceilings had little effect. If the ceiling on shirts was $5, the store retailers simply raised the price of their $2 shirts. The difference between various types of clothing can be rather subjective, and businessmen have naturally taken advantage of this fact during controls.

Upgrading

Upgrading has always been an illegal activity, even in normal economic circumstances. It is defined as the fraudulent practice of selling a product with false grading standards. An example of false upgrading is choice meat sold as prime meat. Thousands of such violations took place during World War II, especially in produce, meat, and poultry products. Upgrading is always a problem under tight controls, when ceilings are far below market levels.

Cash-on-the-Side

Cash payments exceeding the lawful price were common in World War II because cash transactions are difficult to trace. One government official recalls situations in which a person, after paying the legal price for an article, returned and said to the seller, "Oh, by the way, here's that ten dollars I owe you." And there was little the OPA could do, except to check the man's records, petty cash vouchers, and so on. In another case, a seller placed one of his employees on the payroll of the buyer to draw a salary for services not actually done!

In *The Black Market,* Marshall Clinard describes how extensive upgrading and false labeling were during World War II:

> Other seizures on charges of economic violations in 1942 and 1943 included imitation fruit-type beverages sold in a manner to create the impression that they were pure fruit juices; canned sardines labeled as packed in pure olive oil when they were packed in corn oil infused with an olive oil flavor or in unadulterated corn oil; oysters in small containers, incorporating excessive water; "enriched" bread that contained no enriching ingredients; horsemeat from which the dealer had stripped the identifying labels; Japanese crab meat relabeled after importation, "packed in Siberia, Soviet Russia"; domestic cheese stamped with the words "Imported Swiss" or "Switzerland"; storage eggs misbranded as fresh eggs; short-weight retail packages of "nut meats" containing a

187

material proportion of pumpkin seeds; cider vinegar debased with water, ascetic acid, and distilled vinegar; chicken loaf with skin and lung tissue substituted for chicken meat; white poppy seed colored to simulate a more costly variety; waffle and pancake sirup with glucose and corn sirup substituted for cane sirup . . . .

Price ceilings on scarce commodities have tempted unscrupulous concerns to offset by giving short weight or measure. While this type of violation is easy to detect, the field is so tremendous that the constant vigilance of both local and Federal food enforcement agencies is required. One of the principal short-weight items for which many shippers were cited during the Spring of 1943 was potatoes packed in bags. To circumvent the price ceiling by marketing short-weight potatoes meant that the receiver was forced to pay an increased price per pound. The largest number of short-weight seizures involved butter. Also seized in substantial quantities was packaged sauerkraut in glass containers containing a very excessive quantity of brine. Other short-weight or short-volume foods seized included smoked salmon, spiced herring, crab meat, preserves, marmalade, apple butter, canned chicken, peanuts, mixed nuts, olive oil, wheat germ, pimentos, spices, and pickles.

Clinard also writes that increasing the fat content of meat and other forms of meat adulteration were widespread.

Discontinuing Discounts

Elimination or reduction of discounts is not always illegal under controls, but it was generally so during World War II. If discounts were an established business practice, they were not allowed to be dropped unless prices dropped by an equal amount.

Discounting, however, is not a uniform practice, even within a particular business. For example, larger, more established customers may negotiate and receive a larger discount than smaller customers. This practice is perfectly legal as long as the seller can prove cost economies as a result of bulk sales. Interestingly enough, during Phase IV (1973–74), elimination of discounts was common and legal, provided that the "list" price was realistic. Many items sold at bid prices far below "list" prices, so there was plenty of room for increases. Sellers were known to reduce discounts more to some customers than others.

Charging for Common Services

In many cases, items are not sold individually but as part of a package deal. Businessmen can thus elude controls in many cases by raising prices of other goods or services that are part of the package. This is a relatively easy task if these common goods or services are presently selling below ceiling levels or are exempt from controls.

Many examples of this occurred during the Nixon program. In the oil industry, while retail gasoline prices were frozen at June 1–8, 1973, levels, several refiners attempted to increase revenues by raising rents to service stations or requiring extended hours of operation. (Rents were exempt from controls during this period.)

Gas retailers were able to circumvent controls to some extent by engaging in several similar practices. Some of them raised the price of car washes, discontinued trading stamps and self-service pumps, or increased the prices of related items—tires, batteries and accessories.

Another method commonly used was to raise the deposit or down payment for an item even though the full price remained the same. The Cost of Living Council caught on to this practice and outlawed it, ruling that this amounted to a price increase. The elimination of trading stamps at gasoline stations and retail stores was another common practice during the Nixon controls. During the 1971 freeze, the Cost of Living Council ruled that if a retail outlet dropped trading stamps, it would have to reduce prices of all goods sold by the value of the stamps. Doing so is a lot easier said than done, and it was difficult if not impossible to enforce this ruling.

Double Billing

During World War II, OPA officials discovered that a number of companies were evading controls by using a double-billing method. According to this method, a company would send out a legitimate invoice bill for goods bought or services rendered at the maximum legal price, but then send along with it (or a few days later) another smaller bill for the purchase of something

189

never received. Unless the purchaser complained to the government (which meant that his source of supply would be cut off), it was difficult if not impossible to detect this kind of evasive action.

Legal and Quasi-Legal Methods of Eluding Controls

I noted in the previous section how some past methods were deemed unlawful by government controllers. I also showed that under certain circumstances some of these methods, such as eliminating discounts and charging more for related services, were permitted. Now, let us examine legal methods of circumventing controls. Sometimes these methods may be called "quasi-legal" practices, since the question of their legality may be unanswered at this time.

Obviously, the best way to avoid the harmful effects of controls is to be exempt or excluded. This, of course, is not possible for the great majority of businesses, but there are ways to take advantage of the exemptions and exclusions in the law.

The "artificial" creation of new products is one way that has been used time and time again during price controls programs. I noted some examples of this in chapter 5, "The Consequences of Price Controls." New products are very difficult to control in any objective way. During World War II, businessmen found that they were generally able to obtain higher ceiling prices for new products that were hardly distinguishable from older products. Many instances were cited in which *new* manufacturers were given higher ceiling prices than *old* manufacturers for comparable (but not identical) merchandise. In clothing, for example, men's shirts "made out of white sheeting" were given higher prices than regular shirts. The Office of Price Administration became painfully aware of the "new product" ploy and sought to develop a system to determine when a product had been sufficiently changed to warrant being called a different product. Firms were always making slight changes in their products in an effort to create a new one. One example: "Towel racks used to

190

have metal joinings, but now employ wooden dowels." Is that a sufficient change to warrant being called a new product?

The new product technique was especially effective in fashion design. Chester Bowles, head of the OPA, told Congress, "Clothing has been one of the most difficult of all products to control due to style changes. A few extra stripes added to fabrics or a few buttons or trimmings added to the garments and previous ceiling prices no longer applied." The OPA tried unsuccessfully to develop an effective controls program for clothing. Mansfield & Associates wrote of this period: "During the Summer of 1942 new brands of processed foods appeared daily on grocers' shelves at ever-increasing prices. In clothing the style factor alone was enough to make deliberate switching unnecessary. When style was stable, new names were tied to familiar products."

The artificial creation of new products also went on during the Nixon controls period. Specifications in lumber products were sometimes altered to create new products, for example. To avoid this growing problem, Nixon's controllers ruled that (1) prices should be set at cost plus net operating profit on a similar item, or (2) prices should be based on the base price charged by another firm, or (3) prices should be according to "customary pricing policies." The Cost of Living Council also ruled that the acquisition of a product from a new firm would not be grounds for considering it "new." Obviously, these guidelines were rather subjective and left firms in a position to elude controls to some extent.

The agricultural exemption was used in several unique ways to avoid controls at the wholesale and retail level. Remember that the Nixon controls exempted "raw" agricultural products only, and only the *first sale* of these products in June-August, 1973. The *Historical Working Papers* cited one way that distributors got around this regulation: "For instance, freeze regulations exempted the first sale of raw agricultural products. Under one scheme, distributors, wholesalers, and other marketing middlemen would not take title to a product but would pass it along the distribution chain until it reached the retail market. At that point the 'first' sale took place and the price of the product would include a certain percentage commission for each person who had had a part in the distribution and final sale of the product.''

In a similar vein, foreign imports were exempt during the Nixon controls, though not during World War II. The *first sale* of imported goods was exempt, but not future sales. Some kind of arrangement similar to the one accomplished by the produce middlemen could have been carried out with imported products, though I know of no such case. It's also important to note that companies that imported some or all of their products (gasoline, lumber, et cetera) were allowed to charge higher prices.

In this connection, one method of eluding controls was contemplated by oil refiners during the Phase III½ freeze of June-August, 1973. Refiners could have detained crude oil overseas until the freeze was lifted, or refined the crude overseas and imported it as a higher-priced foreign product, or diverted it to processing and used it in a foreign market. This did not take place, however; the sixty-day freeze did not last long enough to necessitate pursuing such policies.

Customized products served as an easy method of avoiding government controls. Under base-period pricing, it was very difficult to control prices of custom products, mainly because each product was by its very nature a ''new'' product. The Cost of Living Council defined a custom product as one that had never been made before or which varied enough from time to time so that no large number of the individual items remained comparable. These ''products'' constituted a substantial portion of American industry: most of aerospace, construction, advertising, publishing, radio and television broadcasting, and even retail trade. Retail trade could be regarded as a customized ''product'' because profit margins varied with volume discounts, credit, free delivery, store surroundings, and so on. I will discuss this issue further when dealing with profit margins.

Seasonal variation was sometimes taken into account in previous incomes policies, and it needs to be if the government adopts any kind of sophisticated plan. During Nixon's Economic Stabilization Program, seasonal variation was allowed if it could be proven to have occurred in each of the preceding three years at fixed dates. Seasonal fluctuations occur in numerous markets, if not at all retail outlets. Some months of the year are known to be better times than others for sales.

"Volatile Pricing Authorizations" were granted by the Cost of Living Council from time to time. Firms had to demonstrate evidence of past price changes due to volatile commodity prices. (Remember the example of cocoa in Hershey's chocolates.)

It is worth noting that some industries that had experienced high rates of inflation prior to the imposition of the Nixon controls were given special allowances during the controls. Jackson Grayson notes that both the health services and insurance companies were used to big increases in prices and premiums, and as a result, during Phase II they were allowed large (though less than usual) increases—more than the typical 2.5 percent allowance set for the whole economy.

Used and damaged goods constitute an exempt area that has been exploited in previous controls programs. One can almost envision a company salesman taking a sledge hammer to every appliance in the warehouse so that they could all be sold as damaged goods. Of course, this kind of reckless action would only come about if controls were so strict that used and damaged goods in fairly good condition sold for more than new merchandise. In some lines, however, it may be cheaper to manufacture damaged products. In clothing, for example, "irregular" pants may cost less to produce, and under controls, therefore, the profit margin on them could be spectacular. Have you ever tried to find the defect in "irregulars" or "seconds"? Sometimes, it is pretty difficult, so the demand for these "damaged" goods could skyrocket if new merchandise is not readily available.

Sometimes it may be possible to make a product into a used good, exempt from controls. One method used in the past has been to *lease* merchandise for a period of time. Then, after the lease expires, the leased product can be sold to the lessee as a used good, and depending on market conditions, at a higher price. This method could be used with any leased merchandise—automobiles, televisions and other appliances, various forms of real property, et cetera.

The question arises, "Why would anyone want to pay more for a damaged or used good than he would have to pay for a brand new item?" The answer lies in supply—there will be few new products available at the unprofitable controlled prices.

The case of steel scrap provides another useful example of how controls have been circumvented. Under Nixon's controls, steel scrap as a by-product of production operations of big firms was subject to price controls, but steel scrap produced from obsolete or worn-out equipment was not. Steel companies therefore emphasized this source for steel scrap.

When steel scrap from obsolete equipment was not available, they often used barter arrangements to elude controls. Barter was discussed in chapter 7 from the point of view of the consumer. But business can also take advantage of barter. In the steel case, scrap under control was sold through barter to obtain scarce reinforcement bars. In other cases, companies would transship scrap from one plant to another (within the same company) to avoid controlled prices at one market location. Then they would buy a similar quantity of scrap at another place at uncontrolled prices, or at higher prices.

Increasing the volume of services is another method that has been used in the past to circumvent controls. During Phase II, a Treasury official complained that some medical doctors were dodging controls by increasing the volume of services—extra X rays, extra blood tests, et cetera. This method, called "overutilization," was largely dismissed as being only occasionally practiced, according to reports in the *Wall Street Journal*. This method is generally limited to businesses and professions that offer several services to their customers, rather than selling a single item. This particularly applies to monopolistic (state-licensed) professions (e.g., doctors, lawyers), who probably more than others can get away with increasing services without too much difficulty.

Getting around Markup Regulations

Under base-period pricing, the government usually allows some form of pass-through of costs according to past markups. One of the most common methods used to get around these markup regulations is through "multiple sales." The same product is sold back and forth between companies with successive applications of markups. The lumber industry in particular took advantage of this method as much as possible during Nixon's program, since there were wide discrepancies in prices due to price controls in the early 1970s.

Escaping the Profit-Margin Test

Profit-margin restrictions have existed in previous controls periods for the purpose of eliminating "excess profits"—and also to indirectly control prices. The profit-margin test could also serve easily as a way of exposing previously confidential cost data of a company to the government, particularly the Internal Revenue Service. Price Commissioner Grayson brings up this point in his *Confessions*. He expresses concern that the IRS could have access to the files of the Price Commission, or that the Justice Department could use the files for antitrust investigations.

I have discussed the effects that profit-margin restrictions can have on a business. Among other things, the business will have a strong incentive to consume its capital if the restrictions are too strict. It will spend more money on business trips, buy gold watches for Christmas presents, and so forth. Needless to say, carrying out schemes to overcome the effects of the profit-margin test should prove extremely beneficial.

The profit-margin constraints set by the Cost of Living Council were based on a base period—the best two of three fiscal years prior to August 15, 1971, but after August 15, 1968. These rules were changed from time to time, but in all cases, the constraints were based on past performance of a business.

It must be pointed out that with a base-period system, some companies will have high profit margins during the base period while others will have low profit margins. The companies with high profit margins during the base period were hardly hurt by the Nixon controls. There was no effort to force profit-margin constraints to go below levels set by past performance. As John Flory states in his contribution to the *Historical Working Papers,* "for some individual firms the base period profit margin was so high that it never represented an effective constraint." One might conclude from all this that the best course of action is to artificially increase profit margins as long as possible before controls are imposed. This would be fine except that there is a penalty for doing so—e.g., the corporate income tax on profits. One cannot ignore the tax effects, but at least this method should be examined.

How does a company increase its profit margins without raising its prices to uncompetitive levels? There are several alternatives: (1) replacing obsolete equipment at a slower rate, (2) divesting itself of an unprofitable business, and (3) eliminating less profitable lines (more and more firms are testing the profitability of individual areas of their operations with an eye to cutting costs and raising overall profits).

After a profit-margin constraint is imposed, what sound methods could be used to soften the harmful effects of the constraint? John Flory does business an excellent service in his paper, "Price Control Mechanisms," in the *Historical Working Papers,* by providing numerous ways to "evade" (his term) the profit-margin test. (*Every* major corporation should have a copy of the *Historical Working Papers.*) Flory writes:

> If, for whatever reason, the firm was about to exceed its base period profit margin and had previously increased prices, it could increase certain costs (e.g., expense accounts, advertising, research and development, or any discretionary cost that could be expensed, but had some future value beyond its normal economic justification) and constrain the profit margin. Thus, a control that was designed to cause price constraint might actually cause unneeded increase in spending, a result which in itself could be inflationary.

However, there is a less expensive way to evade profit-margin constraints, one that is a bit more subtle and harder to detect: increasing sales without increasing profits. To quote Flory again:

> One avenue is to buy raw materials or other component parts or to contract out for services. Suppose Firm A and Firm B wanted to increase their profit margins. Firm A can buy from Firm B component part "a" and Firm B can buy from Firm A component part "b," in each case instead of producing the part themselves. (They can even buy and sell the same part to each other, but that kind of evasion might be too easily spotted.) If each firm made about the same amount of profit on its sale as it lost on its purchase, neither would have changed its true profits. Each would have increased its sale by the amount it sold and so would be able to show a lower ratio of profits to total sales—the profit margin test. Likewise, if each lost about the same amount on its purchase as it made on its sale, neither would have changed its true profits, but each would seemingly have increased its allowable costs. The costs of producing the component parts sold would have been counted only against those parts, but the costs of purchasing the component parts to be used in the final product would be more than the

costs of the produced parts and so would count as cost increases. Thus, each company would have obtained, at no real cost, the legal ability to raise its price.

As Flory points out, this possibility is not remote by any means. "Most large companies regularly buy and sell with other companies in or out of their own industry. All it would take to exploit the evasion possibilities inherent in this practice would be to increase its scale. The oil and fertilizer industries (and perhaps others, too) even buy and sell their finished products back and forth in order to meet temporary local shortages. For companies in these industries, 'paper' allowable costs and the ratio of profits to sales can be virtually set at will at any level they choose."

In the retail trade, Flory demonstrates how retailers can make more money with the same profit margin. In this market, profit margins vary with volume discounts, credit, free delivery, store surroundings, and the like. "A retailer," notes Flory, "could thus voluntarily or involuntarily go down the 'scale' toward becoming a discounter, in order to make more money at the same profit margin. While this process could not be used extensively by the most tradition-bound retail firms, it could be used, at least to some slight extent, by nearly all industry."

In addition to these methods, there were a number of exclusions from the profit-margin rules during the Nixon controls. These included: (1) nonoperating income and expenses (income not derived from ordinary operations, such as royalties, interest income, rents, dividends, et cetera); (2) extraordinary income and expenses (gains or losses from the sale of business assets, casualty losses, expropriation losses, et cetera); (3) public utility operations (which are regulated by state governments); (4) insurance operations; (5) construction operations (under $1 million annually); (6) sale of raw agricultural products; (7) foreign operations—(gross receipts excluded); (8) federal, state, and local income taxes (surprise!); and (9) international air fares and ocean shipping rates (regulated by the Civil Aeronautics Board and other agencies).

These exclusions should be noted carefully, because it will probably be possible to take advantage of many of them in the future. For example, if a company has foreign offices, gross receipts from their source can be excluded from the profit-margin test. Companies should therefore be prepared to shift sales and production operations to foreign plants and offices in case domestic profits become unduly limited by government-imposed profit-margin constraints.

How Important Is Company Size?

I have referred at times to the importance of the size a firm is and how the government will deal with large and small corporations. This is an extremely important issue during controls. Large firms, for example, were required to prenotify the Nixon administration of *any* price increase, and in many cases, this waiting period (sometimes months) was costly. The government controllers had to decide the minimum firm size necessary for prenotification of price increases, reporting and surveillance. They finally decided on $100 million in annual sales. But, according to Jackson Grayson, this tripled the workload of the Price Commission under Phase II. Afterward, Grayson felt that it would have been better to choose a cutoff point of $250 million or more in sales. The Price Commission covered 1500 firms under the cutoff point they chose. If they had chosen the $250 million cutoff point, they would have had to deal with only 500 firms.

The major oil companies provide a good example of the problems involved in prenotification of price increases. Under Special Rule #1, they were required to prenotify for price increases, and this usually involved expensive delays of thirty days or more. What was their alternative? One was, as mentioned earlier, to ship their foreign crude to their refiners in other countries, so that they could increase their prices immediately to offset higher crude costs. One company claimed to have diverted a shipment of foreign crude in the spring of 1973 to avoid the prenotification process.

In addition to the obvious benefit of establishing foreign subsidiaries and offices, businesses should also consider voluntarily breaking up their organizations into several units, all of which would remain under control of the parent company. This, of course, is a serious proposal, and no company should take such a step without considering the risks of administrative and economic problems. By dividing the company into several companies, it may be possible to reduce sales to less than $100,000 for each company, thus reducing the chances of government scrutiny.

The Silver Coin Ploy

One of the most interesting economic developments in the past decade or so is the use of "junk" silver coins in financial transactions. These coins are the pre-1965 dimes, quarters, and half-dollars of 90 percent silver content. Because the economic value of silver exceeded the face value of these common U.S. coins in 1964, the coins ended up in the hands of collectors, hoarders, and speculators. (This is not to disparage the worth of these individuals; it was government policy that led to the disappearance of the coins.) Today these silver junk coins are valued at at least three times their face value. These coins are sold on the commodity exchanges in New York and Chicago at both spot and futures prices. They are sold in bags of $1000 face value. Coin dealers around the country sell them in lots of ten or in quarter, half, or full bags. The market for these silver coins is extremely liquid, and they can be sold or bought with little trouble anywhere in the U.S.

Transactions with the use of silver junk coins can be extremely useful for businessmen facing taxes, inflation, or price controls. This ploy was first brought up as a way of avoiding the payment of taxes, or at least reducing the tax owed to the federal government. René Baxter writes:

> The government's deliberate policy of currency debasement (and the inexorable working of Gresham's Law) has resulted in the issuing of new clad coinage of little or no metallic value to replace the old silver coinage. Fortunately, the old coin is still considered *legal tender*. If you take a $1,000 face value bag to your bank or to the Federal Reserve, they will accept it at *face value only*. The official position of the U.S. government is that silver quarters are still only worth a quarter. This fact leads to a very neat and perfectly legal tax avoidance and anti-inflation measure you can use to protect yourself from the ravages of

big government. Suppose you wish to sell a piece of property which you originally bought for $2,000. Today the property is worth about $7,000 in our new inflated "mini-dollars." You find a buyer, but you insist on payment in *cash*, U.S. silver coin minted 1964 or earlier. The buyer goes into the coin market and buys two bags ($2,000 face value) at $3,500 a bag. He signs your sales agreement, and you sign a receipt for "$2,000 cash, U.S. funds." He pays you $2,000 and he gets the deed. You paid $2,000 for the property originally, and you sold it for $2,000 cash. The fact is, you owe no tax. You have made no profit. Now if you turn around and sell the two bags for $7,000, you'll owe tax on the gain. But you avoid this by either keeping the coin as a long-term hedge, or by making similar cash-value deals with others using the coin in the same way to buy anything you want—from another piece of property to a year's supply of food. Simply calculate the day's exchange rate and pay in cash. Be sure to get a receipt to back yourself up with.

The IRS is aware of this tax avoidance ploy, but the fact is that they can do nothing about it so long as the government continues to accept pre-1965 silver coins as legal tender. The IRS regards this ploy as a case of "substance over form," and has tentatively ruled it unacceptable. There has not been any court case on this matter as yet.

The silver coin ploy may be extremely useful under price controls. A seller, for example, might be faced with a ceiling price of $3000 for a new car. If this price is below what he could get if the market were uncontrolled, he could ask the buyer to purchase a bag of silver coins with a face value of $1000, which costs $3500. The buyer gets his new $3000 car, and the seller gets a bag of silver coins worth $3500. In essence, he has just legally sold the car above the ceiling price. But the official transaction is listed as selling for $1000, U.S. funds.

There are a number of problems with this approach, however, although I believe none of them are impossible to overcome. First, the buyer may be reluctant to engage in such a deal. He knows that the cost to him is $3500, not the ceiling price of $3000, which is what he would like to pay. But if there is a severe shortage of new cars, he may well be willing to buy the car for $3500.

Second, selling a new car at $1000 instead of the legal price of $3000 would undoubtedly raise the suspicions of government controllers, especially if the practice became widespread. But this problem can be solved rather easily. All the seller has to do is ask the buyer to pay $2900 with a regular check and $100 in silver coin, making the total real value of the deal $3250. The nominal, paper value of the deal is at the legal limit, however, $3000.

What would be the reaction of the price controllers to this method? They could argue that essentially the seller is engaging in a tying agreement, which would make the deal illegal. But it certainly would be something difficult to detect without the assistance of disgruntled buyers. Still, controls bureaucrats will no doubt try to monitor such activities.

This method has use for both the businessman and the consumer, as I mentioned in chapter 7. The wage-earner may also be able to profit from this silver ploy under wage controls. If he could convince his employer to pay part or all of his salary in silver coin, he could thereby reduce his salary or wage by a third overnight. Under these circumstances, it would be much easier for the employer to give him a raise, since in nominal terms his wages would be far less than the legal level. There are other fringe benefits to this arrangement: lower income taxes, lower social security taxes (for both the employer and employee), and the possibility that the worker could get food stamps and go on welfare due to his "substandard" wage level! Obviously, the wage-earner would have to sell his silver coins in order to pay his rent, eat, et cetera, and this would mean he would be subject to a capital gains tax. The best alternative to this would be to be paid only partially in silver coins, for use as barter items or long-term hedging, as René Baxter suggests. One of the drawbacks of this idea is that it may be difficult for an employer to justify company expenditures for silver coins.

How Businessmen Profit from Controls

There are numerous ways that businessmen can profit from controls. Some of the obvious ones include withholding products from the market in expectation of decontrol. This is possible because government usually lacks the authority to control production.

An example of profiting from government controls involved

the federal government's support price for peanuts during the 1971 freeze. The support price was raised two days before the freeze. The market price was not allowed to rise along with the support price, at least at first. Manufacturers of peanut butter and related products were forced to accept higher costs, and pressure on profit margins forced them to curtail purchases of peanuts. Peanut stocks grew, nevertheless, due to the increased support price, and the government was forced to buy an estimated $20 million worth of new peanuts.

Middlemen and Arbitrage

The most universal way of profiting from price ceilings is through arbitrage techniques, purchasing merchandise at controlled prices and selling it at uncontrolled prices. It is also possible to profit when all prices are controlled. This is because with a freeze, for example, some prices have higher ceilings than others, even in a local area. This provides great opportunities for middlemen, who purchase at low controlled prices and sell at high controlled prices. One of the chief difficulties for the middleman is to obtain a supply of the lower-priced merchandise, which is generally in scarce supply.

The use of arbitrage techniques by business was widespread in lumber, petroleum, and other products during the Nixon controls, and it came under scrutiny by the government. Wide discrepancies in prices existed in the lumber industry due to wide differences in the effects of controls on lumber firms. Some firms could charge high prices based on costs of imported lumber or the purchase of exempt stumpage. Fully integrated producers or firms under long-term stumpage contracts had only small cost increases and therefore were severely limited in the prices they could charge.

Markups

The successive use of markups is a source of profit for businesses. The "gray market" in steel, which was investigated by the Select Committee on Small Business in 1952, is one of the best examples of how this works. (This scheme works only under base-period pricing, when costs are allowed to be passed along with a customary markup.)

The Korean War created shortages of steel and a dozen other metals. To deal with these shortages and to obtain a profit, many steel companies used a "chain" method of successive markups. One of these operations, called the Daisy Chain, involved a shipment of 74,780 pounds of steel.

Harry Phillips of the Ohio Valley Tool and Die Company, Steubenville, Ohio, was the first link in the chain. He purchased the steel from the Weirton Steel Company and the Fort Pitt Steel Company at prices ranging between $5.20 and $5.80 a hundredweight. He sold the steel to his brother, Matthew Phillips, of the M. & E. Company, New Cumberland, West Virginia, at $7.50 a hundredweight. Matthew sold it to a Pittsburgh broker, Isadore Foreman, at $10. Foreman sold it to the Martin Company of Cleveland at $10.40.

The person who bought it for Martin then turned around and sold a portion of the shipment in the name of Metal Associates at $10.50 to Emergency Steel Service of Skokie, Illinois. Emergency finally sold the steel to an end user, the Daisy Manufacturing Company of Plymouth, Michigan, at $10.95 a hundredweight plus forty cents in phantom freight charges and "federal tax."

Metal Associates sold the balance of the shipment to K. & G. Steel of Chicago at $11.10 a hundredweight. K. & G. in turn sold it to Aldan Steel at $11.95. Aldan sold it to Chevrolet-Indianapolis at $15.45.

Thus, in one series of deals, the steel was bought and sold by six different brokers, and in the other series of deals seven brokers managed to take a hand in extending the "daisy chain." Throughout the transactions, the steel remained in Steubenville, Ohio, until it was sold to the end users, Daisy Manufacturing and Chevrolet-Indianapolis!

To stop this practice (which was called a "gray market" because it was unorthodox though legal), the government recommended a limit to the increase in the price of steel from markups regardless of the number of hands through which it passed.

Needless to say, the federal government did not like the gray market in steel. The Select Committee on Small Business reported that "the gray market in steel has been a vicious and reprehensible thing. The small-business man has not been its only victim. Big business has felt its effects too. The entire economy has suffered. The net effect of gray markets, in steel and elsewhere, has been to inflate prices and to increase the cost of the defense program. In these days when economy is essential to the economic well-being of the Nation, America can ill afford gray markets. They must be stamped out wherever they arise."

I will discuss the gray market in steel and the development of artificial middlemen during controls in chapter 12, "The Black Market." The difference between a gray and a black market is often so slight as to be almost undetectable.

"The Canadian Connection"

The *Wall Street Journal* reported on an interesting development during the Nixon controls that demonstrates the use of the foreign-trade exemption for profitable opportunities. The obvious plan is to sell domestic products to foreign buyers at higher prices. But there are more subtle ways to take advantage of controls.

The *Journal* reported in August, 1973, that Canadian meat buyers had bought more American live cattle than usual during the July-August 1973 period, when the U.S. was having its second price freeze. Some contended that the purpose of the increased buying was to allow the Canadian meat buyers to sell the meat back to the U.S. in processed form at about 25 percent higher prices.

Was this illegal? The Cost of Living Council ruled that reexports on items originally purchased in the United States cannot be sold in the U.S. at prices above ceiling levels. Despite this regulation, it was obviously difficult to trace the origins of the meat. Moreover, the Canadian meat buyers could have completely circumvented the whole issue by simply using the U.S. beef for Canadian consumption and shipping Canadian beef to the U.S. at higher prices!

Chapter Ten

The Landlord Faces
Rent Controls

We already have rent control in the United States. New York City has had it for decades. Other large cities are establishing "tenant-landlord commissions" to keep landlords from "gouging" tenants with higher rents. Some local governments have passed rent-control laws that limit rent increases. (The District of Columbia has such a law on its books, and despite opposition from the mayor and others, it appears that the controls are here to stay.)

Rent controls on a nationwide basis are likely under a generally favorable climate toward national wage and price controls. Tenants have too much political clout for Washington to ignore their demands for rent controls.

How to Prepare for Rent Controls

Landlords and real estate investors should divest themselves of property subject to rent restrictions. They should also stay away from real estate in major cities that is likely to come under regulation.

This is not to say that all real property should be ignored as an investment medium and income-generator. In all previous controls programs, some forms of real estate have either been exempt or have received more favorable treatment. I will discuss these exemptions and exclusions in more detail below (also see chapter 4, "What Kind of Controls Are Coming").

Nonetheless, investors and landlords must be extremely cautious about their real estate investments.

On this subject, investment adviser Gerald Appel writes in *Inflation Early Warning System:*

> Real estate, once a major form of investment for both large and small investors, is coming under pressure now because of the twin threats of rising operating costs (especially for fuel and electricity) and the spread of rent control legislation; landlords are easier to restrict than OPEC. In many parts of the country, it has become a buyer's market for income property—particularly where dangers of rent control exist. In addition, banks, fearful of an economic trend that has been hurtful to small-income property investors, have become increasingly unwilling to provide mortgages on commercial income-producing property.
>
> In the past, income properties have provided excellent vehicles for investors willing to assume the tasks of owning and operating them. Tax shelters, rental income and the authorizations of mortgages on tenant money provided fine appeal. Now, the tide may be turning and, at least until the housing shortage becomes more acute, caution is advised in purchasing any income property for investment.
>
> Regardless, if you plan to go ahead evaluate the following:
>
> 1) Does rent control legislation exist in the area? If not, are there strong, vocal groups priming the area for such legislation?
>
> 2) Is the community receptive to multiple dwellings, or does the prevailing attitude discourage the provision of multiple-dwelling housing? What has been the drift of recent legal action in the area? (Many communities are enforcing restrictiveness indirectly by penalizing landlords, thereby discouraging rental housing.)
>
> 3) What have been the recent price trends for income property in the area?
>
> 4) Never, in the current climate, should you pay more than five times annual rental for small-income properties.
>
> Eventually, housing shortages will force communities to relent their attacks on landlords. But right now rent control is popular legislation.

Taking Advantage of Exemptions

Both the landlord and the real estate speculator can still obtain worthwhile income and capital gains by buying properties likely to be exempt or treated favorably under controls. By entering such markets prior to the imposition of rent controls, these investors will be able to profit even more than usual because of the increased demand for *uncontrolled* real estate properties.

Industrial, farm, nonresidential, and commercial property were exempt from controls during World War II, the Korean War, and the Nixon program. However, there are numerous pitfalls in real estate, even without controls. Remember the bad luck of the real estate investment trusts (REITs) during the 1973–75 recession. But considering the likelihood of food-price controls and food rationing, good farm land might not be a bad investment.

New construction is another exempt area worth looking into, but only *after* controls are imposed. New rental property was exempt from the Nixon freeze of 1971 only if offered for rent for the first time after the freeze started.

Rehabilitated dwellings were exempt with certain restrictions during both the Korean and Nixon controls. This kind of property is initially inexpensive, but once renovated it could easily become subject to future federal or local controls. *Avoid!*

Probably the best category of exempt real estate is single family dwellings. Single family dwellings were exempted under the "small landlord" clause during the Nixon controls and are likely to be excluded in the future. (Note how exemptions are consistently made for the "small" businessman, landlord, worker, et cetera.) Under the Nixon program, a small landlord could own up to four separate dwellings (or up to four units in a rental dwelling) without being controlled. Under similar circumstances, a landlord with large property holdings might consider divesting himself of his large real estate investments and buying up several homes or duplexes. He could use the rest of his capital for more profitable endeavors.

One more exemption is worth noting: units renting for $500 a month or more—the "luxury rental exemption." An investment in this area is really worth pursuing and is bound to be extremely profitable under tight rent controls. Under controls in general, the rich are somehow able to make even more money; this means more demand for penthouses and expensive apartments in large cities. And there is no limit to the number of luxury rentals you can own.

Rent Controls, Political Battles, and Evasive Methods: The Case of New York City

Rent controls have existed in New York City since 1941—on an "emergency" basis. There is perhaps no better example of the kind of political, economic, and financial battle that goes on between landlord, tenant, government, and investor under rent controls. When the liberal and consumer-conscious *New York Times Magazine* prints an article with the headline "Rent Control Must Go" (April 18, 1976), you can bet the problem has reached gigantic proportions. As the author of the *Times Magazine* article, B. Bruce-Briggs, concludes, "we can now see the dark at the end of the tunnel."

Bruce-Briggs' article summarizes some of the methods used by tenants and landlords to serve their own interests in spite of rent controls.

Not too long ago, when rent-control laws were stricter than those in force today, "key money"—the payment of a bribe or fee to an agent, superintendent or previous tenant to obtain a rent-controlled apartment—was a common institution. In effect, this was simply additional rent paid by a tenant who could afford it to someone other than a landlord. . . . Meanwhile, the landlord interest, while weaker than the tenant interest, has not been without influence. Rent-control legislation was never a total defeat for the landlords; they always gained important concessions. The rent-controlled units were kept alive at first by an across-the-board 15 percent increase in 1953 to take account of the inflation of the Korean War and later by a provision for a 15 percent increase if there was a vacancy—an ingenious compromise permitting the residents to retain low rents and only hitting the transients who were more likely to be newcomers and/or nonvoters. Single-family homes were not covered by rent control, and while New Yorkers are not as enthusiastic for home ownership as the rest of the nation, increased prosperity led more of them to buy houses, usually outside of the city limits where land was available. Apartments in two-family houses were free of controls, and this exemption was soon extended to structures with up to six units.

Most important, when the Federal Government abandoned controls and the state determined to continue them in 1947, the new law provided that all new construction would be free of controls. . . .

Rent-control legislation has always provided for increases in cases of landlord "hardship"—proof that he is losing money. Obviously, unscrupulous landlords can easily concoct phony operating expenditures;

208

also, such applications for hardship increases are expensive and time-consuming and thus effectively useful only to the largest landlords, who typically operate in the more settled and prosperous areas.

In the late 1960s, when rent in the uncontrolled sector escalated rapidly, "rent stabilization" was applied to that area, too. After long negotiations, the "Maximum Base Rent" concept was adopted. Bruce-Briggs writes:

> According to a complex formula based on maintenance and operating costs and a fixed profit (and calculated by computer), landlords were permitted to raise rents. . . . The system quickly degenerated into a program that routinely permits the landlords fixed annual rent increases, usually of 7½ percent, hardly enough to keep pace with inflation.
>
> Another innovation of this period was vacancy decontrol. This was a great victory for the landlords. When a rent-controlled or stabilized apartment became vacant, it was decontrolled; a landlord could then charge a market rent to a new tenant. . . . The senior citizen's exemption was invented to protect the elderly from increases. Rents from these people are held at 1970 levels, and landlords get a tax break equal to the permissible MBR increases. . . .
>
> [In 1974,] decontrolled buildings were put under rent stabilization. Worse, new construction since 1968 was stabilized. Twice the city and state have reneged on promises of free-market rents to investors in residential property, a point that has serious implications. With record interest rates and operating costs up 50 percent since 1967, the landlords were clearly hard hit by the fuel price increases of 1974–75, so the Council further muddied these murky waters by adopting a "fuel pass-along" permitting additional rent increases. Today a single building may have apartments that are controlled, decontrolled and stabilized, and senior-citizens' exempted—making it impossible to calculate the return a landlord is receiving. . . .
>
> Today it cannot be seriously claimed that New York offers desirable opportunities for housing investment. The MBR formula provides for 8½ percent return on investment. You can put your money in a savings bank and collect 7.9 percent return with no risk whatever. . . .
>
> With all the investment opportunities in the world, after what has happened to property owners in New York, would *you* invest a penny in city housing?

Cooperative and Condominium Apartments

One method of controls avoidance that Bruce-Briggs ignored in his article is the conversion of apartments to condominiums or cooperative apartments, owned by the tenants. In both cases, New York rent controls are in large part suspended. Of course, not all apartment dwellings are easily convertible to these types of ownership, but under strict controls, it pays to investigate the condominium and cooperative alternatives.

What about the monthly charges on condominiums? During the 1971 freeze, monthly charges to cover costs associated with general maintenance of cooperative and condominium apartments were exempt from the freeze. Due to the forms of ownership, these maintenance charges were considered "operating costs" incurred by individual owners. When the condominium was run by an agent, however, "management services" were subject to the freeze. But "maintenance services" were not and could be increased!

Rent-Control Violations

The Emergency Price Control Act of 1942 had some interesting provisions for rent control. For one thing, it required that each rental-unit owner report the following within sixty days after the act went into effect: (1) maximum rents, (2) grounds for adjusting the maximum rent, (3) minimum services, (4) restrictions on unwarranted evictions, and (5) registration of property.

Below are outlined the major types of violations during World War II, the Korean War, and the Nixon Economic Stabilization Program.

(1) *Overcharging*. During World War II, this constituted a minority of violation cases. Landlords generally try to avoid direct, obvious violations of rent-control laws.

(2) *Indirect overcharges*. Indirect overcharges have always been very difficult to monitor and control. Violations were drawn up as fast as the evasive techniques were discovered. Many of them could never have been predicted. They clearly demonstrated the shrewd, ingenious, and perhaps "unscrupulous" nature of the landlord. In all cases, the maximum rent allowed by law would be maintained and never exceeded. But at the same time the landlord had a handful of devious ways to get around the regulations.

Here are a few examples: payment of rent in advance, increased security deposits, eliminating or decreasing the interest on security deposits, elimination of customary discounts for prompt payment of rent, nonreturn of deposits, separate rental of apartment and furniture in a "furnished apartment," and all kinds of tying agreements. In order to keep abreast of these violations, the government during World War II required the registration of both rent expected and services provided by landlords. Without written proof, it would be extremely hard to prove a violation.

(3) *Tying agreements.* Tying agreements between landlords and tenants have always been the most popular form of rent control evasion. Consequently, tying agreements are quickly banned by government officials. During World War II, complete registration of rental charges helped in policing landlords in most areas, but tying agreements were always difficult to prosecute, especially if the agreement was voluntary and desirable for both tenant and landlord (which was often the case). In many cases, the landlord compelled the tenant to purchase or rent something he did not need. In other cases—and here is where the regulations lost all effect—landlords were smart enough to start selling things tenants needed! All sorts of items were sold—clothing, furniture, an empty lot, a used car, a subscription to a magazine, and so forth.

Former OPA Commissioner Leon Henderson commented on this method: "The most common dodge is the must-buy-furniture requirement. . . . A landlady in Norfolk, showing two Navy officers a moderately priced apartment, announced that to get the apartment, the officers would first have to buy her paintings, a bargain at $300 each. Other forced sales concern kitchen furnishings, bathroom fixtures, supposedly rare plants, and the ubiquitous cat. . . ."

The French are past masters of this technique. They have lived under rent controls since World War I. They use everything from charging colossal "key money" for finding an apartment to selling decrepit furniture at antique prices.

(4) *Payment of utilities.* Landlords have tried to increase their profits by separating utilities from payment of rent, leaving utility bills to their tenants. This is a good idea when heating,

electricity, and water bills are rising as rapidly as they have been in the past couple of years.

However, divorcing utility payments from the rent is easier said than done. It means, for one thing, the attachment of separate meters for each apartment, and many apartment complexes are not set up to permit such drastic changes. In addition, once rent controls are imposed, regulations will likely prohibit the separation of utilities payments from rent. Such was the case in the last controls program. Under freeze regulations in 1971, landlords could not require a tenant to pay for utilities after August 15, 1971, if prior to that date utilities had been paid for by the landlord.

(5) *Evictions*. Under some controls programs, it paid the landlord to use unusual methods to evict tenants from their apartments. Controls kept many tenants from moving for years. By evicting tenants, landlords were thus able to raise rents by certain amounts under certain government regulations or to sell their buildings for a higher profit. Such practices were widespread in New York and during World War II. To combat this, certain methods of eviction were made illegal under past controls programs.

(6) *Fictitious services and charges*. Under rent controls, landlords may actually *increase* certain additional services to tenants in an effort to increase their income. Though illegal, this was common in the past. Tenants would be charged for a quick paint job (whether the apartment walls needed it or not), fixing appliances, and so on.

(7) *Capital improvements*. Landlords would often make superficial "capital improvements" in an effort to increase the legal ceiling on rent. To eliminate this ploy, controllers during the Nixon freeze and Phase II required that "capital improvements" be limited to those defined in the Internal Revenue Code.

(8) *Decreasing services*. During World War II, any substantial decrease in essential services, furniture, or equipment without an equal reduction in rent was considered a rent violation. During the Nixon controls, the general price rule stated that any reduction in services or the product offered for sale constituted a price increase.

Some of the services often reduced were cleaning and maintenance, mowing the lawn, and beautification of the surroundings. Some of the more ingenious ways of decreasing services included: no longer heating the swimming pool in winter or summer, eliminating parking lots or renting them out to tenants or outsiders, failing to replace burned out lights in hallways and stairwells, et cetera.

(9) *Changes in the physical structure.* A radical method of eluding rent controls is the restructuring of apartment dwellings. Examples of this occurred in New York City, where landlords reduced the size of individual apartments so that they could rent out more rooms. Rent controls, like price controls in general, often fail to regulate the size of rental dwellings (though "altering the unit of rent" was a violation in World War II). Thus, landlords are often allowed to decrease the size of apartments, depending on what building codes and local laws allow. A six-room apartment might be subdivided into two three-room apartments.

(10) *Key money.* During World War II, it was illegal to use bonuses, commissions. rewards, and gratuities to obtain an apartment. These things were considered to constitute rent increases. The waste of time involved in searching for an apartment was somehow not equivalent to a rent increase. Such is the logic of controllers!

In any event, this regulation was largely ignored in the larger cities where vacancy rates were extremely low, especially after the war ended. According to Marshall Clinard, "in many rental areas tenants publicly offered rewards to the person locating an apartment for them." To this day, key money is often used as a general business practice to save consumers time in looking for an apartment. Perhaps this will make the use of key money legal during the next round of rent controls.

Profiting from Rent Controls

The most obvious way to profit from rent controls is to invest in or own *uncontrolled* rental properties. These would include single family units (up to four units), commercial real estate, farm land (especially farm land, for reasons stated earlier), luxury apartments that rent for $500 or more, new construction, and so on. The demand for such properties will increase under rent controls.

You must be cautious, however. Not all property that is exempt from controls will prove profitable. A number of other factors are sometimes more important than rent controls: location, taxes, terrain, et cetera.

There are other ways of profiting from rent controls. For example, John Kamin, an expert in real estate speculation and author of *How to Make Money Fast Speculating in Distressed Property* (Pyramid, $1.25), argues that in many U.S. cities there are quality areas where rents are 40 to 50 percent below market levels! The key to profiting in real estate speculation is to move into these below-market areas before rent controls are imposed. Kamin writes:

> In many U.S. cities there are concentrations in key "growth" areas with the public totally ignoring other parts of town. As a result, you can find high rents in some parts of a city and low rents in other parts of the city, even when the neighborhoods are essentially of the same quality. A survey of several cities reveals that you may find good quality neighborhoods with rents as low as 50 percent *below* market and yet even more convenient to the city's hub. . . .
>
> A particular part of a big city will grow. Then developers will go "hog wild" with projects, and build and build in that area of town. Speculators will speculate five, ten miles in that direction, expecting more growth. Result? Growth in one direction has caused a saturation point and speculators have bid prices up high in that particular direction of the city. . . . The real estate market, like all markets, has its cycles, its bull markets and its bear markets. Many cities are now caught in a situation where a particular real estate development in one part of the city has reached its "speculation phase." That means the real estate speculation in that area of town is at the top of the bull market. Developers have overbuilt, rents have skyrocketed, and speculators have bought way out beyond the growth pattern.
>
> Look around you and you may find that in the opposite direction of town the quality of property is just as good—even closer to town, with rents as low as 40 percent to 50 percent of those in developed areas. You may be looking at the next boom area of your town! Smart developers are already discovering this phenomenon—a sort of vacuum effect in real estate speculation. Of course there are some exceptions. Each town will vary so you must survey your own town. For example,

a classic city in the U.S. is Albuquerque, New Mexico, with an air force base on one side and a mountain range on another side and a national park on still another. It's obvious the city can grow in only one direction. But there are few such special situations. Most cities can grow in any direction.

Many people are beginning to move out of the overcommercialized and super-high rent, highly-promoted areas and into the areas which are less congested, yet are even more convenient to work. When the shortage comes, rents will move upward.

Your strategy in the coming real estate crisis should be to seize advantage now while there is still time. If your rents are down, get them up 25 percent to 30 percent—where they should be. Survey rents in other areas of town and anticipate growth patterns for your area or the area where you may wish to speculate. Act quickly before the political economic impact of growing tenant-landlord commissions gains its full effect on the economy.

Are there profitable opportunities once rent controls are imposed? Yes, for the speculator, says John Kamin. He recommends that

> when you buy real estate you should focus your attention on capital gains, not income. You are in to make a lot of money, not small eight or nine percent returns. . . . What if the lid on rent controls never comes off? What if you are hung with rent controls on rentable property for several years? . . . As supplies fail to keep pace (because of artificially suppressed prices), with rental space demanded (by those who are willing to pay a higher price to get what they want), blackmarkets and shortages develop. Under-the-table payments become commonplace. Potential renters turn into buyers; they kick out the present tenants and take over the building for their own use. You saw it happen in World War II. When shortages and blackmarkets like these develop, you can sell buildings at much higher prices than frozen rentals would indicate. Potential renters are suddenly willing to become buyers, just so they can get the space they need.

215

Chapter Eleven

The Investor Faces Price Controls

If my analysis of the economy is correct, price controls will most likely be imposed in a highly inflationary climate. The last time this occurred (1973–75), the stock market was declining precipitously, precious metals were skyrocketing in price, strong foreign currencies were appreciating rapidly against a weak U.S. dollar, and traditional savings accounts and certificates of deposit were losing value every day. These financial conditions may well repeat themselves when price inflation resurges. But will this situation continue under controls or will investment markets react differently?

The Stock Market

How has the stock market reacted during past price controls? This is difficult to answer, mainly because we can never really be sure what causes the stock market to fluctuate. There is always a multitude of major factors that influences the minds of investors. These factors include such diverse things as corporate profits, the rate of inflation, growth or decline in the money supply, balance of payments, interest rates, and various government policies.

The following graph shows the movement of the Dow Jones Industrial Average, an extremely important indicator of the stock market.

As you can see, the stock market does not appear to have

PRICE CONTROLS AND THE STOCK MARKET
Dow Jones Industrial Average, 1929–1975

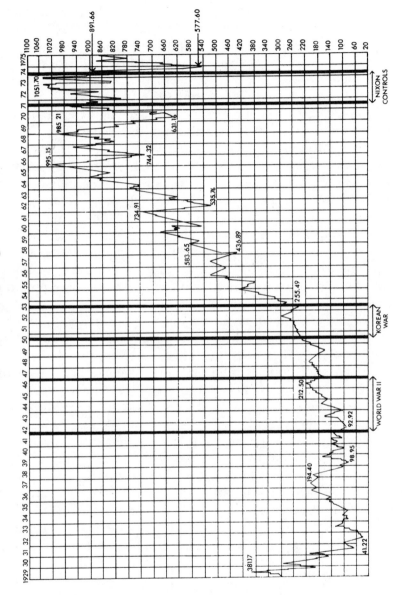

been adversely affected by the imposition of price controls, even over long periods of time. From 1941 to 1946, when controls were generally in operation, the DJIA climbed from 100 to 200 points. From the beginning of 1951 until the middle of 1953, the market rose, from 240 to around 275, not much of a gain, but still upward. The Nixon era was mixed. At first, the stock market continued rising, from 800 to over 1000 points, but then the DJIA dropped back to 800 during 1973–74.

It would be misleading and naive, I believe, to say that price controls were chiefly responsible for the rising stock market during the Korean War and World War II. As I stated previously, the stock market is influenced by many factors, both technical and fundamental. We would be committing the post hoc ergo propter hoc fallacy if we said: price controls were instituted during the time the stock market (Dow Jones Industrial Average) rose, therefore the imposition of price controls *caused* the stock market to rise. We could just as easily say that price controls kept the stock market from rising further than it did. And from a theoretical point of view, this interpretation might be more correct.

Not much is known about the impact price controls can have on the stock market. The Nixon period clearly shows that a rising stock market does not always accompany government wage and price policies. During World War II, many investors felt that corporate profits played a far greater role than price controls in influencing the fundamentals of the rising stock market. Interestingly enough, business profits grew very rapidly during the world war, and at all levels, wholesale, manufacturing, and retail. And, surprisingly, despite the crippling nature of controls, the number of business failures dropped from 1941 to 1945. Even industries in which there were heavy violations of control regulations (e.g., textiles) showed heavy profits. These factors could have been the primary motivations for rising stock prices during the war. Corporate profits also rose during the Korean War, as demand picked up for industrial products and war commodities.

The Nixon controls period is rather intriguing in this respect and may provide valuable guidelines for investors when controls return. Price controls may have played a stronger role during the

1971–74 period than in past eras in terms of their impact on stock market prices. As I mentioned above, leaders of major corporations were elated almost to a man when Nixon announced the ninety-day freeze on wages, rents, and prices. Their chief concern was the exceptional bargaining power of major labor unions, which were getting double-digit wage increases. Business leaders saw controls as a way of keeping union demands down and keeping profits up. The imposition of controls was a psychological victory for big business, and it created a wave of optimism that may have spilled over into the stock market. Also, corporate profits were up in 1972 during Phase II, and this contributed to market optimism.

What brought the DJIA down from its 1000-point peak? Some of the most important factors, according to many stock market analysts and investors, included: the rise in the rate of inflation despite controls, growing shortages, a growing foreign trade deficit, and the first signs of a recession. Business in general was hard-hit by the price controls—short-run victories turned into long-run defeats. Industry suffered far more from shortages, distortions, and declining markets than did other sectors of the economy. And many of the other maladies mentioned here were caused or aggravated by controls.

Market conditions accompanying the latter half of the Nixon controls provide clues to what you should expect when controls are reimposed. Under rising rates of inflation, price controls will cause *immediate* shortages and will hurt industry first. This, coupled with profit margin restrictions, makes it unlikely that corporations will enjoy increasing prices for their stocks.

I do not believe that we will follow the same route that we did under the Nixon controls, when the rate of inflation was declining at the time the regulations were imposed. When controls are imposed at a time of accelerating inflation, stock market investors will be confronted with the worst of all possible worlds: widespread shortages, declining corporate profits, spot inflation, and dollar devaluations. Dividend controls, which could be more unfavorable to stock prices than price controls, will almost certainly be imposed. One bright spot is that with base-period pricing, corporations might have a freer hand with their pricing policies for a period of time, assuming that their base-period years were during a period of high demand (which is likely if controls are imposed after a few years of rapid expansion).

A declining stock market does not mean the investor should completely abandon speculation in stocks. On the contrary, there are several ways of profiting from a bear market, which I discuss below. These methods are considered highly speculative, however, and traditional investors may wish to seek their fortunes elsewhere.

Short-Selling Stocks

In short selling, one *sells* shares of a particular stock, waits for the stock to decline in price, and then *repurchases* the shares at the lower price. The difference in the two prices is profit, not counting the interest charged on the loan from the stockbroker for selling short, commissions, et cetera.

There are some important points to remember about selling short. First, the short sale must take place in a margin account. Second, the short sale must be done on an "uptick." Third, your profit potential is never more than 100 percent, since the price of the stock can only decline so much. Fourth, it is very important to remember that just because the DJIA is declining, not all stocks are declining in price, so your choice of common stock is extremely important. Fifth, when you sell short, you are required to pay out any dividends accrued by the company whose stock you are selling short. Consequently, it is best to pick stocks that pay little or no dividend; this of course severely limits the stocks you can short.

Frankly, I think selling short is highly speculative and should not be a part of your investment strategy during controls, except perhaps if you are a seasoned trader.

Stock Options

The second method of profiting from a bear market is through the wise use of stock options. Stock options, I believe, provide better profit potential for the risk involved than short selling. But they are still a speculative investment and should be limited to risk capital.

A stock option is the right to either buy or sell 100 shares of a particular stock at a specified ("striking") price until a certain time. Not all stocks are permitted to have options, but the number is growing at the exchanges. An option to buy is a *call option,* an option to sell is a *put option.*

To take advantage of a declining stock price, you could purchase a put option, which would entitle you to *sell* the stock at the striking price to the person from whom you bought the put for a period of, say, one year. If the stock price does indeed fall sufficiently sometime during the year, you then *buy* 100 shares of the stock and exercise your option by selling them for the *higher* striking price. Your profit is the difference, minus the cost of the put option and the commission.

Using this method, it is possible to profit by several hundred percent. For example, if the option costs $2000, the striking price is $100, and you eventually buy 100 shares at a price of $40, your gross profit would be $4000 (60 points times 100 shares, less $2000 for the cost of writing the option). You profit 200 percent on your money; you make $4000 with an original investment of $2000. Thus, stock options are potentially more profitable than short selling. With short selling, you are limited to 100 percent profit, but with stock options, you can profit by more than 100 percent.

Of course, if the price of the stock should rise rather than fall, you would not exercise your option. But your loss is limited to $2000. Stock options are therefore less risky than short selling, and less capital is required. But you do have to pay a premium before you make a profit from stock options. Moreover, the price of the stock has to drop quite a bit before a profit can be realized, since you first have to cover the cost of the option premium. Finally, put options can be illiquid at times.

Stock options can be used for all kinds of situations, not just in bear markets. In fact, a *straddle* can be used to make a profit in cases where you feel that the price of stock is going to move, but you are uncertain about which way it will go.

Price controls will probably provide many such instances. Indeed, price controls will inflict more harmful effects on certain companies than others. I mentioned, for example, that smaller companies will fare better than larger corporations in terms of government harassment and monitoring. Also, companies involved in manufacturing "vital" products will face stricter controls than other firms. There is no doubt that these selective measures will affect the stocks of some companies more than others. Some companies will undoubtedly improve their earnings throughout the controls period, either because they market *uncontrolled* merchandise and services or because they will cater to the needs of government or businesses that require more of their services (e.g., economists, price-controls consultants, paper companies, and, perhaps, brokers). Thus, some businesses will prosper not because they are allowed to raise their prices, but because they are able to expand their services.

It should also be pointed out that stocks listed on foreign stock exchanges may provide excellent investment opportunities, assuming that they are not saddled with price controls, too.

The Bond Market and Interest Rates

The outlook for interest rates under price controls depends on a number of factors. In a highly inflationary climate, interest rates are likely to be relatively high in the short run. The introduction of wage and price controls is not likely to change this situation. Credit controls may be imposed as a concession to certain vested interests (e.g., labor), but the government has traditionally emphasized the use of monetary and fiscal policy to control interest rates. Failing to keep interest rates down, however, may bring strong pressure for artificial credit restrictions.

In either case—credit controls or no—the investor should avoid at all costs putting his money in *long-term* bonds and other debt instruments. If he does so, he will be locked in to relatively low interest rates. If he tries to liquidate his investment prior to maturity, he is likely to take a loss. It would be far better to place funds in such extremely liquid short-term debt instruments as ninety-day Treasury bills and money-market funds (Dreyfus, Capital Preservation, Kemper, and the like).

222

The Commodity Futures Market

The commodity futures market faces a unique situation under wage and price controls. The stock market has always been allowed to fluctuate freely in price because stocks are neither capital goods nor consumption items. In the past, controllers have seen no necessity for placing ceilings on stock prices. With commodities, however, it is a different story. Many of the commodities traded on the futures market are basic products in the economy—wheat, corn, beef, copper, and many more. Farm commodities have been exempt from controls under previous programs, but what if they are not in the future? Some commodity markets have been subject to controls in the past--metals, meats, and others. The commodity futures market was supposedly exempt during the Nixon controls, but *spot,* or *cash,* markets were not.

The *Wall Street Journal* reported on June 21, 1973, during the second Nixon freeze: "Currently, commodity futures traded on organized exchanges aren't covered by the freeze. But deliveries of commodities against future contracts are, and under the government's rules, such deliveries can't be made at prices higher than the freeze levels unless they are exempt as raw agricultural products." Elaborating, the *Journal* said that "if a price on a contract made prior to the freeze and calling for delivery during the freeze is *above* the freeze price, both buyer and seller must adhere to the freeze rate. The seller may decline to deliver the contract, but the buyer doesn't have to accept delivery at a date after the freeze."

The basis for concern over the commodity futures market was the growing disparity between futures prices and delivered prices, artificially created by price controls. Cash, or spot, prices were controlled, but futures prices were not. This was especially evident in the following markets during June, 1973: crude soybean oil, soybean meal, iced broilers, frozen pork bellies, platinum, palladium, silver, gold, copper, silver coins and propane. If the futures prices were allowed to rise well above cash prices, the Cost of Living Council foresaw the possibility of "artificially increased demand" for cash prices of all commodities—to 100 percent of the ceiling price. The Council was also deeply concerned over the possibility of widespread violations of the ceiling price for delivered goods. It also feared a potentially heavy loss for hedges if the "cost of buying a futures contract to cover an earlier hedge rose substantially." Finally, the Council feared new speculation on the part of "spreaders" who saw a "sure deal" with the cash price fixed at the ceiling level and the futures price continuing to rise (a clear case of profiting from the government's controls).

As a result of these concerns, and on the request of the Commodity Exchange Authority, trading in soybean, soybean meal, and soybean oil futures was suspended for one day on June 21, 1973. The Authority also requested that July, August, and September soybean and soybean meal contracts be limited to *liquidation only* (in other words, no new positions were to be taken) unless sellers planned to deliver.

A week later, the Authority issued more details of the new regulations on the futures market. Commodity futures were to be covered by the freeze starting the first week in July, 1973. The ceiling price was set based on the highest price at which at least 10 percent of the volume of the commodity was traded in the nearest future between June 1–8 (the base period). The nearest future generally meant July. The day these regulations came out, June 28, 1973, the futures prices of *all* commodities fell (take note, traders!).

Iced broilers, frozen pork bellies, platinum, palladium, silver, copper, and silver coin futures were all covered by the new freeze orders in June, 1973. Rulings applied only to July and August contracts, since the freeze was only to last sixty days. The *Wall Street Journal* commented that "market sources fretted it could be extended to other deliveries if the present measures proved ineffective." Since futures prices exceeded the ceiling levels, trade in certain 1973 futures was *terminated* (except for liquidations): July copper, July and August silver, and July mercury contracts. Also, specific ceilings were placed on platinum and silver coin contracts. A ceiling was also imposed on July lumber futures. As a result of these actions, even prices of unregulated commodities were affected adversely; cotton futures and Maine potato futures fell in price.

Legal Problems

Naturally, this situation raised a number of legal questions. If the government had not made allowance for liquidations, the old story of a commodity futures trader waking up one morning with 5000 bushels of wheat dumped in his front yard might have come true! (Actually, to be more realistic, the trader would have received a warehouse receipt.) But since there are always equal numbers of "buying long" and "selling short" contracts, there was no real problem with the liquidation of contracts.

Investment Dangers with Commodity Futures

Even though there appeared to be little problem in liquidating futures contracts, many commodity speculators *did* face losses because of the sudden liquidation of their contracts. For example, a trader selling silver short would take a loss if liquidation occurred after the price had risen. Thus, many investors were caught in a loss position by the arbitrary actions of the government.

This kind of situation can be avoided when controls are re-imposed. The day price controls are announced, commodity traders should avoid markets subject to such government manipulation. One way to elude controls on the commodity futures market is to shift funds into trading on commodity exchanges in Canada, London, and other foreign markets, or to shift to commodities and currencies that are not controlled.

A permanent wage and price freeze in the U.S. would have a devastating impact on the commodity futures market, and problems similar to those just mentioned would become widespread. Both cash and futures prices would be controlled directly or the commodities would be closely regulated by the government. Futures markets would not be required.

Such a sterile situation occurred during World War II. Memberships in the old Chicago Butter and Egg Board (now the Chicago Mercantile Exchange) and the Chicago Board of Trade became practically worthless by the end of the war. Some sold for as little as $100 each. Today those memberships are worth around $100,000 because of their income-producing potential. What made the difference?

During the wartime controls and price ceilings, the market was not allowed to operate freely. Much of the country's capital and resources went into the production of war material. Rationing and price ceilings virtually eliminated the market's role as an efficient distributor of the country's resources. How could there be a futures market for a product that would have the same price six months or a year from now? The same thing occurred with silver and gold bullion. Their prices were fixed by the U.S. government until recently, and until prices were allowed to fluctuate, there was no futures market for either of them.

Fortunately, a permanent freeze is highly unlikely. Government controllers will eventually shift toward a method of "formula price," allowing average prices to move up a specified amount. Under such circumstances, commodity futures would likely become exempt to a large degree. Traders should then be on the lookout for profitable spread opportunities as the cash price is regulated and allowed to rise somewhat (though always below market levels), while the futures price is uncontrolled. This is highly risky, of course, and should be limited to experienced commodity speculators.

Gold and Silver

Price controls will undoubtedly prove favorable for gold and silver prices, but just how favorable is uncertain. It is certainly true that gold was in a strong bull market throughout the last controls period, 1971–74, but this was a result of other more powerful influences, I believe. Gold had been artificially controlled below free market prices for decades; the 1971–74 period reflected a period of catching up. Other very important factors were the worldwide rates of inflation and the instability of markets and governments. Price controls in the United States and elsewhere no doubt played a significant role in the growing demand for gold bullion and coins, but they were not overriding influences.

With inflationary pressures mounting, the demand for gold will increase. This does not mean that the price for gold will skyrocket, however. We cannot ignore the supply side, and if the U.S. Treasury and the International Monetary Fund sell off some of their gold from time to time, the price of gold may flounder. Still, I am inclined to believe that gold will rise in price when double-digit inflation returns. And the demand for gold can only increase as a result of the reimposition of wage and price controls. The enactment of such income policies is regarded by many international investors and speculators as a clear sign of weakness. Governments impose controls either for the purpose of reducing a balance-of-payments deficit or to repress the domestic rate of inflation (or both). In either case, the policy concerned is a temporary, artificial course of action that may help in the short run, though it may hinder the country's economy in the long run. The institution of controls is a point-blank, public announcement to the world that the government's monetary and fiscal policies are failures, unable to control inflation, foreign exchange imbalances, and other economic troubles. On the other hand, such an announcement is bullish for gold, known for its quick response to political and economic instability.

Silver is, in a sense, the "poor man's gold," but there is a major difference that all investors should recognize. Silver is primarily an industrial metal, while gold is chiefly a precious monetary metal. Silver does seem to react favorably to bad news, but it reacts even more to general market conditions and industrial demand. No investor should look to silver as an investment solely on the basis of price-controls legislation. Industrial demand for the silken metal may well be high when controls are introduced, so this means that silver may have already risen in price. If gold and silver are subjected to price ceilings, the *legal* market for the precious metals may well dry up in the United States. Then the best places to buy gold and silver would be Europe and Canada. Swiss banks offer particularly good services for storing gold and silver—if you are willing to make large purchases.

Collectables

Under price controls, inflation is no longer reflected in the regulated industries and markets. This does not mean that inflation disappears. Rather, it begins to appear in the uncontrolled industries, the "inflation-reflecting industries." I have mentioned some of these areas above: antiques, rare books, coins, stamps, paintings and other art objects, fine wines of vintage age, and other collectables. Collectables—this is where investors can count on excellent returns and a sure hedge against inflation.

On this subject, Gary North writes in *An Introduction to Christian Economics:*

> Thus, it would pay investors to become at least moderately skilled in purchasing goods in these areas (highly differentiated products on the collectors' markets). They can put such knowledge to work before the population at large begins to comprehend what is going on. The old rule for success holds true: get there "fustest with the mostest." As inflationary hedges for private, family protection, they cannot be surpassed. It takes a certain degree of skill in selecting the proper mixture of hedges, and prospective investors should work in those fields that they know best. Maybe now you can put your wife's talents as an antique "nut" to work; she, in turn, will have to grant you your full credit for having developed your taste for expensive imported wines. Bernard Mandeville's early eighteenth century classic, *Fable of the Bees,* convinced Adam Smith of the fact that private vices can be converted into public virtues; we may find that governmental policies of inflation and price controls can convert our private vices into private virtues.

It is interesting to note that collectables did extremely well during the last round of price controls. Inflation was no doubt a major factor in the increase in prices for antiques, stamps, numismatic coins, and so on. Many of these areas of investment did well throughout the 1973–75 recession. Remember, though: a collector needs to be selective.

Coins

Regarding the collection of coins, it is important to distinguish between bullion-type coins and numismatic coins. Bullion coins are primarily sold for their gold or silver value, and they are traditionally priced slightly above the bullion price. Examples of these coins are the South African krugerrand, the Mexican 50 peso, the British sovereign, the Austrian 100 corona, and the Hungarian 100 corona. The premium fluctuates between 5 and 30 percent. The reason for this is that these coins are still being minted.

Numismatic coins are no longer being minted and are rare. Consequently, their premium over bullion value is usually very high, sometimes over 1000 percent. The U.S. St. Gauden's 20 dollar gold piece is an example of a numismatic coin.

Bullion coins and numismatic coins will serve two separate, distinct purposes under controls. Bullion coins may be controlled—remember that silver "junk" coins were given price ceilings during the Nixon controls. But they may serve well as barter coins if controls become oppressive, as I discussed in chapter 7.

Numismatic coins, on the other hand, will be of interest to the collector and investor, who will hold them for appreciation and capital gain. They might be used in barter arrangements on a limited scale, but in such cases the chances of taking a loss would be great, since so much depends on the expertise of the buyer, the kind of coin, the condition of the coin, and so forth. Furthermore, the high price of all numismatic coins precludes their use in exchanges for basic essentials and small items.

Diamonds

Diamonds are collectables that will most likely remain un-controlled. There are pitfalls, however. Like numismatic coins, they require expert judgment when buying and selling. Also, many diamond purchasers make the tragic mistake of buying diamonds at the retail price and selling at the wholesale level, resulting in a substantial loss. Diamonds should be bought at the wholesale level and sold at the wholesale level or at auction. Under these conditions, diamonds are bound to prove an excel-lent prospect for "inflation-reflecting" investment during price controls.

Foreign Currency Profits during Controls

Foreign currencies did not provide much opportunity for profit from price controls during the Nixon program because most major currencies were fluctuating at the time.

During World War II, it was a different story. Newspapers recounted many instances of foreign currency "profiteering" by American servicemen abroad. The problem arose when the War Department decided to pay U.S. soldiers with local foreign currencies. This was done because many foreign government officials were complaining that American soldiers were creating quite a disturbance in the local currency markets by selling their U.S. dollars in the illegal black market.

American servicemen found that they could not use up all the local currency and requested that they be allowed to channel any surplus pay back to the States or be allowed to set up savings plans. The Army promoted these savings plans. The exchange rates between local currencies and U.S. dollars were fixed at official (below-market) levels. There was no limit on the exchange of local currencies into U.S. dollars. Exchange profits were made because the military exchanges gave out U.S. dollars to soldiers at a fixed rate below market rates. Thus soldiers could take the local currency in wages, exchange it for dollars, sell the dollars in the local black market for local currency, take the local currency back to the military exchange for more dollars, and on and on. Some soldiers even went so far as to request their parents to send back their savings in dollars. These profitable opportunities turned up in China, North Africa, Italy, France, Germany, and in the islands of the Pacific.

Similar situations can occur even today with fixed exchange rates. In fact, one of the purposes of arbitragers is to seek out such markets. I discovered one such situation when I was in Colombia several years ago. As far as I know, it is still possible to duplicate it. In Bogota, I took a $1000 check to the First National City Bank and asked for U.S. dollars instead of Colombian pesos. After receiving the $1000, I flew to the Colombia-Venezuela border, drove across the border into Venezuela, and purchased Venezuelan bolivars with my $1000 at an exchange rate of about five bolivars to the dollar. (For purposes of clarity, all exchange rates used here are approximate.) With my 5000 bolivars, I went back to Colombia and bought pesos at the exchange rate of five pesos to the bolivar. I then had 25,000 pesos. If I had exchanged my $1000 directly for pesos at the official exchange rate of about twenty pesos to the dollar, I would have only received 20,000 Colombian pesos. But by going through another currency, the bolivar, I was able to gain 5000 more pesos. In one day of exchanging currencies, I profited 5000 pesos, or $250, with an original investment of $1000! The only thing that is keeping me from taking a million dollars down to Colombia and repeating the whole thing over again (resulting in a gross profit of $250,000) is that it is extremely difficult to convert Colombian pesos back into dollars.

Chapter Twelve

The Black Market

When most people think of the black market, they probably think of the drug-pusher, the fence, the smuggler, and the mafia. Under normal circumstances, such characters play a major role in black market activities. By normal circumstances, I mean a free market except in areas deemed socially undesirable by the government—illicit drugs, stolen goods, et cetera. Under these conditions, the black market remains relatively small in comparison to all the goods and services exchanged in the country.

Wage and price controls can radically change this situation. Under government price-fixing, black markets can be created in virtually all areas of the marketplace, in nearly every product. No longer is the illegal market one of illicit drugs and stolen goods. It becomes possible to sell meat, potatoes, and shoes at prices exceeding the legal limit, and some of our friends may sell or buy merchandise at forbidden prices.

America's Black Market in World War II

Though the situation in the United States was never as grave as it was in postwar Germany, nevertheless the black market was extensive. It existed in practically all commodities by the end of the war, and there were acute problems in twenty-one major commodities. Black markets existed in coffee, meat, poultry, potatoes, onions, sugar, grains, cigarettes, liquor, apparel, lumber, waste paper, consumer durables, gasoline, fuel oil, used cars, tires, building materials, industrial materials, scrap metal, and rent.

Large and small manufacturers became involved in illegal channels to obtain much-needed supplies. Almost every wholesale dealer in sugar was found to be in violation of government regulations on rationing and pricing.

The Office of Price Administration estimated that 3 to 5 percent of the nation's $27 billion food budget went into the black market. As much as 20 percent of meat supplies and 5 percent of gasoline went into illegal channels.

Commenting on the black market during the war, *Fortune* magazine had this to say:

> In the U.S. in 1946, the historians will write, it was possible to get anything you could imagine—for a price. The black-market quotations were fairly level across the land, too; for $7.50 you could get a pair of nylon stockings in any city; for $1 to $1.50 you could buy a pound of butter. It was said and not denied that if OPA really enforced the law, all the building-materials businessmen in Boston would be in jail. In the South, 1,250,000 pounds of black-market sugar went to the highest bidders—the moonshiners. Throughout the U.S. trucks were sold by "tie-ins"; for as much as $1,000 over the ceiling price the customer got some extra piston rings or two front fenders. Carpenters' nails were scarce, with the ceiling at $5 a keg in twenty-five keg lots, they were selling at two or three times the ceiling price. . . . The black market in farm machinery was one of the wildest: used tractors, OPA-priced at $2,000, sold at $3,400. Lumber got around the OPA everywhere by a variety of new grading methods; one lumber buyer grumbled: "If you can pick up a board by both ends without breaking it in the middle, it's No. 1 Select."

Gasoline provides one of the best examples of how troublesome the black market became under price controls and rationing. (This summary should also prove helpful in anticipation of another energy crisis.)

Rationing of gasoline began in December, 1942. Pleasure driving on Sunday was banned. The task for government controllers was immense; through rationing, they had to reduce gasoline consumption in 1943–45 by a full one-third compared to consumption in 1941. Consequently, there were extensive thefts, counterfeiting, overissuance of gasoline rations, et cetera.

The black market in gasoline extended from coast to coast. A cozy relationship developed between legitimate gasoline dealers, public officials, and the underworld. Dealers received more gasoline if they presented more coupons. So they had a great incentive to obtain illegal coupons.

In *The Black Market,* Marshall Clinard writes:

> By June of 1944 there had been over 650 robberies of local boards involving 300 million gallons in coupons, and about the same time a campaign against counterfeit coupons enabled the identification of over 132 different types of gasoline counterfeits and yielded 13 printing presses used to print counterfeits. One such press was running an order for 15 million counterfeit A gas coupons and for 1.5 million counterfeit shoe coupons when found. In one case a racketeer with a prison record for robbery was found illegally in possession of 38,000 gallons in counterfeit gasoline coupons, 25,000 gallons in genuine fuel oil coupons, and 437 counterfeit shoe coupons, as well as a loaded automatic, two shotguns, and burglary tools.

Who Ran the Black Market?

From the preceding quote, one might be inclined to view the black market as an operation run by the underworld. Interestingly enough, this was *not* the case in World War II. Under price controls, the overwhelming proportion of black marketeers were from the legitimate business community. Clinard says that, contrary to public opinion, "the black market cannot be attributed to gangster and shady elements in business." And former OPA Commissioner Leon Henderson said, "Criminal racketeers of the gangster variety have relatively little place in the wholesale chiseling now going on. They do not control our slaughterhouses, lumber mills, textile centers, and automobile agencies, nor do they have any interest in our retail stores and railroads. Current racketeering is largely in the hands of men and women with whom we have always done business."

Even the meat black market largely operated through ordinary business channels. One government official stated that "the black market consists of numerous violations, none of them committed by the Capone-type conspirator or meat bootlegger, but rather by established members of industry. . . ."

After studying the black market in meat in Detroit at the end of the war, one expert concluded:

First and most important, the meat black market was not a clandestine criminal organization parasitic upon the industry. It did not hijack meat at various stages in the normal flow and sell it through blind pigs known to fortunate customers. It was most definitely not an excrescence upon the industry composed of racketeers coming from various criminal fields, or perhaps surviving from the prohibition era. Had this been the case, effective detective work could have uncovered it, and OPA would indeed have been remiss in not doing so.

Of the thousands of meat black marketeers proceeded against criminally, civilly, and administratively, the writer knows of none who were gangsters. Of the several hundred defendants in the Detroit area, only two had a previous criminal record, but neither of these could in any way have been regarded as a gangster. Neither of the convictions was for activities related to meat, and both had been committed outside of Michigan some years previously. Actually, then, the violations in this industry were committed by persons more or less well established in the different levels, from slaughterers to wholesalers and retailers. And the violations ranged from hardly more than traditional sharp practices to the most studied and deliberate attempts at conspiracy.

Clinard, who worked for the OPA, reports that less than one black market violator in ten had any criminal record in those cases where criminal prosecution was pursued. The black market radically changes its character under strict price controls and rationing, shifting out of the realm of the underground and into the new routine of industrial channels.

Sanctions against Black Marketeers

Criminal sanctions and punishment have always been fairly harsh against black marketeers, *except* under price controls. Sanctions seem to have become progressively less severe, from Diocletian's death penalty to imprisonment during World War II to simple fines under Nixon's program. Studies made of the prosecution of violators in World War II reveal that government enforcers were reluctant to prosecute and that the courts were even more reluctant to punish.

This reluctance was based on a number of factors. First, the majority of violators in these cases are not gangster types, but are members of the business community. Second, price control violations involve acts that would, in many cases, be considered perfectly legitimate during normal times. If you think about it, it is a radical change for businessmen to charge less than what the market dictates, but under price controls, that is what government expects. Finally, controls programs are almost always regarded as "temporary" measures (except in Communist countries), and the courts are unlikely to jail someone when in short order a similar act will be completely legal.

Under most price-controls programs, it seems that the black marketeer can operate on the assumption that he will likely escape prosecution and punishment. As Clinard observed, the climate favors the black market: "Those who wish to violate should now know how to do it, and may proceed on the premise that the possibility of detection is limited, the penalty slight, and the disapprobation of other businessmen almost nonexistent."

How the Black Market Works

Today, profiteers in the black market are pretty brazen. A Mr. David Randall (a pseudonym?) recently wrote *The Black Market Manual*. Randall explains the basics of the black marketeer, whom he glorifies in his book:

> Morals, smorals, the black marketeer is a hero in my book. . . . Namely, I buy from the well-off and sell to the needy (who are even richer). . . . Of course there are shades of gray in all operations, to be sure, but whether wheeling openly in white markets or dealing clandestinely aboveboard in gray ones, both situations exist in advance of severe shortages that typically characterize black markets. The onus on the term "black market" or "under-the-counter selling" is not, believe me, as bad as having the Black Plague; history repeatedly bears this out. And to pretend that commodities of all sorts are not sold, from time to time, in violation of "official" prices is the height of naivete in the business world. . . .
>
> All three shades of market operations serve a purpose. They balance off the irregular effects of supply and demand, while physically fulfilling very real consumer and manufacturer needs.

The Black Market Manual describes numerous ways of profiting in "gray" markets, as well as black markets. The difference is one of legality only. Both involve taking advantage of shortages. In the black market, the profiteer charges prices above the legal ceiling. In the gray market, there is no legal ceiling, but sales are not made through normal business channels.

I mentioned the gray market in steel in chapter 9. During the Korean War, there was a tremendous shortage of steel due to the war and government controls. Small businesses were the first to feel the pinch. In a short time, they started to receive telephone calls and circulars from "steel brokers" offering hard-to-get steel. These unknown steel brokers usually sold the steel at three or four times above the regular warehouse price. No questions were asked, such as the source of the steel. The Senate committee investigating this gray market said that "a considerable amount of steel was escaping from normal channels of distribution and finding its way into the gray market." It was a gray market because the higher prices were still considered legal because of the existence of loopholes in the controls legislation (such as the use of successive markups, e.g., the "Daisy Chain").

Brokers would often set up dummy companies. "It was apparent," reported the Senate committee, "that many of these individuals with no business assets except a telephone and a desk had parlayed hard-to-get steel into a multimillion-dollar business."

Going from the gray market to the black market is only a matter of one step as far as technique is concerned. The idea is always to line up buyers with sellers, with the middleman taking the commissions. Randall describes how one person did this during the 1974 energy crisis:

> Take the published case of 23-year-old Stephen Prine. Just out of college and starting out on his own in October, 1973, with no more than the Yellow Page directories and a lot of persistence, Prine worked 16-hour days to match up Company A's needs with Company B's surplus. He pocketed the difference in prices between the two in commissions. Skipping the Shells and Mobils, he went straight to the likes of Adobe Refinery in LaBlanca, Texas for his source of oil supplies. After his first six months he had amassed over $5.2 million in gross sales, secured a $500,000 loan and incorporated the business.

The mail order business can also serve as a lucrative way of profiting through the black market, although it is a hazardous course because it is so visible. Mail order firms have in the past minimized this public exposure by using only direct mailings rather than display advertising in magazines and newspapers. In 1943, for example, a mail order firm started marketing household

237

wares and house furnishings, which were in short supply. They sold at prices twice those being charged by other wholesalers. Many retailers purchased from the mail order company because of the shortages, despite the fact that the company was operating illegally (all firms were required to apply for OPA approval on their prices prior to posting them).

Rules of the Game

Black market brokers live by some basic rules. The cardinal rule is: do not buy any product unless it has already been sold at a higher price. Randall outlines this and five other rules in *The Black Market Manual:*

1. Rarely commit yourself to the purchase of a commodity you haven't already sold elsewhere at a higher price, unless you're fully prepared to take physical possession of it.

2. Never handle the type of commodity you couldn't store at mother's; it's probably too hot to handle.

3. Secrecy and aloneness are part and parcel of this game. Your big expense is the telephone, much of it long-distance, in trying to match sellers with buyers. Remember, your word is your bond.

4. The company with the surplus goods does not wish to make itself known. It could be bad for its reputation, and besides, it might be only quasi-legal to boot. Your job is to arrange the deals, not bring together bosom buddies.

5. Never, never fall in love with a particular commodity you're selling. As with owning Penn Central stock, you may be its last lover before it falls completely out of bed.

6. Always assume the attitude that you're getting out of (not into) business; this way you'll remain flexible and loose.

Economics of the Black Market

Why do price controls inevitably lead to black markets? What is the nature of black markets? Do they solve the problems created by price controls or make them worse? What determines black market prices?

Basic economic principles can help answer these questions. In chapter 5, I discussed the consequences of price controls. Using

SHORTAGE UNDER PRICE CONTROLS

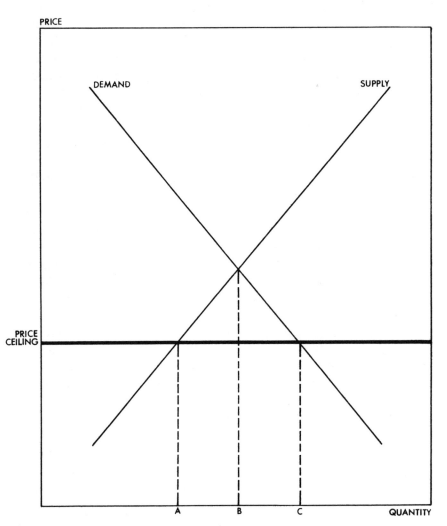

economic principles, I showed that shortage is the child of controls. The above graph shows the supply and demand for a particular product and the effects of a price ceiling below the free market price.

Two events take place as a result of a price ceiling below the free market price. First, suppliers offer less of the product because their return is less. Thus, instead of offering the amount B, they only offer the amount A. Second, at the low price ceiling, consumers desire to purchase more of the product. The people who bought before now want to buy more, and new customers also enter the market for the first time to boost demand. Thus consumers now demand the amount C. The difference between what suppliers are willing to sell (A) and what consumers desire to buy (C) is the shortage (C minus A).

This graph also demonstrates why black markets are almost inevitable under such circumstances. Look at the demand curve. This represents what consumers are willing to buy at different prices. Under normal free market pricing, the demand for the product is represented by the *demand curve above the line B*. Under a price ceiling, the demand for the product expands to include *all of the demand curve above the line C*. As you can see from the graph, this means that nearly all consumers are willing to pay a higher price. And more than half are willing to pay the free market price. This is a tremendous incentive for black marketeers to enter the market and sell the product at forbidden prices—especially when consumers have to wait in line to obtain the merchandise at legal prices.

There are two basic problems facing the black marketeer. First, he has to find sources of supply outside regular channels. He must be willing to sell at illegal prices and to operate under the fear of being caught. All of these factors mean that he will incur higher costs. Second, consumers may not wish to purchase from the black marketeer because of the illegal nature of the transaction.

As a result, the black market is characterized by a reduced supply curve and a reduced demand curve. The following graph illustrates the supply and demand situation of a black market compared to supply and demand under normal conditions.

In this graph, the supply and demand curves facing the black marketeer are simply superimposed on the normal supply and demand curves from the previous graph. As you can see, the black market price will not necessarily be above the free market price (i.e., the price the product will sell for when controls are lifted). The supply and demand curves can be drawn such that the black market price can be above, below, or equal to the free market price.

240

SUPPLY & DEMAND ON THE BLACK MARKET

Actually, the whole distinction of black market and free market is a kind of chimera. There is no scientific way of determining whether the black market price is above or below the free market price. The fact that a black market exists means that there is no free market. More correctly, the black market is the only market. It is futile to keep discussing what will happen to prices when controls are lifted, whether they will reach black market levels, or whatever. The only conclusive statement that can be made is that prices will definitely rise when the legal ceiling is lifted.

Black markets can *never* eliminate shortages created by controls. All they can do is alleviate the shortage problem. There will still be people lined up to buy at legal prices. Given the costs confronting the black marketeer and the prices consumers will be forced to pay, the quantity supplied by the black market is limited by the market's very nature. In the graph, the black market does *not* provide the amount X. In reality, it only offers amount X minus A to consumers. The amount A is what is available to consumers at the legal price. The black marketeer is limited by production to that which is between the amounts A and B. Under no circumstances could he supply more because this would mean that his supply would exceed free market output, a clear absurdity. Thus it should be obvious that shortages are alleviated but not eliminated by black markets.

This analysis provides some helpful suggestions to government controllers (they need all the help they can get). Should price enforcers concentrate on penalizing sellers in the black market or buyers in the black market? What if they penalize only the seller? Using the black market graph, what we would be dealing with is the black market supply curve and the free market demand curve, since there is no penalty to consumers for paying above-ceiling prices. These two curves would cross at a point such that the result would be *higher prices and increased supply*.

What if the government chose to penalize only the buyers? Then, we would be dealing with the black market demand curve and the free market supply curve. Where they intersect on the graph demonstrates that the results of such an enforcement program would be *lower prices and increased supply*. Clearly, from the point of view of the consumers and the economy in general, the best course of action (next to decontrol) would be to penalize the buyer rather than the seller. Unfortunately, the policy has practically always been the opposite in the past. The government always seems to impose heavy penalties on the black marketeers, while failing to impose restrictions on the buyers.

Rationing will not eliminate the black market under most circumstances. Even though people may no longer stand in line for the goods they need, they nevertheless will desire more than they are getting. Their demands will still be unsatisfied, and this fact is the basic bread and butter of the black marketeer. Moreover, ration coupons will provide an excellent source of profit for the black marketeer, as was the case in World War II. Counterfeiting, stolen coupons, and the illegal selling of coupons have all been serious problems in the past.

One way to alleviate this problem is to permit the free exchange of coupons. Essentially, this "white market" technique amounts to a way of redistributing income in favor of the poor without creating the additional problems of overissuance, enforcement, and so on. Counterfeiting would likely still be a major problem, however.

Chapter Thirteen

What Now?

In discussing this book with an economics professor, I was told not to worry too much about wage and price controls. Why? Because, he responded, controls would never become too severe. If they ever did, shortages would become so widespread that the public would demand that they be lifted immediately. Democracy works! So, argued the professor, if controls are reimposed, they would only be on a limited basis, creating little distortion. The government could be expected to take a "pragmatic" and "reasonable" approach, responsive to the people.

I wonder if our government leaders have really changed so radically from the days when, for example, the Allies maintained severely tight Nazi controls in Germany after World War II. Sure, the government has learned some lessons about wage and price controls. And, admittedly, the government failed to renew price-controls authority in 1974 after a sudden surge in double-digit inflation.

But, the government has not always been "reasonable," even in the recent past. During the Nixon controls, businessmen facing bankruptcy were still denied relief from controls. And few observers would call the government's Phase III½ (the second freeze) "pragmatic" when severe shortages occurred in meat and other products. Furthermore, what about today's price ceilings on natural gas and, in New York City, rent? Can these be the products of "reasonable" government policy? Hardly.

Frankly, I am not convinced that government can be expected to react rationally and reasonably in the face of an economic crisis. In fact, the imposition of controls is never a rational act from an economic point of view. Because controls always result from a political decision, one can never be sure how far the government will go. Historically, the government has more often than not *increased,* not decreased, its power when faced with an economic crisis, whether inflation, depression, or shortages. "Decontrol" is always a painful decision. It is much easier to either expand government intervention or, at least, postpone decontrol.

What will the government do if there are widespread shortages created under its price-controls program? No one knows for sure, but certainly immediate decontrol is not the likely response. The government could, for example, argue that controls are not working and should be tightened. And if that does not work, then the government could blame businessmen for withholding supplies from the market and nationalize them for the "good of the public." These alternatives have all been used in the past and must never be discounted.

But whether controls are limited or severe, there is no doubt that they will eventually be reimposed. President Carter has said that he wants stand-by authority to impose controls, power similar to that granted President Nixon in 1970. As Gary North points out, such legislation signals the inevitability of controls in the near future. You should take immediate action to insulate your affairs from the harmful effects of controls.

As usual, the great majority of people will not follow the advice given in these pages until it is too late. This should be to your advantage, however. If I were to outline the basic lessons of this book, they would be:

First, certain actions need to be taken prior to the imposition of controls. This especially applies to businessmen, who may be required to establish a "customary business practice" in order to circumvent controls.

Second, it pays to be in the best financial shape possible in order to make necessary purchases and weather the coming economic storm.

Third, since the utility of money is partially destroyed by controls, those in possession of "critical necessities" will be able to survive better than others. Stocking up with the products suggested in this book is absolutely essential. This precautionary measure will minimize the temptation to participate in illegal markets.

Fourth, income-earners will need to rely on more than one source of income.

Fifth, controls distort the patterns of economic activity. Artificial shortages and financial hardships will arise in many areas. But at the same time, profitable opportunities for businessmen, employers and investors will arise in uncontrolled areas.

Your motto should be: Hope for the best, but prepare for the worst. That's the best insurance you can buy.

Suggested Readings

Throughout this book I have referred to a number of books and periodicals that have provided me with extremely valuable information and advice. Some of the books are out of print, but may still be obtained at bookstores, at your local library, or through the Library of Congress.

Economics

Man, Economy and State, Murray N. Rothbard. This two-volume textbook is the clearest and most logical presentation of economic principles I have ever read. Unlike all other economics textbooks, this one begins with a simple Robinson Crusoe economy and slowly develops the basic principles of a modern economy. It is the only theoretical presentation that is entirely consistent with economic growth, savings, and the free market. Unfortunately, Rothbard and his monumental work have largely been ignored by the economics profession. (Nash Publishing Co., Los Angeles, California, 987 pages; $30 hardbound, $10 paperback.)

What Has Government Done to Our Money?, Murray N. Rothbard. A short, but excellent booklet explaining the mysteries of money and how the government has caused inflation. (Rampart College, Santa Ana, California, 62 pages; $2.)

The Case for a 100 Percent Gold Dollar, Murray N. Rothbard. Another booklet by Rothbard offering a clear-cut alternative to fiat money. Rothbard argues that a return to a pure 100 percent gold standard will assure "the end of inflation, and with it, of the business cycle." (Libertarian Review Press, Alexandria, Virginia, 43 pages; $2.)

America's Great Depression, Murray N. Rothbard. Not only does this book review the true causes of the Great Depression of the 1930s, but it provides an excellent explanation of business cycles in general. (Sheed and Ward, New York, New York, 361 pages; $12 hardbound, $5 paperback.)

University Economics, Armen A. Alchian and William R. Allen. A superb and enlightening treatise on microeconomic principles. The section on macroeconomics, unfortunately, does not match Rothbard's. (Wadsworth, Belmont, California, 857 pages; $13.95.)

Price Controls

Historical Working Papers on the Economic Stabilization Program, August 15, 1971 to April 30, 1974. Written and compiled by about a dozen analysts who worked for the Cost of Living Council, this two-volume set (the third volume is a statistical section) abounds with solid information on the Nixon controls program and advice to future controllers. This is perhaps the best government source on what to expect under the next round of wage and price controls. (U.S. Government Printing Office, Washington, D.C., 1538 pages; $14.40 for the first two volumes.)

Confessions of a Price Controller, C. Jackson Grayson. The former chairman of the Price Commission describes in detail what happened under Nixon's controls program. An excellent portrayal of government in action. (Dow Jones–Irwin, Homewood, Illinois, 265 pages; $8.95.)

Remnant Review. Gary North's newsletter, published every two weeks, specializes in monitoring and giving advice on price controls and related problems. If you want the best counsel on how to prepare for price controls and cope with them when they are imposed, this is where to find it. (P.O. Box 1580, Springfield, VA 22151; $65 a year.)

The Black Market

The Black Market, Marshall Clinard. Clinard worked with the Office of Price Administration, Enforcement Department, 1942–45. His book is by far the most comprehensive study of World War II price violations. Surprisingly objective. (Patterson Smith, Montclair, New Jersey, 410 pages; $14 hardbound, $4.50 paperback.)

The Black Market Manual, David Randall. Overpriced for its size, this booklet is nevertheless a good compilation of black market techniques. (Clinton Publishing Co., New York, New York, 61 pages; $15. Black cover, naturally.)

Investments

You Can Profit from a Monetary Crisis, Harry Browne. A bit elementary and already out of date, Browne's book is still valuable in exploring profitable avenues resulting from government intervention into the economy. (Macmillan, New York, New York, 397 pages; $8.95 hardbound, $2.25 paperback.)

You Can Profit from the Coming MidEast War, John Dublin. Basically the same principles used in Browne's book applied to an international war scenario. Dublin's emphasis is on speculation in the commodity futures market. (Dublin Publishing Co., New York, New York, 91 pages; $10 paperback.)

99 Ways to Make Money in a Depression, Gerald Appel. Many of Appel's recommendations may apply during price controls, so this book is worth examining. (Arlington House Publishers, New Rochelle, New York, 238 pages; $8.95.)

How to Make Money Fast Speculating in Distressed Property, John Kamin. Solid, useful information on real estate speculation. (Pyramid Books, New York, New York, 170 pages; $1.25.) Up-to-date recommendations from John Kamin can be obtained through his excellent newsletter, *The Forecaster* (19623 Ventura Blvd., Tarzana, CA 91356; $75 a year).

International Shortage Reporter (30 West Pasadena, Phoenix, AZ 85013; $38 a year, 18 issues). This newsletter calls itself the "newsletter of counter-economics, black markets and underground business." It provides numerous present-day examples of shortages and how to profit from them.

Index

Agriculture. *See* Food co-ops, Food prices, Food storage
Alchian, Armen A., 248
Antwerp (Belgium), 69
Apparel industry, 111, 191
Appel, Gerald, 206, 249
Arbitrage, 202
Auctions, 162–63

Balabkim, Nicholas, 120
Bankruptcy, 97, 178
Barter, 73, 156–58, 194
Baruch, Bernard, 71
Baxter, René, 163, 199–200
Belgium, 55
Big business, 49, 83, 135, 137, 198–99, 219
Black markets, 10, 18, 26, 232–43
  in Germany, 29, 72–73
  government approval of, 141
  in Korean War, 77
  sanctions against, 235–36
  in World War II, 76, 232–36
Bond market, 222
Bonuses, 168–69
Bowles, Chester, 75, 138, 191
Brookings Institution, 43–44, 46
Browne, Harry, 249
Brozen, Yale, 117
Burns, Arthur F., 19, 45, 81, 101
Business cycles, 62–65
Businessmen:
  employees of, 169, 201
  favoring controls, 52–53, 219
  freedom of, under controls, 95–96
  small, 105, 118–19, 137, 198–99, 237
  under controls, 30, 85–86, 136, 178–204

Canada, 19, 55, 80
"Canadian Connection," 204
Carter, James Earl (Jimmy), 245
Cash-on-the-side, 187–88
Chamber of Commerce, U.S., 52
Churches, 153–55
Cigarettes, 73–74
Clinard, Marshall, 98, 138–40, 187, 213, 234–36, 249
Clothing industry, 111, 191
Coins, 158–59, 228–29
Coleman, Philip D., 129
Collectables, 174–75, 227–29
Commodity futures markets, 100–1, 223–26
Competition, 41–42
Congress, U.S., 43
Consumers, 145–63
  dealing with controls, 145–46
  preparing for controls, 11–12, 22–23, 146–47
Continental Congress, 70
Controls (*see also* Price controls):
  bureaucracy under, 77, 127–30
  ceilings, 75, 81, 88, 91, 97, 118–21, 186–87
  in China, 74
  consequences of 109–26, 238–40
  constitutionality of, 27–29, 131–35
  cost of, 86, 128
  dividends, 83, 107, 219

251

econometric studies favoring, 45–47
effects on business, 21–22, 29, 85–86, 120–21
effects on prices, 110–13
failure of, 69–70, 75, 93
history of, 67–86
on interest, 68, 107
in Korean War, 77, 127, 184, 202–4, 218, 237
in Latin America, 81
on production, 70, 95–96, 110
profiting from, 24, 201–4, 213–15
on profits, 72, 91–92, 106, 124
public support of, 53–55, 85
rent, 24–25, 53, 84, 103–5, 108, 125–26, 142, 206–9
return of, 41–42, 44–45
selective, 48, 71
shortages under, 48, 85–86, 88–90, 179, 219
stand-by, 12, 40
success of, 45–47, 76, 83, 90
on trade, 84, 96–97, 99–100, 124
on wages, 78, 164–77
in Western Europe, 77–80
in World War I, 70–71
in World War II, 54, 74–76, 91–93, 95, 97–98, 105–6, 111, 120–21, 125, 135–39, 166, 168, 183, 185, 187, 190, 210–11, 213, 215, 218, 225, 230, 232–36
Cost of Living Council, 29–30, 42, 83–84, 92, 98, 105, 127, 171, 182, 189, 193, 195, 204, 223–24
Cost-plus pricing, 71, 78–79, 92, 108, 136, 191
Cost-push inflation, 49–52, 108, 113–16
Council on Wage and Price Stability, 40
"Customary business practice," 136, 183
Custom products, 99, 192

Damaged goods, 100, 193
Decontrol, 85, 94
Diamonds, 229
Diocletian (Roman emperor), 68
Discounts, 113, 181–82, 188
Dividends, 83, 219
Double billing, 189–90
Droitsch, Roland G., 45
Dual-pricing, 21, 118
Dublin, John, 10
Dunlap, John T., 99

Econometric studies, 45–47
Economic Stabilization Act of 1942, 75
Economic Stabilization Act of 1970, 39, 43, 82, 97
amendments to, 83, 91, 105–6, 166–67
Emergency Price Control Act of 1942, 75, 210
Employee Stock Ownership Plans (ESOP), 167
Energy crisis, 17, 91, 94, 117
Environmental Protection Agency, 149
Equilibrium models, 111–13
Erhard, Ludwig, 73
Eucken, Walter, 123
Evasion and illegal methods, 23–24, 30, 71, 183, 185, 189
penalties, 68, 72, 137–42
rental property, 24, 210–13
Exemptions under controls, 97–106, 108, 197–98
agricultural commodities, 20, 75, 90, 97–99
art, 102–3
damaged and used goods, 161–63
foreign goods, 160–61, 192, 204
oil, 101–2
rent, 103–5, 206–7
securities, 100
small business, 101
wages, 75, 105–6, 164–65

Federal Registry, 103
Federal Reserve Board, 59–61, 65
Flory, John, 92–93, 195–97
Food co-ops, 152–53
Food prices, 55–56, 75, 84, 90, 97–99, 191
processed and raw, 98–99
Food storage, 149–52
Ford, Gerald R., 130
Foreign currencies, 229–31
Formula pricing, 92–93, 106, 226
France, 79
rent controls in, 19, 126, 211
rollback of prices in, 90
Freeze, 48, 54, 77–82, 84–85, 88–90, 99–100, 106–7, 108, 118, 170–71, 202, 210, 212, 226
effects of, 21, 111–12, 113–18
"General Max," 75
purposes of, 90

Friedman, Milton, 14, 27, 31, 45, 51, 59,
    125
Fringe benefits, 105, 166–67

Galbraith, John Kenneth, 19, 29, 47–52,
    56, 101
Gasoline rationing, 94–95, 148–49, 233
Germany:
    controls in post–World War II, 29,
        72–74, 109, 120, 170
    Nazi controls, 71–72, 95, 184
Gold and silver, 226–27
Gold and silver coins, 158–59
Government, 135–42
    controllers in, 130
    reliance on, 130
    waste in, 32–34
Gray markets, 77, 202–4
Grayson, C. Jackson, 40, 41, 48, 53, 54,
    83, 92, 98, 101, 128, 136, 140, 182, 193,
    195, 198, 248
    recommendations by, 108
Great Britain, 68–69, 123–24, 186

Haberler, Gottfried, 51, 109
Hammurabi, Code of, 67
Heller, Walter, 19, 48, 101
Henderson, Leon, 31, 120, 211, 234
Historical Working Papers, 42–43, 45, 54,
    92, 191, 195–96, 248
Hitler, Adolf, 71
Hobbies, 174–75
Hoover, Herbert C., 71
Houthakker, Hendrik, 54

Inflation, 44–45
    causes of, 56–61
    prospects of, 56
    runaway, 65
    under controls, 46
Inflationary recession, 59, 81
Interest rates, 222
Internal Revenue Service (IRS), 22,
    27–28, 141–42, 195, 200
Investors, 25, 216–31

"Jawboning," 78
Juries, 133–35

Kahm, H. S., 175
Kamin, John, 162–63, 214–15, 249

Keezer, Dexter M., 166
"Key money," 208, 211, 213
Kosters, Marvin H., 109

Labor unions, 49, 51, 53, 75, 78, 107, 116,
    219
Lanzillotti, Robert F., 46
Latin America, 19, 81
Litman, Simon, 69

Mail order business, 176–77, 237
Mansfield and Associates, 94, 124, 191
McCracken, Paul, 31, 114
Meany, George, 53, 107
Meat, 98
Mendershausen, Horst, 72
Merit increases, 106, 168–69
Miller, Roger Leroy, 118
Mises, Ludwig von, 121–24
Money supply, 59–61, 84
Moonlighting, 175–77
Mormons, 154–55

National Association of Manufacturers,
    52, 85
National War Labor Board, 75
Netherlands, 79
    seige of Antwerp, 69
New products, 190–91
New York City, 125, 208–9
Nixon, Richard M., 17, 39, 82, 128
Nixon's Economic Stabilization Program,
    129–30, 140–42, 191, 218–19
    bankruptcy during, 29
    hurt by, 17
    Phase I (Freeze), 82, 118, 166, 182, 212
    Phase II, 82–83, 98, 105, 109, 136, 166,
        181, 182, 193, 194, 212
    Phase III, 83–84
    Phase III½, 83–84, 98, 117, 182, 192
    Phase IV, 85–86, 111, 130, 142, 167,
        181, 188
North, Gary, 145–46, 153–54, 155,
    157–58, 159, 168, 169, 170, 172–75,
    228, 248

Office of Price Administration (OPA), 49,
    75, 95, 138–39, 151, 183, 187, 190, 191,
    233
    price violations under, 24

253

Office of Price Stabilization (OPS), 77, 184
Okun, Arthur M., 44

Paper industry, 111, 179
Patman, Wright, 66
Pay Board, 53, 83, 105
Payments in kind, 169–70
Perry, George L., 44
Petroleum, 99, 101–2, 132, 142, 147–49, 189, 198
Prenotification, 198
Price Commission, 40, 83, 98, 101, 183, 195, 198
Price controls (*see also* Controls):
  circumventing, 120
  constitutionality of, 27–29, 131–35
  courts on, 27
  morality of, 27
Profits, 72, 91–92, 106
Profit-margin test, 91–92, 124, 195–98
Promotions, 106, 168
Proxmire, William, 39, 43
Puritans, 70

Randall, David, 236–38, 249
Rationing, 49, 91, 93–95, 98, 226, 243
  certificate type, 93
  coupon type, 93–94
  of food, 151
  of gasoline, 148, 234
  in Germany, 73, 93
  in Great Britain, 93
  of meat, 98
  problems with, 94
  in U.S., 75, 93, 148
  value, 93
Recessions, 62–64
Reimann, Guenter, 120, 184
Rent controls, 53, 84, 103–5, 205–15
  in France, 126
  in New York City, 104–5, 125–26
Repairs, 159–60, 172–73
Roberts, Blaine, 46
Rollbacks, 70, 71, 90
Roosevelt, Franklin D., 75
Rothbard, Murray N., 62–64, 247–48
Ruff, Howard, 150, 152

Samuelson, Paul A., 44–45, 126
Santayana, George, 19

Scherer, F. M., 185
Schumpeter, Joseph A., 41, 124
Seasonal variations, 116–17, 192
Service industries, 194
Shortages, 48, 88–90, 145–46
  businessmen facing, 15–16, 120, 179
  effects of, 22
  preparing for, 11–12
  types of, 145–46, 179
  under runaway inflation, 26
Short-selling (stocks), 220
Silver coins, 159, 199–201
Simon, William E., 95
Small business, 118–19
Socialism, 14, 22, 121–24
Soviet Union, 95
Steel industry, 116, 171, 202–4, 237
Step increases, 106
Stigler, George, 125
Stock market, 216–22
Stock options, 220–22
Stone, Richard, 125
Subsidies, 75, 96

"Truck wage system," 170
Trudeau, Pierre E., 80
Truman, Harry S., 76
Tuition, 100, 182
Tying agreements:
  in business, 184–85
  combination sales, 71
  in rents, 25, 183–84, 211

Unemployment, 44–45, 56
  under controls, 46
Upgrading, 139, 187
Used goods, 100, 161–63, 193

Vocations, 172–75
Volatile prices, 193

Wage-earners, 23, 201
Wages, 75, 78–79, 83–84, 115–16, 164–77
Wage Stabilization Board, 166, 168
Weeden, William B., 69
"White market," 94, 148, 243

Yakus v. *United States*, 131